P9-DHS-132

THEORIES OF BIBLIOGRAPHIC EDUCATION

Theories of Bibliographic Education
Designs for Teaching

EDITED BY

Cerise Oberman
Katina Strauch

R. R. Bowker Company
New York and London, 1982

To my Mom and Dad and Laurie
—C.G.O.

To Bruce and Raymond and Mom and Dad
—K.P.S.

Published by R. R. Bowker Company
1180 Avenue of the Americas, New York, NY 10036
Copyright © 1982 by Xerox Corporation
All rights reserved
Printed and bound in the United States of America

Library of Congress Cataloging in Publication Data
Main entry under title:

Theories of bibliographic education.

    Bibliography: p.
    Includes index.
    1. Library orientation. 2. Searching,
Bibliographical. I. Oberman, Cerise, 1952– .
II. Strauch, Katina P., 1946– .
Z711.2.T49   025.5'6   82-4270
ISBN 0-8352-1506-7   AACR2

025.56
T343

Contents

Preface

Along with many others, we have for some time looked for a theoretical foundation in our teaching. But there has been very little literature that presents both theory and design for library instruction programs. This book, therefore, is intended first, to remedy the absence of theory-based instruction literature. Second—and possibly more ambitious—this book attempts to signal a shift in emphasis from tool-based learning in bibliographic instruction to the potential of bibliographic education, with its emphasis on conceptual-based learning.

Librarians are acutely concerned about and interested in finding and applying theoretical foundations to current instruction practices. Both formal and informal discussions among practitioners seem to center on such questions as: Is there a theory of or for bibliographic education? What education theories have direct application to library instruction? Is librarianship able to develop its own theoretical base from which the teaching of research methods can be drawn? These and other questions are addressed in this book. For the basics of library instruction, a companion volume is *Learning the Library: Concepts and Methods for Effective Bibliographic Instruction*, by Anne K. Beaubien, Sharon A. Hogan, and Mary W. George (Bowker 1982).

There is a broad range of essays collected here, intermingling the theoretical threads of information structure and education principles. As a whole, they exemplify the diversity of thought and intellectual fervor in the current instructional community.

Each of these nine original essays is written by a practicing librarian or library educator who has explored the theoretical basis of his or her teaching efforts. The contributors have, where appropriate, given concrete examples of teaching for the benefit of other librarians. These essays, of course, do not represent the entire body of theoretical literature as it relates to bibliographic education. Rather, they are a sampling of current thought and practice: exploring the theoretical foundations of a science of bibliography (Keresztesi); searching for evidence as a means of instruction (Lindgren); teaching library research as metaphor (McInnis); using development theory as the basis for problem-solving (Mellon); exploring the theoretical basis for the self-instructional workbook (Berge and Pryor); stimulating reasoning skills through the adaptation of Guided Design theory (Oberman and Linton); contrasting the structures of scientific and humanistic literature (Smalley and Plum); using self-instructional motivation technique through computer-assisted instruction (Williams and Davis); and developing independent researchers through understanding of information structures (Frick).

It is our hope that these essays provide a beginning. For the practicing instruction librarian, this book offers a diversity of theories currently being applied in a wide range of instruction programs. They are meant to provide both information and inspiration. For the library school student, this book presents an opportunity to become immersed in the idea and importance of constructing an instruction program around a theoretical approach. It provides for theory as a forethought to instruction rather than an afterthought.

Above all, this book represents the first step in the building of a documented, theoretical base for bibliographic education, a base that allows for the development and maturation of this educational component of librarianship.

We would like to acknowledge the help and cooperation we received from the library staffs at the College of Charleston, South Carolina, and Walter Library, University of Minnesota, Minneapolis. A special thanks to our typists, Mary Catherine Barber and Jan Roseen, and to our families.

Cerise Oberman
University of Minnesota

Katina Strauch
College of Charleston

THEORIES OF
BIBLIOGRAPHIC
EDUCATION

1

The Science of Bibliography: Theoretical Implications for Bibliographic Instruction

MICHAEL KERESZTESI

The field of library science, as reflected in the academic curriculum, contains three major ingredients. The first concerns the library as an organization with its primary focus of service and management. The second could be called the "politics of librarianship." Here, the emphasis is on social and institutional aspects, mainly legislative, budgetary, cooperative, professional, and community-centered concerns.

The third ingredient is more diffuse and more difficult to define. It revolves around the handling of the human record—the literary, artistic, historical, philosophical, scientific, and popular materials produced since the beginning of writing. There is no ready-made generic term to describe this particular domain of library science. Some have used the vague expression "bibliothecal matters," implying that only those activities connected with handling the human record are truly pertinent to the social mission of librarianship. Others refer to "epistemological aspects," alluding to the fact that librarianship has something to do with knowledge, although techni-

1

cally the term has more philosophical than library-related connotations. Still others, in discussing the library's role, would use "substantive" to describe its function of making available to the public the books, periodicals, and other vehicles of information.

Thus, if language indicates a condition, we may infer that this third ingredient of library science is of central importance. And so, it is all the more perplexing that we lack the appropriate terminology to cover it. Is this lack accidental or is it due to difficulties with concepts, which need to be addressed?

The semantic confusion does seem to reflect actual conceptual problems. In contrast to earlier eras, we do not have at this time an unequivocal conception of the librarian's role as it concerns the human record.

Library science, like other academic fields, has been going through an evolutionary process propelled by constantly shifting paradigms, or models, which develop around new insights, needs, and priorities. They mobilize a discipline's intellectual and material resources for new tasks, setting new directions and goals and strategies to reach them.

Library concerns once revolved only around custodianship, and in many parts of the world this "custodian model" still predominates. In such a pattern, the librarian's relationship to the human record is clear. Professional activity is organized around gathering, arranging, and preserving intellectual materials on all subjects. Operating in this model, library science is generally and globally oriented and develops a universal taxonomy, an all-encompassing classification system, and a variety of inventory techniques for handling the human record. The "general" and "global" orientation indicates that, in its relationship to the human record, librarianship employs externally generated categories to impose order and structure on the world of knowledge. The effect is manipulative, rather than substantive. In historical perspective, the literature of the profession shows extensive preoccupation with matters of classifying and technical processing.

Today, with the advent of the "information age," we seem to have slipped into a new pattern. The library's function is being transformed from that of a public warehouse of cultural goods to one of a social dynamic institution of communication and knowledge dissemination.

Although the urge to provide guidance to the user has always been present in one way or another in American library practice, the rise of the bibliographic instruction movement in the 1970s can be viewed as a new service direction in the wake of shifts from the traditional role model. This process has been taking place without anyone articulating how, and in what respect, the librarian's relationship to the human record has changed or should change. The increasing pressure to scale down our "generalist posture" as it concerns the world of knowledge and to move toward narrow subject specializations could perhaps be regarded as evidence of an emerging new relationship. Although this trend alone may not be very helpful in formulating a new orientation in specific terms, the signals are sufficiently clear to suggest a shift of focus from preservation to "content." The term *content* refers not only to the intellectual matter contained in the human records themselves (in contrast to the material object in which it is encoded), but also to the internal logic in the physical organization of the library.

Thus, the information age urges the profession to concentrate on content to maximize the social utility of libraries. This has also been the motivating force behind the beginning bibliographic instruction movement, which has matured to seek solid theoretical foundations for the new roles and models of library service that it has been advocating. The quest for such foundations indicates that we should examine closer the "third ingredient" of library science.

The Need for New Conceptual Tools

Content-centered library practice is synonymous with what is today generally considered "information service." Providing information service requires conceptual tools to indicate how librarians should perceive content and how they should communicate and interpret it to the user. Library activity that aims at a purposeful manipulation of content, rather than of the physical object, will depend on the service apparatus that is available to access content. Thus, it is not unreasonable to claim that in the information age the librarian's relationship to the records is determined to a large extent by the nature of the information apparatus contained in the libraries. This apparatus is being expanded and refined constantly by the commercial, professional, scholarly, and government publishing industry and is given greater mechanical maneuverability by electronic technology.

The growth of information apparatus and its increasing sophistication have created a qualitatively different environment for service in libraries, but they have not essentially altered the librarian's relationship to knowledge itself. This relationship remains synoptic, indirect, and external because it affects not the depth, structure, and substance of knowledge, which are the realm of the scientist, the scholar, and the subject specialist researcher, but it affects access to that knowledge. Scientific work is concerned with access to content only to the extent that such access can contribute to the solution of a particular problem. There is a clear division of labor and roles in relation to the records, that is, the literature of a discipline, between scientists and scholars on the one hand and librarians on the other. Scientists and scholars are trained for professional practice involving application, concrete problem-solving, research, and, in the academic world, teaching. These are activities that require substantive uses of the content of the records, as well as its augmentation by the scientist's and the scholar's own empirical, theoretical, and methodological contributions. The huge escalation of the quantity of research and the mandate to acquire expertise in particular domains compel professional practitioners to seek increasingly narrower subject specialization.

On the other hand, the pressure for librarians to acquire narrow subject specializations in specific disciplines at the expense of a global stance in relation to knowledge is a misdirected effort. Librarians should not compete with scientists and scholars in their own fields. The librarian should gain expertise in accessing both general and discipline-generated specialized knowledge. To do this, the librarian must focus on the instruments of access to that knowledge. This is a different kind of expertise, which is complementary to the scientist's knowledge. Librarians and scientists are truly partners in a joint enterprise.

Confusion about the nature of this partnership on the part of both groups probably has historical roots. Library science as a distinct disciplinary field presented itself to the world as a form of applied management, a concept that is explicitly conveyed in the field's Latin-based designation, as, for example, *bibliothéconomie* in French. The dominance of administrative and political aspects in library school curricula, fostered by the heavy influx in library education of former library administrators and practitioners, contributed to the public and academic image of library work as an exercise in "glamorized housekeeping." To the extent that housekeeping needs necessitated it, the "substantive" or "intellectual" components of library science were developed. Classification and cataloging are a case in point.

The study of the instruments that create and organize access to knowledge has been traditionally relegated to courses in general and to subject reference. Schools often require only the general reference course for a professional degree. Frequently taught by practitioners in the form of an item-by-item survey of reference works, the courses could not provide a conceptual framework necessary to understand the art and craft of information toolmaking and the capabilities and functions of the products in the knowledge-producing and disseminating process.

Pitted against a background of ingrained misconceptions, the bibliographic instruction movement must equip itself with new tools of concept and theory in its struggle to make the most social use of libraries, particularly in the area of education. Since bibliographic instruction involves the advocacy of bibliography, the building of theoretical foundations must begin with a re-examination of the concept of bibliography.

Redefining the Role of Bibliography

A common conceptual difficulty connected with bibliography stems from the term signifying both the art and the craft as well as the artifact. In practice, the word has become pervasively associated with some kind of listing of books and other forms of published writings or with enumerating materials in other recorded formats. Used principally as a finding and verification tool in library practice, bibliography has been considered a product of specific inventory practices in the literature of a particular field. The vital role attributed to such functions of bibliography can be explained by the demands of library work that were operational in the "librarian as custodian" or the "library as cultural warehouse" pattern. During this long historical period, the focus of bibliographic craft was on eliciting individual specifications and production information for discrete physical units of intellectual materials in order to facilitate their selection, acquisition, organization, and storage. Prevailing to this day, this narrow focus has diverted attention from the broader implications of bibliography.

As already noted, library work in the information age demands greater concentration on content. To expand the concept of bibliography to encompass content is to ask that, in addition to identification and production data, bibliography should also be concerned with other categories of information elements in a particular body of literature. The accumulated knowledge of a discipline collectively resides in its literature; so the information embedded in that literature is a basic cognitive unit. It is not knowledge in itself, but it is a building block of knowledge. And knowledge is constructed by subjecting clusters of relevant information to complex intellectual operations, leading to cogent and verifiable formulations.

Simultaneously with this process emerges an intellectual activity, the aim of which is not to produce valid formulations, but instead to isolate and extract data from a literature of homogeneous information clusters and subsequently to format and package that data in response to specific needs. Inasmuch as contemporary scientific knowledge is the product of a vast and complex social enterprise, immense layers of disparate information building blocks underlie its many-sided structure. These units may relate to concepts, theories, postulates, paradigms, terminology, methodology, and formulas. Furthermore, they may deal with people, events, organizations, institutions, and various mechanisms active in a discipline, or they may address numerous other manifestations of a discipline's life. Together with inventory and enumerative products, the organized presentation of such informational units in the form of reference works or electronic data systems constitutes the information apparatus that serves a scientific discipline or scholarly field in the same manner that the array of weaponry serves the logistical objectives of an army on the move.

The conception of bibliography as a comprehensive apparatus created to meet specific information needs makes it evident that because it is anchored in the subject literature, it is intimately linked to the life processes of a particular discipline. Its nature is determined to a high degree by the maturity level of the discipline it serves.

Thus, we need a more unifying view of bibliography, which holds that bibliography as an intellectual pursuit must concern itself with the total process of how an information apparatus evolves through its interaction with the discipline or field it serves, and how this process creates the end products, the inventory artifacts, together with the printed and electronic information instruments.

This broad interpretation is not totally alien to bibliographic tradition. Bibliographic travail in literary scholarship, musicology, art history, and certain other fields has gone beyond the mere inventorying of the works of individual creators. The scope of inquiry in these fields has extended to a work's origin, circumstances of birth, tracing its influence, and gauging its impact. In librarianship, however, the conceptual evolution of bibliography in modern times seems to have been arrested in the inventory stage.

A unifying concept of bibliography is now necessary because knowledge cascading from the many-faceted, multitiered, institutionalized knowledge-producing and disseminating systems of today's scientific disciplines is much more difficult to access than the knowledge that flowed from individual thinkers and writers of past centuries. The task of teaching general and subject reference in a meaningful way also demands a unified theory of bibliography. The proliferation of reference works has reached a point where the traditional item-by-item survey is impossible. But perhaps most imperatively, an ordered image of the bibliographic universe is essential if instruction librarians are to make the internal world of scientific and scholarly disciplines intelligible to library users.

Scientific Disciplines as Knowledge-Producing and Disseminating Systems

A functional analysis of scientific discipline structure sheds light on the internal processes to which bibliography is intrinsically linked. The major role that bibliography plays in these processes can be seen when the word *bibliographic* is understood as describing any action along the research path that results in the production of a record. An example would be the designing of a project that is subsequently submitted in the form of a proposal to a funding agency in response to a "request for proposal" that appeared in a recent issue of a foundation's newsletter. The proposal itself, as well as the newsletter, are "bibliographic" products. Similarly, the informal communication of an interim research report among peers at a college, the presentation of the same report in more polished shape at a conference of the professional association, the submission of an article for publication in a journal, or the invitation to a researcher to testify as an expert at the hearings of a congressional subcommittee are all actions with obvious bibliographic implications because they generate records. The key point is that, although the research work, the professional association's conference, and the congressional hearing are not themselves "bibliographic events," they come under the scope of bibliography when the nature of a bibliographic tool is considered or an answer is sought to the question of how an information apparatus evolves through interaction with the discipline it serves.

Defining a scientific discipline as a "knowledge-producing and knowledge-disseminating system" implies that its mission is to produce knowledge in the area it has staked out for exploration.[1] It follows that new knowledge discovered through research must be communicated initially to members of the profession by means of established channels and must be accepted by those members. Eventually, new knowledge will reach society through journalistic, educational, and other avenues of transmission. Further consideration maintains that in order for a scientific or scholarly discipline to be productive, it must gain society's approval. This approval is symbolically granted when the discipline is embraced by the university. There is no bona fide scientific or scholarly discipline in the United States today outside the university.

A systemic conception of scientific disciplines has a complex mechanism of many components, each with an important role to play. Without meshing these components into a working entity, research and new knowledge production would be inconceivable at our present stage of scientific, economic, and political development. At the center stands the scientist, scholar, or researcher, individually or, more likely, as a member of a team, ready to launch a project, carve out a piece of reality to observe, to experiment with, to gather data on, to establish new facts, discern new patterns, formulate new theories, reveal new truth, or reaffirm or disprove earlier assertions.

Before this process can begin, however, a thorough search must be made in the accumulated records, that is, in the literature of the discipline, to see if this exploration has already been done, to avoid wasteful duplication. The search of literature also brings to light the state of knowledge of the subject. Obviously without the physical existence of the records in libraries, and without organized access to them provided by the bibliographical apparatus and the services of librarians, the research capability of a scientific discipline would be gravely impaired, if not completely obstructed.

Carrying out even the most humble research involves considerable sums of money. At the start of the process are the funding agencies, the contractors and consumers of research—government, public, private, and philanthropic—which have given vast sums to turn the wheels of our gigantic research machinery. Among them, the university occupies a special position because of its commitment to nonprofit-bearing fundamental research, aimed solely at broadening the theoretical base of a discipline. Government-sponsored research has assumed such proportions that publishing and marketing the scientific and technical report—literature amounting to hundreds of thousands of items—requires a special agency and a distinct bibliographical mechanism.

Obviously, the participation of contractors and consumers of research in the knowledge-producing and dissemination process is chiefly indirect. Nonetheless, they are vital components of the system and greatly influence bibliographic activities. It is noteworthy that in recent years a whole information edifice has sprung up to monitor both grant flow and funding.

In the next stage along the research path, the scientist must devise the instruments, tools, and operational methods to conduct experiments and gather data, or select among existing ones. In the social sciences, for example, a huge pool of processed survey data is available for researchers for secondary analysis, making their own data-gathering superfluous. Sociologists and economists may resort to the monumental compilations of macrodata, such as demographic and economic censuses. But existing instrumentation can also provide the researcher with applicable methodology and procedure, usually embodied in manuals and handbooks, or that supply the standardized terminology, nomenclature, and formulas contained in subject dictionaries. Today, researchers in many fields are largely relieved of the burden of toolmaking, a task taken over by an arm of the professional association, the government, or specialized publishers. What needs to be emphasized here is, first, that toolmaking is an important contributory element in the system, and second, that much of this instrumentation is a standard feature of reference collections in research libraries.

The university is the linchpin of the whole system. The department or school is the discipline's seat, marshaling activities around research, teaching, and service to the profession and community in that order. The university performs three key functions. The first involves the professional preparation of future practitioners in a discipline, and the granting of officially sanctioned credentials without which they could not practice. The second function is organizing and institutionalizing research within the university in specialized centers, institutes, and laboratories. Attracting large government and private grants, many universities have now become veritable knowledge factories. The third function is establishing channels of information dissemination.

The bibliographic implications of the academic enterprise are far-reaching. A large number of specialized journals and a huge body of scientific report literature emanate from university research centers, institutes, and disciplinary departments, along with a stream of program-related reference materials, such as catalogs, syllabi, course texts, brochures, and reading lists. An important vehicle for publishing activity is the university press, whose main business is to provide an outlet for the narrowly focused monographic literature growing out of Ph.D.-related research and for the academic writing of the faculty. Without the university press, the market would be very limited. Indicative of the scope of this publishing program are many monumental ongoing scholarly series spanning several decades and numbering in the hundreds of volumes. The school or department as organizer, and the university as a forum of regional, national, or international conferences, seminars, and symposia, with the university press as publisher of the papers and proceedings, all play their part in the bibliographic process. In fact, many academic departments have been serving as specialized bibliographic workshops, assuming the responsibility of producing a whole galaxy of key bibliographic tools.

Along with the production of new knowledge, the researcher's most important obligation is to communicate the findings and implications of the research. Beyond the informal contacts within the college circuit are the formalized instruments of communication: published reviews, articles, studies, essays, reports, conference papers, and monographs. The vehicles are journals, magazines, bulletins, newsletters, pamphlets, numbered series, Festschriften, and others, which together constitute the vast intellectual circulatory system that keeps a discipline alive. Concurrently, another circulatory mechanism carries the new ideas, the research results, and discoveries across the discipline's boundaries into the intellectual bloodstream of the larger society. The transmission is performed by the printed and electronic popular press, by the lay-level science magazines, and through the simplified interpretations of mass-produced nonfiction books and public lectures. At some point in the process, the new ideas and discoveries are incorporated in textbooks and are eventually restated and integrated into canonical knowledge and presented in subject encyclopedias, dictionaries, or handbooks. The time lag between a new discovery and its entry into the public domain of a record can be considerable, and much can obstruct the flow of information. Both phenomena are of serious concern for bibliography.

Finally, the professional organization occupies a pivotal place in the internal life of a scientific or scholarly discipline. Apart from acting as a social and political arm of organized practitioners, the professional association provides a forum, a sort of tribunal of peers to which new research is presented, debated, validated, or rejected. Scientific knowledge is a matter of consensus among practitioners, and the nature of scientific knowledge is such that judgments can seldom be considered final. The documented evidence of these activities is embodied in the association's official journal, its reports, the minutes of the plenary and committee sessions, its manifestos, and the annual reviews of the discipline's current literature. As the political arm of the profession, the association defines its position vis-à-vis other professions and government policies as well as its stand on public issues, especially with regard to funding policies, which may involve forming a lobbying force to influence legislation. The association also gives the discipline a social framework for group and individual interaction, with membership rosters, comprehensive or classified directories, and biographical dictionaries as their expressions in bibliographical terms. (The elements of scientific disciplines just discussed are shown graphically in Fig. 1-1.)

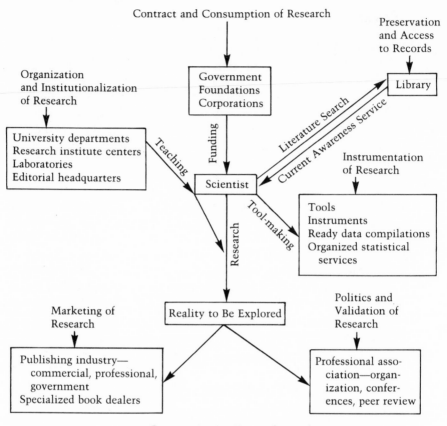

Figure 1-1. Scientific disciplines as knowledge-producing and disseminating systems.

Among the many other tasks a professional organization sets for itself, one is to see, most usually through an explicitly mandated committee, that practitioners in the field are adequately furnished with bibliographical accoutrements to ply their trade. As a matter of policy, extensive bibliographic publishing programs are maintained, with abstracting and indexing services constituting the main tributary in a vast system of commercial streams.[2]

Through the convergence of these various roles, the professional association may contribute to the emergence of a hierarchy within the profession, with the result that certain members are rewarded with research funding and job and consulting opportunities. A philosophically homogeneous group within the professional association can be elevated to office and implicit high scientific authority, thereby gaining influence over the intellectual and political orientation of a discipline, at least for a period, and ushering in a new paradigm. Such developments have implications for bibliography; they signal interest areas for research, with the emergence of previously obscure research nodes and scientists, and with anticipated growth of literature in those subjects.

In this model of scientific disciplines, research looms large as the central activity, but research cannot occur in isolation from forces that influence the execution of a research task. Bibliography, therefore, must view a discipline as a many-tiered system of linkages in which each productive and supportive action engenders corresponding effects in the discipline's literature and the information mechanism that provides access to it. The interrelations between research and bibliography become obvious when scientific disciplines are examined in an evolutionary matrix.

Scientific Discipline Patterns of Evolution

The natural sciences, the humanities, and the social sciences vary a great deal in origin, maturation processes, and final organization into full-fledged modern disciplines. But despite the diverse time points regarding the first widespread application of empirical, critical, and analytical methods to answer discrete questions or to solve specific problems, the history of the various scientific and scholarly domains suggests certain common characteristics. Disciplines go through several stages of development marked by certain characteristics in the epistemological orientation, methodological concerns, the social and organizational makeup, modes of communication, and the forms and quantity of literature produced. In an abstract model, these evolutionary periods can be designated somewhat arbitrarily as (1) the pioneering stage, (2) the elaboration and proliferation stage, and (3) the establishment stage.

The pioneering stage

The birth of many scientific disciplines can be traced to some great thinkers, or a pioneering intellectual who burst upon the

scene with original ideas, profound insights, startling propositions, or illuminating new theories. Today, a new scientific
movement is more likely to be initiated by dissident groups
branching off from the mainstream of an established discipline. It may remain identified with the parent organization,
operate in a subfield of it, or it may strike out on its own,
laying the foundations for a new discipline. In earlier times,
pamphleteering was the usual method of spreading new ideas;
today, every conceivable medium becomes involved—lectures, articles, interviews, books, conference and seminar
papers. At this stage, the struggle to attract attention and
followers may exceed any other effort.

Initially, the followers are known to one another and communicate informally in person, by letters, by telephone, or by
computer in college. But as followers multiply, they must
formally organize. To keep the band of followers together and
ensure ideological purity, the beginning discipline starts a bulletin or newsletter that eventually may grow into a full-sized
journal, serving as a rallying point for and mouthpiece of the
group. At first, the newsletter and the journal may be ignored
by indexing services, but later may be picked up by a "catch-
all" indexing tool. Expenses are covered by the founder if he
or she is independently wealthy, or by individual contributions, or by a public or private grant. To illustrate their inter-
relatedness more clearly, Table 1-1 summarizes the social and
epistemological events in the early life of a discipline, with its
corresponding bibliographic responses.

The elaboration
and proliferation stage

The transition from the pioneering stage to the elaboration
and proliferation stage may be blurred, and the speed of the
process may vary from discipline to discipline. Changes are
due primarily to growth and accumulations in all spheres.
The number of followers multiplies. Workers in the sprouting
discipline appear all over the world, forming national, regional, and international associations. Interaction among the
people in the field becomes structured and formalized through
meetings, conferences, and committees. They no longer all
know one another personally. There is now a need for international directories, biographical compilation, launching printed
proceedings, publishing minutes, annual reports on the activi-

Table 1-1 Phase I: The Pioneering Stage
(Struggle for Attention, Recognition, and Converts)

Events and Developments	Modes of Communication and Bibliographic Responses
1. The "great thinker," "prophet" emerges	1. Pamphleteering; individual contacts, letters, touring, lecturing; use of all accessible channels to communicate new ideas, discoveries; to champion new solutions to old problems
2. Group of dissidents branch off from mainstream of an established discipline	2. Special panels, satellite meetings at conferences of parent organization, minutes of meetings, manifestos, position papers, minority reports
3. Efforts to propagandize, persuade, convert	3. Polemical writings, abundance of fugitive materials: appeals, circulars, and so on
4. Small band of followers group together who know one another personally	4. Communication informal; personal correspondence; exchange of papers; invisible college
5. Efforts to keep in touch and maintain ideological cohesion	5. Bulletins, newsletters
6. Attempts to gain scientific legitimacy	6. Followers place articles in established journals, publish books, present papers at conferences and seminars
7. Financing through own effort, perhaps through philanthropy	7. Grant proposals, annual report to the sponsor

ties of the organizations and sessions of committees, and the studies of various constituent bodies.

Since more people now work in the subject area, there are more contributions to the literature. The growth of the literary output triggers chain reactions in several directions. Although earlier writings were mainly topical or problem-specific, now there is also excessive preoccupation with methodology. The one-unit subject matter of the discipline breaks into subfields, each spawning its own journals with increasingly narrow specialization. There may be so many of them that special indexing and abstracting services develop to cover them. Along with the journals, there is also such a luxuriant outcropping of monographic works that highly focused subject bibliographies are needed. With the many disparate contributions and the uncoordinated use of terminology, semantic confusion may arise, requiring a standard usage and nomenclature by means of approved dictionaries in the discipline.

By this time, the founder and the first generation of pioneers may have already left the scene, and the scientific and intellectual community may begin to recognize the significance of their contributions. Their celebration may find expression in Festschriften, publication of their memoirs, and perhaps their inclusion in a general encyclopedia. Also, the time may have come to establish the state-of-the-art, or perhaps synthesize the existing knowledge and accomplishments in an ambitious subject encyclopedia. Table 1-2 illustrates the workings of this stage.

The establishment stage

In this stage of its evolution, the discipline's collective energies are directed toward gaining scientific legitimacy, which paves the way to the university. The admission of the discipline to the university is the final evolutionary step because it symbolizes academic respectability. The discipline becomes part of the scientific establishment. Once in the university, the discipline is organized into an academic department, where entry, teaching, and educational qualifications are rigidly formalized, with highly structured curricula, requirements, and examinations. To ensure uniformity in coverage and transferability of credits, standards are formulated, and criteria for evaluating the educational program are laid down by accrediting agencies. Graduate training is introduced with theses and dissertations and related in-depth bibliographical explorations as end products.[3]

Table 1-2 Phase II: The Elaboration and Proliferation Stage (Struggle for Scientific Legitimacy and Acceptance)

Events and Developments	Modes of Communication and Bibliographic Responses
1. Followers multiply, spread all over the world	1. Membership roster, national directory, international directory
2. Practitioners of the discipline no longer all know one another personally	2. *Who's Who;* biographical directory
3. Interaction among the people in the field becomes structured and formalized	3. National association formed; committees, conferences, symposia, published proceedings, papers, reports, studies, yearbooks, official journal

Table 1-2 (cont.)

Events and Developments	Modes of Communication and Bibliographic Responses
4. Formal international organization established	4. Formal ties with UNESCO or other U.N. agency; *Yearbook of International Association* and conference; separate international journal; international subject periodicals directory
5. Subject matter becomes more and more complicated; discipline breaks up into subfields; preoccupation with methodology	5. New invisible colleges; new modes of research; separate journals with narrower focus
6. Concern for training of future practitioners	6. Standards or guides; textbooks, handbooks; proceedings and laboratory manuals
7. Total literary output very large; monographs proliferate	7. Book reviews multiply; guides to subject literature; collected works of most representative writing; classified bibliographies; global coverage
8. Attempts to bring out new monographic works in a systematic fashion	8. Publication series; monumental collection of related works
9. More journals; periodical and report literature expanded	9. Specialization in indexing and abstracting services
10. Privately or philanthropically sponsored; special research institutes established with own bibliographies; information centers; databanks	10. Institute's library catalog published in book form; guide to databanks; lists or annual books of the institute's publications
11. Terminology and nomenclature diversifies; semantic confusion ensues	11. Standardization of terms; glossaries; specific subject dictionaries
12. Time to survey field	12. Synthesis; standardization of article writing
13. Need to systematically evaluate new contributions and interject new research results and discoveries into body of accepted knowledge	13. Annual review of literature, regular library services
14. Codification of established knowledge achieved in discipline domain	14. Subject encyclopedias
15. Founder and pioneers generally have left scene; recognized by scientific and intellectual worlds	15. Memoirs, collected works by authors, biographies and encyclopedias, author bibliographies

Another major event marking this phase is the institutionalization of research in centers, laboratories, bureaus, and institutes, with professors holding joint appointments in the department and the center. Stratification within the discipline progresses. The strong departments lure the "stars," the nationally known experts who can attract contracts, get consulting assignments, and are often invited to testify before Congress in connection with pertinent legislative matters. Federal and state governments, foundations, and corporations move in to commission, sponsor, or stimulate research.

Sustained programs can relentlessly push back the frontiers of research, and in the wake of new explorations, more and more complex spheres of reality may open up for investigation. Reflecting this trend, the subject matter and methodology grow more intricate. The field may further subdivide, and each area could in turn spawn new branches, crossing over to and sometimes fusing with other fields.

With the proliferation of programs in the colleges and universities, the student market may look lucrative enough for some publishers to specialize and eventually monopolize discipline-related textbook, monograph, and reference publishing. Similar trends may take place in the channels of distribution both for new and old books. Secondhand book dealers often build fine stocks of retrospective, out-of-print, and rare materials to meet the needs of libraries and private collectors. The catalogs of such publishers and book dealers are cherished instruments of bibliographers and acquisitions and reference librarians. The bibliographic implications of the establishment stage, as the discipline moves into the university, is shown in Table 1-3.

The insights gained from this look at the historical evolution of scientific disciplines permit certain generalizations. First, the evidence shows an intrinsic connection among bibliography, the information apparatus, and a discipline's internal processes. For every major event and development in the structure, size, or orientation of a discipline, there appears to be a corresponding bibliographic response. Parallel with diversification in the life of the discipline is a comparable trend toward sophistication of the bibliographic apparatus. This trend is perhaps most apparent in the "content side" of bibliography, that is, information retrieval rather than in the inventory aspects of the field. The principle that seems to be at work here is that quantitative changes in the manifestations

Table 1-3 Phase III: The Establishment Stage
(Achievement of Academic Respectability)

Events and Developments	Modes of Communication and Bibliographic Responses
The discipline moves into the university.	
1. Autonomous departments organized.	1. Catalogs, bulletins, self-study documents.
2. Educational program, requirements, qualifications rigidly formalized.	2. Directories of programs, commercial and professional; standards of accrediting agencies; textbooks; reading lists.
3. Structured curricula developed.	3. Departmental bulletins, announcements, syllabi, reports.
4. Graduate and doctoral programs introduced.	4. Theses, dissertations, special indexes and abstracts.
5. Research institutionalized in centers, laboratories, institutes.	5. Databanks, data archives, research bulletins, and reports; bibliography of center's publications; research manuals; directories of research institutes; subject bibliography series put out by the center's or institute's library.
6. Stratification of the discipline, strong departments attracting "stars" who can bring research grants, get consulting assignments.	6. Specialized biographical directories, *Who Knows What*; directories of consultants.
7. Federal government contracts research.	7. Proposals; technical reports and research monographs published, announced, and marketed by federal government outlets; database on ongoing research; government abstracts and indexes; congressional hearings at which research scientists testify as experts; bibliographic guides to government publications.
8. Foundations, industry sponsored research.	8. Foundation directories.

of a discipline will cause qualitative changes in bibliography. For example, an excessive growth in research activity and literary output necessitates the construction of special thesauri to replace the crude subject organization of the literature by broad headings. Or the fusing of some disciplinary subfields brings in its wake the application of facet indexing in several major abstracting tools in the social sciences.

Second, the evolutionary patterns of scientific disciplines

reveal a direct relationship between the maturity level of a discipline and the sophistication level of bibliographic and reference tools. Accordingly, if we knew what stage a discipline has reached in its structural development, we could tell by extrapolation what kind of bibliographic and reference works it probably has at that point. And conversely, by reviewing its existing information apparatus, we can predict approximately how far the discipline has advanced in its evolutionary process.

Third, and most important, the models outlined above indicate recurring patterns and regularities that can lead to theoretical formulations. They tell us that bibliographic and reference works in printed or electronic format grow out of the specific information needs of a discipline. They are calibrated to various types and levels of research problems. With this insight, the jumble of bibliographies, guides, indexes, abstracts, databanks, catalogs, checklists, dictionaries, directories, encyclopedias, almanacs, and various data compilations in the library fit into a recognizable pattern. Once they are so recognized, the users can make some sense of it all and are aided in moving directly to the tools that are necessary to a specific area and level of research.

Emerging also from the evolutionary model is a panoramic view of the landscape, which shows how the specific species of the research and bibliographic literature come into being out of the many operations of the system. The rationale for their existence is shown by their role in the knowledge-producing and disseminating process. This rationale becomes obscured when a literary specimen is looked at in isolation. To understand the literature of a discipline, one must be able to conceptualize the vast and complex mechanism that has been pouring forth abundant varieties of intellectual goods in the name of the advancement of knowledge.

Developing collections of subject literatures for research and graduate education requires that all documentary and literary products emanating from the activities of each component of a discipline be brought together and organized in the library for use. This means all communication organs, reports, journals, monographs, texts, publications of academic departments, research centers, institutes, and university presses, proceedings of meetings and conferences, annual reviews, various reports of the regional, national, and international professional associations and bodies, documents of pertinent government agencies, publications that flow from the respective organs of international organizations, releases issued by funding agencies, and bibliographic instruments and reference tools in printed and electronic format. In a word, it means every important piece of record through which a discipline as a system manifests itself. All these products together constitute a "research collection" or "collecting in depth." The task of collecting in depth and organizing access to the collection commits the librarian to a discipline intellectually in the same manner as the practitioner, but in a different framework.

Conventional wisdom holds that the only way to ensure credibility for the librarian's intellectual commitment is to earn a master's degree in the particular discipline. Since graduate programs are designed to train entry level practitioners, the subject knowledge is only marginally relevant to librarianship, which is a professional practice in its own right. Librarians who are committed to subject disciplines, either as collection builders or information and instruction specialists, need a different kind of knowledge for the pursuit of their service and professional objectives.

The Topography
of Scientific Disciplines

Scientists and researchers are trained for practice involving analytical and diagnostic skills, the expert application of methodology, and the marshaling of resources for problem-solving and research. Their requisite knowledge of a discipline's subject matter, therefore, must be structural, intrinsic, deep-reaching, and anatomical.

But what kind of subject knowledge is relevant to the professional pursuit of the librarian's service and instructional objectives, working in the same disciplinary area? The answer becomes evident in the model shown in Fig. 1-2.

Investigation can be directed at four topical clusters, referred to as "dimensions" (Fig. 1-2). Each dimension relates to a specific aspect of a discipline. The first dimension is epistemological, pertaining to a discipline's key concern, the creation of knowledge, and it encompasses everything in conjunction with the subject matter, structure, scope, boundaries of the field, methodologies, instrumentation, and the nature

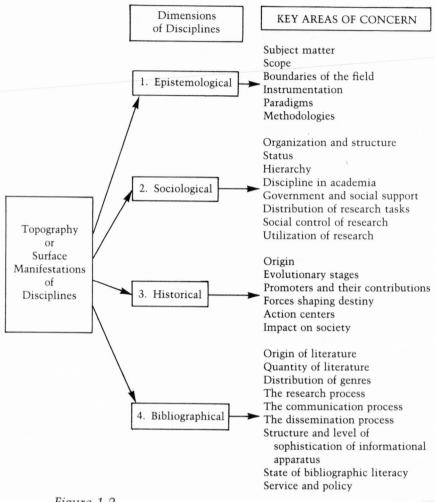

Figure 1-2.

of primary research resources. But the focal point of study is the paradigm, the central organizing force that sets the direction for the discipline's quest for knowledge. It can be probed by questions. For example, What are the core problems of the discipline at this particular point? What knowledge is needed? How can it be obtained? How can the norms and criteria for evaluating new knowledge products be selected?

The second dimension is sociological (Fig. 1-2), which centers attention on the discipline as a group and organizational phenomenon. Of particular interest are questions concerning institutionalization of the discipline, status and structure of the profession, professional organizations and their role, internal hierarchy of the discipline, its place in the academic world and among the professions, government and society support, distribution pattern of research tasks among universities and research centers, ethics of the profession, social and professional utilization of research, and, last but not least, politics of the profession.

The third dimension in Fig. 1-2—historical—grows out of the premise that in addition to being an organized intellectual force and a sociological phenomenon, a discipline is also a process that is set in motion at one point of history and then progressively moves toward maturation. Thus, disciplines have a life and chronological growth. The most relevant questions in the framework of the historical dimension would inquire into the origin of the discipline, where and under what circumstances it emerged, who were the promoters, what were their contributions, and what pressures and influences shaped its destiny throughout the ages. The maturation of a discipline raises questions as to whether it has reached the highest stage of evolution, where the "action centers" have come into being and why, what impact the discipline has exerted on society, and so on.

A primary area of concern under the fourth dimension in Fig. 1-2—bibliographical—is the research, communication, and knowledge dissemination process, together with the origin, quantity, and distribution of the subject literature by genre. The most critical aspect is the information apparatus; how it meets the discipline's needs, the structure and sophistication level of bibliographic access, the capabilities of reference tools, the state of bibliographic literacy, service and policy considerations on local, national, and international planes, to highlight only a few key issues. These are only samples of the numerous questions and topics involving inquiry into the four dimensions of disciplines.

On the whole, such questions are answered. Many of the topics highlighted here have been addressed and partially explored. Philosophers of science are keenly interested in the epistemological dimensions of scientific disciplines. Some of the problems surrounding the organization of disciplines have been dealt with in a subfield of sociology. Intellectual historians have been probing into the evolution, role, and social impact of science and scholarship. In all these cases, the scholars' and scientists' interests may coincide with those of librarians, but their vantage point, focus, and purpose differ a great deal.

The exploration of the bibliographical dimension is a special case and should be the natural task of library science, but writings are relatively scarce in the literature of library science from which to extract a cogent body of knowledge. What material does exist comes from a few original thinkers, some trained in other disciplines, or was generated in isolation at a few special conferences and symposia.[4] The treatment of bibliographic matters in library science literature is pervasively pragmatic and descriptive, giving a splendid account of the trees, but blind to the forest.

Only since the early 1970s has information science begun to examine bibliographical phenomena in a broad theoretical framework. Information science, as an emerging discipline with an undefined territory somewhere between library science, computer science, communication science, sociology, and mathematics, has made valuable contributions toward the analysis of bibliographical phenomena. But since it communicates in an often esoteric language and operates without a socially defined institutional base, its theoretical formulations cannot at present provide guidance for pragmatically oriented librarians.

Separate spheres of investigation—the epistemological, sociological, historical, and bibliographical dimensions of disciplines—point to the fact that there are two kinds of discipline-related knowledge. One bears on the depth, internality, and substance of the subject matter, which can be regarded as the "structural manifestations" of a discipline. This is the realm of the practicing scientist, scholar, and researcher. The other knowledge is not intrinsic to the substance; it consists of "surface" or "topographical manifestations." Topography is the domain of bibliography; no other discipline has staked a claim to it so far. The fact that topography is not central to the scientist's interest does not mean that it lacks its own dignity, unity, integrity, and even grandeur. Moreover, the study of the topography of disciplines can become the core of bibliography, once it is consciously embraced as being its own patrimony, giving its subject matter substance, depth, and internality. In a sweeping sense then, bibliography can be conceived as knowledge about knowledge, a metascience with a specific mission.

Historically, professional work in special libraries and in the field of documentation has focused on "content" much earlier than in academic, public, or school libraries. This early focus gave rise to information science in the United States and to informatics in Europe after it received a decisive impetus from emerging cybernetics.

Evidence shows, however, that information science has slipped into certain investigative areas belonging legitimately to library science, simply because these areas were left unattended. This has been mainly due to the generally technical orientation of library education. It is no credit to the discipline of library science that the bibliographic instruction movement is finding the intellectual terrain of librarianship practically devoid of appropriate theoretical and conceptual tools to guide it.

On another plane, it would not be unreasonable to make a case for the field of bibliography, as it is portrayed here, not only to reclaim "the occupied territories" from information science, but also to fuse the cognitive ingredients, theoretical and conceptual components, and intellectual concerns of the two divergent streams of the information profession, library science on the one hand and information science on the other, into the unitary discipline of bibliography, where they would all belong logically.[5]

To achieve its goals, bibliographic instruction must move into the curriculum on all levels of education, a task that requires close collaboration between librarians and faculty. Presently, this is often hindered by the inability of subject-expert faculty to understand what librarians can contribute to the educational process beyond procuring and managing the materials needed for instruction. Whenever a librarian demonstrates some disciplinary subject knowledge and wishes to contribute to the teaching of that subject, this is generally viewed by faculty as intrusion in a sovereign domain.

Obviously, the necessary collaboration between librarians and faculty ought to begin outside the library in the subject discipline itself by dividing the intellectual labors among themselves: the faculty concentrating on the "core" or "substance," and librarians focusing on the "topography" of the same field. The result will be a sense of true partnership. Then bibliographic instruction, that is, the conveying to faculty and students what bibliographic scholarship discovered and learned "about" the intricate processes in the topography of a discipline manifest in the records, literature, and information apparatus, will become a natural extension of this joint venture in the library.

What the library education establishment and the profession at large must clearly see is that to bring about this idyllic condition, we must not seek the solution in the acquisition of degrees in practice-oriented subject disciplines, but by preserving proudly our generalist posture, we should cultivate our own garden. To renounce this would be to admit to the world that apart from managerial and political concerns and manipulative techniques in information retrieval, library "science" has little intrinsic intellectual substance and that it must seek substance outside its own field. The first step in the right direction would be to give priority to this "third ingredient" of library science both in library education and research.

Notes

1. Michael Keresztesi, "Bibliographic Instruction in the 1980s and Beyond," in *Directions for the Decade: Librarianship in the 1980s*, ed. by Carolyn A. Kirkendall (Ann Arbor, Mich.: Pierian Press, 1981), pp. 41–49. Some of the formulations presented here were extracted from this paper.

2. A spot sampling revealed that six major bibliographic instruction tools in the fields of business and economics, three in physics, and one in political science were produced and serviced by professional agencies. See *Ulrich's International Periodicals Directory*, 20th ed. (New York: Bowker, 1981).

3. The extent of commitment of academic departments and related research centers to the production and maintenance of bibliographic services is evidenced by the fact that in business and economics, for example, seven major tools, as well as four in philosophy and political science, originated in university presses. These same patterns exist in most scholarly and scientific disciplines.

4. See B. Montgomery, ed., *The Foundations of Access to Knowledge: A Symposium*, Frontiers of Librarianship series, no. 8 (Syracuse, N.Y.: Syracuse University Press, 1968) and *Access to Literature of Social Science and Humanities*, Proceedings of Conference on Access to Knowledge and Information in Social Sciences and Humanities, New York City, April 5–6, 1972 (Flushing, N.Y.: Library Science Department, Queens College Press, 1974).

5. This concept is cognate with Jesse Shera's social epistemology, an idea expressed in "An Epistemological Foundation for Library Science," *Foundations of Access to Knowledge*, pp. 7–25.

2

The Idea of Evidence in Bibliographic Inquiry

JON LINDGREN

There is no single correct approach to the complex problem of defining a body of educational theory and implementing an accompanying methodology for the purpose of instructing library users. Similarly, librarians cannot agree on even basic nomenclature to describe efforts at bibliographic instruction. Therefore, we can expect to discover only partial solutions that will help to build a strong tradition of user instruction, and an increasing and maturing fund of knowledge upon which to draw. This chapter is a contribution to such a fund and does not claim the discovery of a panacea to solve our instructional ills.

Educational Theory

Topsy Smalley perceives that present library instruction tends to hinge on teaching "strictly technical skills," such as "the how-to of using *Readers' Guide* and other indexes."[1] In her 1977 article, she reacts against that state of affairs with an alternative: "An understanding of principles and methodology would set the intellectual structure within which we could begin to think about generating effective and creative instructional programs."[2] Although these few words do little justice to the depth of Smalley's analysis, they nevertheless shift our attention from teaching students the mechanics of library use to the teaching of "a conceptual framework of principles."[3]

Having made this shift, we can recognize that certain educators have laid down some basic educational theory that has been almost universally endorsed. Probably the oldest concept in the entire history of education is one that gained widespread prominence early in this century in the progressive education theories of John Dewey. According to this theory, learning should be an active process requiring engagement with the material or information at hand. Commonplace as it is, this idea forms one of the cornerstones of my thesis on teaching bibliographic theory, for the more we can integrate the research process with the subject material and its uses, the more substantial and durable our instruction is likely to be.

Another, less obvious cornerstone derives from an observation by Patricia Knapp in her seminal work on the Monteith College Library Project at Wayne State University. Knapp observed that "they [students] have a basic misconception of the function of information inquiry, that is, they look for and expect to find 'the answer to the question' instead of evidence to be examined."[4] Knapp's comment still rings true: Students come to the library to research a topic and locate enough source materials that they can use to write a paper of appropriate length. The more general the topic, the more readily at hand is the requisite quantity of resource material. Consequently, many students seem to succeed rather well academically without any instruction in proper use of the library.

Even when the topic is narrowly defined and faculty have placed demands for a high caliber of resources in the bibliography, the straightforward suggestion of useful subject headings, indexes, and a bibliography or two normally suffice to lead students to an abundance of resources. So why not merely write a prescription for each student that includes subject headings, indexes, and bibliographies appropriate to his or her topic? This reference advice would be easier to deliver than our present teaching, and if diligently acted on by students (an area we do not much consider our business), it should greatly improve the undergraduate library research carried out on our campuses. The teaching faculty could only applaud that result.

Understandably, faculty are not as a rule sensitive to the need for bibliographic instruction beyond the mechanical prescriptive approach mentioned above. They may disparage the work they are receiving from students, but they are more likely to find fault with the quality of student prose than with either the conception of topic or the suitability of bibliographic entries. A study of the educational literature of various disciplines only occasionally reveals a concern for improving research assignments, let alone the teaching of comprehensive strategies of library research. Largely as a result of the faculty's concerted focus on the subject content (as opposed to the processes of undergraduate scholarship), many students regard the research project as a somewhat artificial enterprise—one that requires stolid perseverance in gathering information above active intellectual pursuit.

Bibliographic instruction theory

The academic library contains a reference apparatus that enables much better handling of information sources than students commonly use, and it is the functioning of that apparatus in the process of intellectual inquiry that provides a theoretical foundation for library instruction. If we agree with Dewey on the futility of passive methods of learning, with Knapp on the ineffectiveness of the "find-the-answer" approach to library research, and with Smalley on the shortcomings of teaching technical skills, we can find a workable alternative in Knapp's concept of teaching the library as "evidence to be examined." In so doing, the intellectual structure of our teaching is placed on a solid functional base, one that is highly integral with the uses of information. So, the reference apparatus, that is, sources for overview, synthesis, access, and evaluation, are invaluable aids in handling information, but teaching the specific functions of this apparatus in consulting the human record has been more or less neglected. As a result, we have not progressed very far toward understanding how one can "learn how to learn" in the library. This lack hinders our best efforts to build collections, improve bibliographic control, and increase the means of access to information.

Librarians who teach the use of the library must investigate, develop, and disseminate ways in which reference and information access resources interrelate with intellectual, and not mechanical, processes of library research. In so doing, we will come to see that the theoretical foundations for our teaching and the contents of our teaching are one and the same. Although Smalley suggests that the theoretical foundation should be formed on the "basic precepts of librarianship, precepts of which we are informed,"[5] I must disagree. Rather, we must concentrate on uniting the *processes* of gathering information with the *uses* of that information. It is this dialectic that we should attempt to communicate to our students. To pervert Marshall McLuhan's maxim slightly, our medium should be our message. How we teach becomes what we teach.

Nearly every statement of the goals of education will emphasize that education is not strictly the learning of a body of information; equally important is the mastery of approaches to knowledge and the way knowledge is used. Such statements often emphasize the transitory state of current knowledge and the need to continue education after formal academic training. The subject-oriented disciplines respond to that challenge by teaching their own particular methods of disciplined inquiry. This organizing principle has been especially important even in the last couple of decades, during which traditional lines of demarcation between subject fields have eroded as a result of the growth of interdisciplinary fields and area studies.

Beyond the introduction of methodology courses into the curriculum, there has been little recognition of the importance of an even more fundamental level at which methodology can and should be approached. In conducting library research, the professional scholar's focus remains on the subject content and on acquiring comprehensive information on a topic. If students base their approach to research on that model, they will be poorly prepared to conduct reasoned inquiry on the limited scale of the beginner because they will likely become captive to the notion that intellectual rigor somehow equates with the compilation of more and more information about smaller and smaller topics.

That this is a prevailing mode of student thinking about library research can be easily illustrated. Students have little difficulty with the idea of topic size and its relation to library materials. Too large a topic means too many resources to contend with; too narrow a topic results in lack of resources. But there are problems with the concept of *shaping* a topic and using library reference resources in topic selection. Knapp's call for teaching library resources as "evidence to be examined" suggests the key idea behind shaping a topic.

The Idea of Evidence

The mere notion of "evidence" implies the underlying existence of a question or argument that forms the basis of the research inquiry. Indeed, students sometimes are taught to frame their research proposal around a series of questions to be answered. As Knapp points out, however, students should not focus so much on getting "the answer to the question" as on the evidence to be examined. In other words, "shape" in a research proposal lies not with the specific question or even list of questions to be addressed, but with the concept of argument (or thesis, in the liberal sense of the word). Without this perspective, the student too often remains a passive collector of information, no matter how sophisticated and detailed the sources or how artfully they are assembled. Such an assemblage of information may serve to inform the student on subject content beyond the classroom and the assigned readings, but it lacks the sense of intellectual engagement with the material. A tradition of our culture is that "truth" is not permanent, static, impersonal, and objective; rather it emerges from the dialectic of argument. The active use of library resources, especially reference resources, must be understood in the context of their contribution to the ongoing dialogue.

Argumentation is only one of the four traditional forms of discourse—the others being exposition, narration, and description. But, since narrative or descriptive writing is seldom appropriate to research writing, the research paper normally uses the argumentative or expository mode, or some combination of the two. Students typically assume that a library research paper forestalls argument in favor of exposition, and this assumption leads them to produce papers that are characteristically bland, shapeless, amenable to plagiarism, and lacking the stamp of a caring, engaged intellect.

Although the argumentative form is not itself a be-all and an end-all in the research process, it can be a useful corrective to the prevailing expository mode for beginning researchers.

Later, as students gain experience with the forms of argument, that corrective can be tempered toward the subtleties of shaping a vigorous and original thesis. According to one popular authority on writing, Sheridan Baker, all good writing possesses an "argumentative edge."[6] Most student research papers do not.

Models for Teaching Library Resources

Some concrete examples of the ways in which library resources can be taught as part of the process of identifying, shaping, and resolving disputed questions or arguments are shown in the following models (further examples in Appendix, pp. 41–46).

Overview sources

The first order of business in finding an appropriate topic for a research paper is to look for evidence of significant disputes, and this initial step points up the need for overview on a topic. Faculty in their academic research presumably originate the theses of their research writings on the basis of broad experience and training in a subject field. This background knowledge most often obviates the need for any kind of overview on a topic; thus the process by which an advanced scholar frames a research question is by and large an inductive one. Students, on the other hand, often lack a sense of how their topics of inquiry have been approached in the past. They have difficulty discriminating between important questions and less important ones. Faculty do not usually perceive that this is so, and thus scarcely understand the potential usefulness of overview sources to student researchers.

For instance, the typical student lacks knowledge about the various abstract concepts within which a topic is embedded. A student doing research on a topic such as "modern religious cults" may possess little background understanding of the concept of religious freedom (either historical or philosophical), may not understand the relationship between society and deviant group behavior, and may have little sense of the legal role of government in protecting minors who may be victims of certain religious cults. Yet, need for this kind of background dealing with abstractions relevant to the topic (religious freedom, group deviance, government as protector) can begin to be satisfied somewhat with reference resources such as specialized encyclopedias for the humanities or social science, for example, *The Dictionary of the History of Ideas*. Students can be instructed in ways of seeking this kind of overview, but the important educational principle is making the connection between the subject matter and the function of the reference resource.

The more traditional concrete (as opposed to abstract) type of overview is also important. A student researcher is normally tempted to use the first resources (usually books) located on a topic, but a research project is usually better begun by establishing an initial "overview" perspective on the topic at hand. "Overview" is, of course, a relative concept, for it is possible to gain an overview of a narrow, specialized subject as well as a broad one. Furthermore, different sources of overview can function in complementary ways. They can, for example, summarize historical background, survey various disciplined approaches to the topic, synthesize previous researchers' findings, evaluate current developments or trends of thought, set forth basic concepts and nomenclature, expose interdisciplinary connections, and identify standard or "classic" documents or statements on the topic. The range of possibilities for gaining different kinds of overview on any given topic is, therefore, practically limitless. At the end of this chapter is a listing of overview sources with some specific examples.

Having located sources for overview on a topic, how can a student then be taught to find specific disputed questions or arguments that pertain to a general topic? The answer lies in searching for evidence. For example, in a single column from the *New York Times Index 1980*,[7] under the heading "Education and Schools—United States," one may find, in addition to a current overview of U.S. education, 10 or more disputed questions. The material below shows the actual wording of the one column in the *Index*.

Article on growing use of computers and computer programs in grade-school classrooms to engage students' analytical faculties; illustration (Winter Survey of Education) (M), Ja 6,XIII.10:5

Article on Washington Watch, program established by 2 Washington area schools and National Network of Complementary Schools, nonprofit organization supported by 27 private and public high schools; network, only such program in nation, is creation of administrators from Phillips Academy in Andover, Mass, and Beverly Hills High School in Calif; was organized in '74 for students whose interests go beyond programs at their own schools; average time spent at a host school is 6 weeks (Winter Survey of Education) (M), Ja 6,XIII,10:5

•Various studies show that after decade of public skepticism, it has become clear that compensatory education programs such as Project Head Start help children perform more effectively in school and in later life; illustration (Winter Survey of Education) (L), Ja 6,XIII,13:1

•Article by Rosalie S Lawrence, who teaches third grade in Pleasantville, NY, asserts teachers today need to borrow techniques of show biz to gain and keep students' attention, observing that students, as preschoolers, 'were spoon-fed a highly saturated electronic diet of color, music and accelerated action;' cartoon (Winter Survey of Education) (M), Ja 6,XIII,23:3

Article by Samuel J Gulino, who is principal of Green Fields Elementary School in Commack, NY, discusses 'back to basics' movement in education; drawing (M), Ja 6,XXI,14:3

Edward B Fiske discusses issue of social scientists' role in shaping of policy in US education; cites impact and views of University of Chicago sociologist Dr James S Coleman (L), Ja 8,III,1:1

•Fred M Hechinger discusses Edward B Jenkinson book 'Censors in the Classroom: The Mind Benders,' analysis of rise of censorship in school libraries (M), Ja 8,III,4:1

Education Secretary Shirley M Hufstedler appoints Richard Beattie as transition chief; gives education lobbyists progress report amid some complaints that she has moved too slowly to fill key posts in her dept; has until May 29 before $14 billion Education Dept must legally come into existence; says she wants to beat deadline and is aiming for date in early April; presides at swearing in of William L Smith as 24th and last US Education Commissioner, post that will be abolished in new dept; Hufstedler portrait (S), Ja 10,20:1

ABC Video Enterprises vice pres Herbert A Granath says company will produce educational programming on video cassettes or disks for National Education Association (S), Ja 13,49:1

•J Harrison Marson, Dean of Student Affairs at Union College and new president of Middle States Assn of Colleges and Secondary Schools, discusses question of Federal and state intervention into arena of assessment of quality education; portrait (M), Ja 13,XI,6:5

Analysis of how NJ's Congressional delegation voted on key issues in '79 shows that on Carter Administration bill to create Cabinet-level Education Department, delegation voted 9 to 4 in favor, with 2 absent (S), Ja 13,XI,9:5; comment on how Connecticut's Congressional delegation voted on Pres Carter's bill to establish Cabinet-level Dept of Education (S), Ja 20,XXIII,11:1

Letter opposes making Martin Luther King Jr's birthday school holiday (S), Ja 21,22:4

•Study by Center for Study of Responsive Law, Ralph Nader organization, explores growing presence and role of business corporations in classroom; observes that as school budgets strain to keep up with shrinking resources and expanding educational demands, Amer corporations find they can plan increasing role in bridging gap—while at same time instilling product-recognition in young students; not all of efforts are self-serving; Burger King has developed highly acclaimed teaching kit on fire safety that is devoid of any company sales pitch other than small logo identifying sponsor; similarly, Singer, IBM, Milton Bradley and Xerox, among other companies, widely distribute free math and vocabulary teaching kits, games and posters unmarked by any commercial message; illustration (M), Ja 23,III,1:4

*16 leaders of Christian evangelical wing urge passage of school-prayer bill under study by HR Judiciary Committee; evangelical preachers include Jim Bakker, Jerry Falwell, James Robison and Pat Robertson, who reach millions of Americans through their TV ministries and who say they will encourage their viewers to write to their Congressmen (S), Ja 24,II,10:5

President Carter proposes to increase spending for social and urban programs, including limited expansion of Head Start program (S), Ja 29,II,11:5

*Article discusses potentialities of television as tool to help children to read (M), F 2,14:5

Fred M Hechinger discusses debate between advocates and opponents of corporal punishment in schools (M), F 5,III,1:5

*US Education Secretary Shirley Hufstedler says she is suspicious of literacy tests given in some states to guarantee that public school students can read and write (S), F 10,19:1

School administrators, teachers and counselors around US have initiated specific programs designed to help students whose parents have divorced, as increasing number of youngsters are forced to face up to their parents' failed marriages; in some schools counselors or school psychologists work with children individually; in others, administrations have hired specialists to help sensitize faculty and staff members to needs of children (M), F 19,III,1:1

*Lawrence (NY) Schools Supt Dr Lawrence Roder article contends that it is insufficient to teach today's young people only the basic skills of reading, writing and arithmetic; warns that US population is not being educated and challenged in critical areas of higher reasoning: seeking relevant information, asking questions, analyzing, evaluating and making rational judgments (M), Mr 2,XXI,16:1

*Teaching of 'values,' which became popular several years ago in wake of moral unrest surrounding Vietnam and Watergate, is still making slow but steady inroads into American elementary and secondary schools; hundreds of teachers a year take courses at Harvard Univ and Carnegie-Mellon Univ and elsewhere in values education, and Edwin Fenton of Carnegie-Mellon, leading proponent of trend, estimates that as many as 10,000 American teachers have attended at least a 1-day workshop on topics such as . . .

The asterisks (not part of the actual *Index*) indicate 10 of the disputed questions that are entirely suitable as topics (listed below) for a research paper.

Public skepticism of compensatory education programs vs. positive results shown by various research studies.

Should teachers become entertainers in order to motivate students to learn?

Problem of censorship in school libraries.

Should assessment of quality (of) education fall under jurisdiction of federal and state governments or remain under traditional authority of accreditation agencies such as the Middle States Association of Colleges and Secondary Schools?

Should school systems offset financial strains by encouraging business corporations to supply free classroom instructional materials, with or without commercial message?

School prayer issue.

Use of television as tool to help children read.

Question of validity of use of literacy tests by the states to guarantee that public school students can read and write.

Insufficiency of back-to-basics skills movement.

Teaching of values movement in the public schools.

The disputed question approach to topic shaping holds obvious possibilities for social science research. Although many partisan sides can agree that a particular problem exists, the projecting of potential solutions yields divergent points of view and conflicting interpretations of evidence. Similarly, the humanities are amenable to the argumentation approach, and a reference source such as *Contemporary Literary Criticism*, which is a survey of current research on writers, reveals an overview of the mainstream of critical opinion about a writer's work, or conflicting critical views on specific matters of literary analysis.

Beyond the approaches to overview and the kind of disputed questions they are shown to reveal, students can be instructed in the use of other kinds of library resources to provide evidence of viable argumentative topics. For example, congressional committee hearings, reports, and prints address disputed questions with an eye toward decision-making. Should we scrap the MX missile? Should we institute national health insurance? Should we allow the development of ski areas on public lands? These and hundreds of other examples readily available in congressional documents show the dialectical method of dispute, with all the kinds of supporting evidence that are used in any reasoning process: expert authorities, survey research, case studies, and empirical research, along with rhetorical skills. Students who are instructed in the techniques of using library resources to locate argumentative topics will at least have multiple opportunities to become intellectually involved in resolving an argument. As that begins to occur, the differentiation of appropriate resource materials from inappropriate ones is more likely to lend purpose to a research project, leading to the greater likelihood that a student will achieve a unique synthesis of those resources.

Using abstracts and reviews

With periodical literature, students can be instructed in using abstracts to scan a topic's literature as it pertains to a disputed question. Again, the use of these reference resources is not initially oriented toward the accumulation of information on a topic. It focuses instead on the rapid survey of the intellectual uses of the information. The emphasis is on the efficiency of abstracts to reveal evidence on various sides of a question, exposing methods of disciplined inquiry, discovering counterarguments, identifying other researchers on the topic, and, in general, creating awareness of the dialectic by which knowledge advances in the scholarly disciplines. After working with abstracts in some depth, a student can look back over the research process and see how even a current article from *Woman's Day* may have its roots in the published scholarship.

Somewhat a counterpart to the use of abstracts for approaching the periodical literature is the use of book reviews to survey the monographic literature. Combined retrospective indexes, citation indexing, improved Wilson indexes, and various specialized abstracts such as *America: History & Life* and *Religion Index One: Periodicals* have enhanced access to scholarly book reviews during the past decade. Students need to be taught not only the means of access to book reviews, but the unique contribution to the handling of evidence on a disputed question that book reviews can make. For example, reviews usually will quickly reveal the strengths and weaknesses of a book's presentation, how it compares with other works, and the methodology used. Obviously, since book reviews are evaluative, that concept of evaluation of resources can lead to the learning of other techniques of evaluation, including the recently developed kind of evidence supplied by citation indexing, use of annotated bibliographies, and biographical details that can provide evidence of an author's credentials.

Subject access

A traditional problem area in user instruction is the teaching of effective use of the subject catalog. The usual approach is to teach a sequence of technical skills that are largely mechanical and are unrelated to the intellectual processes of gathering evidence. Yet, there are possibilities for relating this process to the search for evidence.

Students can be instructed first in the process of identifying "elements" of a topic. For example, if a student is shaping a topic around the disputed question of whether the federal government should adopt stricter regulatory measures in controlling the violence shown on television because of the likely pernicious effects on children, the student may be taught to identify four primary elements pertaining to the topic: (1) goverment regulation, (2) television, (3) violence, and (4) children.

From the *Library of Congress Subject Headings*, the student can then derive lists of potentially useful headings, one for each element of the topic (see Table 2-1).

The student can then be taught to rearrange the headings in a hierarchical order, from specific to general, in order to efficiently exploit the subject catalog. The list of headings can provide an equally useful basis for consulting a variety of indexes.

The principles of subject access that can be taught in this way include the following:

1. Subject headings access to information in books is limited since headings describe the whole book or its major contents. Therefore, although the most specific headings should yield the greatest quantity of pertinent information, more general headings may also lead to sources with useful information.

2. Considerable depth and originality of thinking can be aroused in a research investigation by bringing the information pursuant to one element to bear on another. In the above example, an understanding of the development of the moral sense in children should spark some original insights regarding the influence on children of televised violence. (This kind of integration of learning from disparate avenues of inquiry is the sort that research assignments are intended most to foster.)

3. The syndetic nature of the subject catalog enables a "pyramiding" of potentially useful points of access to information. This should help the student to gain a sense of the dimensions of a topic, some of its nomenclature, and its relationships with other affiliated lines of inquiry.

The goal of this approach to subject access, then, is focused, not on an attempt to explain the card catalog, but instead on

Table 2-1 Elements of a Topic: From LC Subject Headings

Government Regulation	Television	Violence	Children
Administrative agencies	Television	Violence	Child development
Administrative agencies—Rules and practice	Television broadcasting	Aggressiveness (psychology)	Child psychology
Independent regulatory commissions	Television—Law and legislation	Violence research	Aggressiveness in children
U.S. Federal Communications Commission—Rules and practice	Television—Psychological aspects	Violence in art	Imitation in children
Administrative law	Television and children	Violence in television	Moral development
	Television programs for children	Violence in mass media	Socialization
	Mass media and children	Hostility (psychology)	
	Television audiences		
	Television broadcasting—Social aspects		
	Television industry		
	Television broadcasting of news		
	Television programs		
	Documentary television programs		
	Mass media censorship		
	Mass media—Moral and religious aspects		
	Mass media—Psychological aspects		
	Mass media—Social aspects		
	Mass media and children		

the intellectual analysis of a topic and the use of the subject catalog to explore the evidence from available materials. A topic that does not yield several elements is probably too broad an undertaking, lacking in texture and shape.

Of course, not all undergraduate library use centers on the task of writing a research paper. Indeed, one of the goals of library instruction ought to be the blurring of the distinction between research and nonresearch writing. Libraries obviously contain information pertinent to intellectual pursuits of shorter range, for example, the verification or denial of factual premises and the evaluation of evidence. These are the types and scopes of library research activities that are particularly appropriate to assignment-related user instruction.

Suppose, for example, that a student reads in a *Washington Post* editorial that:

> *[gasoline] conservation laws don't work unless they are reinforced by rising prices. When the price of gasoline rose in 1974, gasoline consumption fell. Then, for four years, the price of gasoline in real terms, adjusted for inflation, steadily fell and consumption rose sharply again. When the price suddenly began to rise again in 1979, fuel consumption again dropped.*[8]

Various sources of statistical access could enable a student to assess the argument very well. These sources could include, for example, *American Statistics Index; Statistical Abstract of the United States;* U.S. Federal Highway Administration, *Highway Statistics; World Almanac;* and *MVMA Motor Vehicle Facts & Figures.* As a result of analyzing the *Washington Post* argument, the student would find that the available data do not support the argument as convincingly as the writer would have one believe; indeed, the data is ambiguous and points up the complexity of the argument.

Conclusion

This chapter attempts to blend some theoretical principles regarding the instruction of library users with enough concrete examples, suggestive of some possible applications of those principles, to show that the theory has not totally departed from the real world.

The proposed theory subordinates the teaching of the library as a system of mechanical functions in favor of teaching a more organic concept of the library as a functional organ of communication. Librarians who teach (along with everyone else) have persisted too long in taking a rather literal-minded, therefore limited, approach to library use, along the traditional lines of question/response. By viewing library research as a quest for evidence to be examined, we can do greater justice to the research process. The necessary corrective lies in attempting to find new ways to engage library users with the functions of the various components of the library reference apparatus as they enhance and support the research process. This approach is typified nowhere more clearly than in the discussion of topic selection and shaping, which process, it would seem, can constitute nearly half the work of executing a library research project.

The principles suggested here rest firmly within the tradition of integrated library instruction, which has been developing for some time. Although little or nothing has been discussed here regarding the specific techniques of instruction, it seems that the ideal teaching format is one that follows a brief presentation of concepts or principles with lengthy workshop experience. In this way, the need for students to explore the mechanics of library use can be adequately met.

Appendix

Because of the diversity of types, the range of possibilities for gaining different kinds of overview on a topic is practically limitless, and with imaginative use of the library a rich variety of sources is available. The following list of overview sources only suggests a tentative structure in which those possibilities may be arranged, with specific examples to arouse the imagination.

General summaries

Encyclopedias. General encyclopedias, such as the U.S.-published *Encyclopaedia Britannica, Encyclopedia Americana,* and *Academic American Encyclopedia,* are the most obvious sources of overview on a given topic, and they usually provide brief, highly selective bibliographies as well. Also available are the other national general encyclopedias, for example, *Great Soviet Encyclopedia, Chamber's Encyclopedia*

(Great Britain), and *Larousse* (French), with their particular national/geographic emphases.

Specialized encyclopedias cover nearly every subject area, usually in more depth than general encyclopedias, yet sometimes with broad interdisciplinary coverage, for example, *International Encyclopedia of the Social Sciences* (17 vols.) and *McGraw-Hill Encyclopedia of Science and Technology* (15 vols.). More often, coverage is narrower, as with the following:

> *Encyclopedia of American Economic History* (3 vols.)
>
> *International Encyclopedia of Psychiatry, Psychology, Psychoanalysis, and Neurology* (12 vols.)
>
> *Encyclopedia of American Foreign Policy* (3 vols.)
>
> *Encyclopedia of Chemistry* (1 vol.)
>
> *Grzimek's Animal Life Encyclopedia* (12 vols.)
>
> *Enciclopedia dello Spettacolo* (Theater and Stagecraft, 10 vols.)
>
> *International Encyclopedia of Higher Education* (10 vols.)
>
> *Twentieth Century* (20 vols.)

This listing only touches the surface of specialized encyclopedias typically available in an academic library.

Abstract Concepts. A library researcher may easily overlook possible sources of the various intangible elements pertaining to a topic. Most specialized encyclopedias of the type listed above provide some coverage of abstractions, such as "imperialism," "evolution," "laissez-faire," "alienation," and "realism"; yet, certain other sources are especially prominent for their depth of discussion of the invisible world of ideas, such as the following:

> *The Great Ideas: A Syntopicon of Great Books of the Western World* (2 vols.)
>
> *The Encyclopedia of Philosophy* (8 vols.)
>
> *Encyclopedia of Religion and Ethics* (13 vols.)
>
> *Dictionary of the History of Ideas: Studies of Selected Pivotal Ideas* (5 vols.)
>
> *The Annals of America: Great Issues in American Life: A Conspectus* (2 vols.)
>
> *Illustrated Encyclopedia of Mankind* (esp. vols. 16–20)

Historical Background. The development of virtually any area of human inquiry has been documented by historical accounts. In addition to·the encyclopedias above, likely sources of historical background are general histories (of varying relative scope), chapters from books, and articles. Examples:

Topic	Source
1. U.S. labor	Reedy, *Brief History of the American Labor Movement*
2. Roman comedy	Berthold, *A History of the World Theater*, pp. 170–209

Current Developments. Yearbooks most often provide updated information on a variety of topics. Some yearbooks are adjunct publications of encyclopedias, for example, *American Annual, McGraw-Hill Yearbook of Science and Technology,* but many are not, and some of these are quite narrow in their subject focus. The following are examples of the many possibilities.

Topic	Source
1. U.N. involvement with Palestinian question in the Middle East	*1976 U.N. Yearbook,* pp. 228–248
2. World oil market	*Yearbook of World Affairs, 1978,* pp. 76–92
3. Public broadcasting	*Editorial Research Reports,* 1981, vol. 1, pp. 309–328

Almanacs of the general variety (for example, *World Almanac*) are well-known sources of specific data, but they can also yield overview information in the form of summaries of current social and political developments, and also comparative data covering a period of years. A few specialized almanacs, such as the *Canadian Almanac, Congressional Quarterly Almanac,* and the *Almanac of American Politics,* provide their own special kinds of overview. *News summaries* of various types are available for a variety of purposes, for example:

Topic	Source
1. Abortion issues	*New York Times Index* (brief summaries of articles on a topic)

Topic	Source
2. Political developments	*Keesing's Contemporary Archive*
3. Congressional ethics	*Congressional Quarterly Weekly Reports*
4. Environmental issues	*Environment Reporter*

Recent periodical articles of a general nature can be useful sources of current information on a topic, for example:

Topic	Source
1. Future of coal as energy source	*Scientific American*, January 1979
2. Current technology in the field of medicine	*New York Times Magazine*, August 5, 1979
3. Solar energy	*New Yorker*, April 23, 1979 and April 30, 1979 issues

Reviews of research

Obviously, the "general summary" sources mentioned above can often be expected to refer to both past and current published findings of researchers. Nevertheless, several kinds of library resources point more precisely in that direction. *Bibliographies* will normally yield insights into the way a field is organized and the thrust of previous research. *Annotated bibliographies* and *bibliographic essays* accomplish even more for the beginning researcher by putting past research into perspective and, in many instances, by evaluating the importance of individual works. *Annual reviews* perform the same function on a periodic basis. Following are some examples:

Topic	Source
1. Universalism/Unitarianism	*Religion in American Life:* Vol. IV, *Critical Bibliography of Religion in America*
2. Response of critics to the works of Anthony Burgess	*Contemporary Literary Criticism*, Vols. 1, 2, 4, 5, 8, 10, 13, and 15
3. Effects of urban population density	*Annual Review of Sociology*, Vol. 4

Book reviews of important works on a given topic may constitute a uniquely important introductory framework for a given research area, both by providing useful comparisons with other work on the topic and by exerting evaluative judgment. In addition, contending interpretations by author and reviewer very often will quickly unfold important and substantive questions suggestive of possibilities for narrowing and focusing a research paper topic. Following is an example:

Topic	Source
Higher education in the United States	*Book Review Digest* (latest edition, subject index under "Colleges and Universities" and "Education, Higher")

Abstracts of research studies are published in many, if not most, fields of study, and they are usually organized by topic. Despite its being a fairly random approach to the secondary literature of a field, browsing through abstracts can provide an overview sense of current research trends as well as brief summaries of specific published research studies. This approach to surveying periodical articles is roughly equivalent to (although more efficient than) browsing for book resources in the stacks.

Miscellaneous sources that
yield their own "gestalt"

Just as a picture is sometimes worth several hundred words, the engaged intellect can often assimilate a complex of information into an overview pattern, giving rise to questions that arrest the attention. *Statistical publications* such as the *Statistical Abstract of the United States* contain raw data from which may emerge generalized patterns that are half-perceived, half-created in the inquiring mind. Example:

Topic	Source
U.S. petroleum production, imports, and consumption during the past 60 years	*Historical Statistics of the U.S.* (Bicentennial Edition), p. 593

Atlases, which convey multitudinous information visually, also convey impressions that can lead to endless further analysis. Atlases with specialized subject focus relate to almost any aspect of social, economic, and political activity. On the following page is an example.

Topic	Source
Religious congregations during the American Revolution	*Atlas of Early American History*, pp. 36–39 or *Historical Atlas of Religion in America*

Chronologies of past events are useful for communicating a general sense of the flow of important activity—political, social, artistic, economic, scientific, and so on—taking place in a given time period or geographic location. Example:

Topic	Source
Romantic period in literature	*Timetables of History* or *Annals of English Literature* or *People's Chronology*

Indexes serve the primary purpose of locating information precisely, but a secondary use may be to suggest patterns of development. For example, *The Monthly Catalog of U.S. Government Publications* serves as an index to government documents, but a perusal of the index illustrates in an inimitable way the priorities of the American national government. For another, one can gain a feeling for the spirit of the times (for example, a particular decade) by scanning the entries found in the *New York Times Index* for those years.

Notes

1. Topsy N. Smalley, "Bibliographic Instruction in Academic Libraries: Questioning Some Assumptions," *Journal of Academic Librarianship* 3 (November 1977): 282.
2. Ibid.
3. Ibid., p. 283.
4. Patricia B. Knapp, *The Monteith College Library Experiment* (New York: Scarecrow, 1966), p. 283.
5. Smalley, "Bibliographic Instruction," p. 282.
6. Sheridan Baker, *The Complete Stylist and Handbook*, 2nd ed. (New York: Harper, 1980), pp. 6–8.
7. © 1980 by the New York Times Company. Reprinted by permission.
8. *Washington Post*, January 13, 1981, p. A-14.

3
Do Metaphors Make Good Sense in Teaching Research Strategy?

RAYMOND McINNIS

There is no reason why librarianship as a scientific discipline cannot build its own theory, based on . . . metaphorical models.[1]

By converting ideas, products of the mind (mentifacts), into material objects "out-there," we give them relative permanence, and in that permanent material form we can subject them to technical operations which are beyond the capacity of the mind acting by itself.[2]

We are forced to employ models when, for one reason or another, we cannot give a direct and complete description in the language we normally use. Ordinarily, when words fail us, we have recourse to analogy and metaphor. The model functions as a more general kind of metaphor.[3]

47

248084

This chapter discusses theoretical and conceptual foundations of a library instruction system designed to help students develop research strategies. The original concepts were
presented in *New Perspectives for Reference Service in Academic Libraries.*[4] In that book, the focus essentially is on the
literature of what is known more or less as disciplined or
systematic inquiry and is frequently called scientific literature.

If presented in certain analytical perspectives, this literature
falls into patterns or structures. Using a literature's structural
patterns, it is possible to help students develop ways of knowing about a research topic and, in turn, help them develop
strategies to investigate that topic further. Thus, it can be
argued that this approach contains both cognitive and heuristic features or devices.[5]

My convictions about the soundness of the concepts and
procedures in *New Perspectives* were strengthened by expressions of approval and endorsement from both students and
instructors. They indicate that, following the presentations,
the results of student research efforts are improved, which
makes those concepts firmly grounded in actual experience.

Theoretical support for the concepts comes from a variety
of sources, in particular, writings on the history and philosophy of science by Thomas Kuhn, Michael Polanyi, and Eugene
Garfield.[6] Parallels are found in the discussions of these
writers and their critics and my experience with helping students develop research strategies, especially on the underlying
structures of scientific literature, on how scholars acquire the
craft skills of inquiry, and on other related characteristics of
disciplined inquiry that fall into the broad field labeled "research." The concepts in *New Perspectives* also contain ideas
from cognitive psychology and the sociology of knowledge.[7]

In this chapter, these concepts are refined by showing that
they can be embedded in some of the theoretical literature of
metaphor.

The library instruction system is based on the idea that any
body of scientific literature has both a substantive and a bibliographic structure, each in logical relation to the other. Bibliographic structure refers to the manner in which individual
studies are embedded in the literature of the same field. Substantive structure is the shape of the subject matter that
evolves from the cumulation of contributions in a field as a
consensus is achieved. Bibliographic structure forms a frame-

work that supports the substantive structure of that literature.

Central to these arguments is the proposal that library reference materials, as intermediary sources, form a third structural component. Together, these concepts make up a three-part literature matrix. This literature matrix is a metaphorical representation of actual bodies of scientific literature. The structural characteristics of literature networks can be presented more concretely by showing them symbolically as models. Ideas that support this argument are contained in the theoretical literature of metaphor.

There is little evidence that librarians have examined the theoretical literature of metaphor in relation to theory building.[8] There is, however, compelling evidence that much of what is presented below about the function of metaphor would help to develop a general theory of library reference work as a subfield within the larger discipline of librarianship. Likewise, theoretical foundations of bibliographic instruction must embrace a general theory of library reference work.

The Concept of Metaphor

What is the purpose of bringing up metaphor in a discussion about a theory of teaching library research strategy? Before answering this question, we need a definition of the concept of metaphor.

According to the *Harper Dictionary of Contemporary Usage*, "a metaphor is a way of writing or speaking figuratively and of describing something in terms of something else."[9] Put simply, to use a metaphor is to transfer the meaning of one thing to another thing. Most frequently, "transfer" occurs when, in our desire to make something more concrete, we speak of the abstract thing as if it is a physical entity. "Because of inflation, costs of books are 'ballooning' rapidly to unbelievably higher levels." Theoretical conceptions of metaphor are not, however, limited to its commonly understood function as figures of speech designed to help our understanding. Instead, metaphors are universally applied in a wide variety of functions, formal and informal.

Almost synonymous with the concept of metaphor are the two concepts of paradigm and model. Indeed, without being imprecise or losing meaning, metaphor, as a descriptive word, is often a legitimate substitute for either concept. Paradigm, introduced by Kuhn in *The Structure of Scientific Revolutions*, refers to those "universally recognized scientific achievements that for a time provide model problems and solutions to a research community."[10] Almost universally applied in the sciences, model designates any one of a range of things, which, E. A. Gellner states, "form a kind of continuum." For Gellner, models can range through five types: (1) physical, (2) conceptual, (3) a simplification of the first two, (4) "a tendency to call any theory whatever a model," and (5) which is similar, "any proposition whatever, whether theoretical or not, either is or represents a model."[11] Says Abraham Kaplan, "Models have been defined as 'scientific metaphors.' "[12]

Pervasive nature of metaphors

Metaphors figure broadly in our lives. George Lakoff and Mark Johnson argue that in addition to permeating our language, metaphors permeate our everyday thoughts and actions. "Our ordinary conceptual system, in terms of which we both think and act," they claim, "is fundamentally metaphorical in nature." And they further explain their notion about the metaphorical nature of our concepts; concepts govern our "everyday functioning," they "structure what we perceive," they help us determine "how we get around in the world," and they help us "relate to other people."[13]

Given these understandings, Lakoff and Johnson are able to say that "our conceptual system ... plays a central role in defining our everyday realities." "Our conceptual system is largely metaphorical," they argue, "... the way we think, what we experience, and what we do everyday, is very much a matter of metaphor."[14]

Master metaphors

Educators have long known how powerful metaphors are as teaching and learning devices.[15] Recently, psychologists have come to attach greater importance to the role of metaphor in human thinking.[16] Says Richard Snow, a psychologist interested in theory construction for research on teaching, "man is constantly observing his environment, labeling subjects, events and ideas and relating them to one another."[17] "The basis of scientific creativity," Snow argues, "is found in the production of metaphor."

C. S. Lewis, a literary critic, observed that:

On the one hand, there is the metaphor which we invent to teach by; on the other, the metaphor from which we learn. They might be called the Master's metaphor, and the Pupil's metaphor. The first is freely chosen; it is one among many possible modes of expression; it does not at all hinder, and only very slightly helps, the thought of its maker. The second is not chosen at all; it is the unique expression of a meaning that we cannot have on any other terms; it dominates completely the thought of the recipient; his truth cannot rise above the truth of the original metaphor.[18]

For the psychologist Theodore Sarbin, metaphors constructed to achieve these purposes are examples of Lewis's "master" metaphors. They are, Sarbin says, "the beginnings of cosmological theories," and according to him, Stephen Pepper's concept of root-metaphor marks the master's metaphors for world views.[19] Each of Pepper's classes of world views comes from a basic or root-metaphor. The purpose of a root-metaphor is to provide a framework that helps us understand specific experiences that occur in the real world.

Root-metaphors can also serve as "pupil" metaphors, in Lewis's sense. These are metaphors we construct for objects or events that otherwise we cannot understand. Faced with something for which, either by analogy or similarity, we have no ready-made category or class, we attach it to something we do know. Thus, when out of curiosity we turn our attention to such metaphysical questions as, What is the substance of the world? or What is the essence of creation? or What is humankind? we must invent metaphors to at least represent satisfactory explanations.[20]

Significance of root-metaphor

Pepper defines his root-metaphor concept in the following way: When we seek to understand something, we look for clues about it that we can recognize. Common sense, he says, plays an important role in the process. Once we recognize something, we seek to understand other parts "in terms of this one."[21]

Like Pepper, Snow states that "by creating an analogy between some aspect of teaching and other known things, concepts, or roles, it is possible to elaborate ideas about teaching by playing out the analogy's implications."[22] "Such analogies," Snow says, "are not meant to be closely reasoned or binding in detail, but merely to serve suggestive, hypothesis-generating purposes."[23]

In Pepper's root-metaphor concept, the "world views" of philosophers fall into one of six classes: (1) animism, (2) mysticism, (3) formism, (4) mechanism, (5) contextualism, or (6) organicism. Pepper regards the first two classes as having insufficient scope or noncommunicable categories.[24]

The third root-metaphor, formism, has its origins in Greek philosophy, but it has predominated during most of the modern era. For Leona Tyler, formism is scientific; operations take place by observing and classifying phenomena. With mechanism, the fourth root-metaphor, the machine presents the model, linking together in cause-and-effect relations all parts for analysis.[25]

Pepper's fifth root-metaphor, contextualism, has as its base the historical event, complex, unique, unrepeatable. Not necessarily in the past, the event can be in the present. In this sense, Sarbin argues, "history is an attempt to re-present events, and to bring them back to life again."[26]

General systems theory

The root-metaphor of Pepper's sixth world hypothesis "is the integrated organicism within which everything is related to everything else."[27] Tyler believes that Pepper's sixth world hypothesis has been superseded by the extensive development of Ludwig von Bertalanffy's general systems theory. In systems theory, Tyler says, "the entity to be studied is a set of interacting units rather than separate objects, bits of behavior, or cause-effect linkages. Everything in a system is related to everything else, and these internal relationships are different from those between any of the parts and things outside the system's boundary. Change in one part of a system changes this whole pattern of relationships."[28]

Contextualism

The first four root-metaphors are analytic types of theories, but contextualism is grounded in synthesis. In contextualism, the categories are *change* and *novelty, quality* and *texture,* each further subdivided. "It is the categories that govern scientific work by their control over what is to be observed about events being studied."[29]

In formal experimental situations, "the criteria of truth for contextualism are the successful working out of plans based on the observations, the verification of hypotheses, and quantitative confirmation of the conclusions drawn from the observations."[30] In less formal situations, such as developing research strategy skills in the academic library, similar sorts of criteria apply when judgments are made about the "truth" or quality of results. As Pepper indicates, contextualism is actually the same system as pragmatism.[31]

Although contextualism is predictable in general terms, conditions of specific events shift constantly so that merely integrating the conditions of an event will alter the context of a future event, even if the new event seems similar to a preceding one. "The texture of an event, argues the contextualist, can be understood by noting the integration of the conditions of the event within the context of the event."[32]

The contextualist metaphor need not be a mirror image of whatever it is designed to represent. In a phenomenological sense, it allows a certain amount of inconsistency or anomaly.

Pepper claims that "disorder is a categorical feature of contextualism."[33] Concepts of contextualist categories, he argues, must be framed in such a manner that "order" and "disorder" are not inconceivable in our perception of a "particular situation" or a "particular condition." Says Pepper, "order may have come out of disorder and may return into disorder again—order being defined in any way you please, *so long as it does not deny the possibility of disorder or another order in nature also*. . . . The ineradicable contextualist categories may thus be said to be *change* and *novelty*."[34] Pepper refines the "change" and "novelty" contextualist categories into *quality* and *texture*.[35] In analyzing events from "quality" and "texture" perspectives—that is, in the context noted above of a "particular situation" or a "particular condition"— Pepper notes that an event's quality is "roughly its total meaning" and that an event's texture is "roughly the words and grammatical relations making it up."[36] "The two are not separable," Pepper says, "though in different events, one or the other may be more prominent." Sometimes we attend more to "the total meaning," sometimes "to the words."

John Ziman's descriptions of the untidy, tentative nature of scientific literature seem particularly apropos as an illustration of the idea about an exchange of "order" and "disorder."[37] Particular situations or particular conditions are often similar for us in our workaday worlds as reference librarians.

As reference librarians, we recognize the inconsistency and anomaly of information and knowledge in publications. To paraphrase Thelma Freides, reference materials "are not fixed and immutable." Thus, when teaching research strategies with reference materials, many statements must be qualified because of the materials' inconsistencies.[38] We know through experience that shifts from "order" to "disorder" and back to "order" among reference materials can and do occur rapidly and unpredictably. Examples are the specialized encyclopedia that is not replaced rapidly enough with a new edition or the periodical index that suddenly ceases publication. In addition, patterns of research strategy may be altered with the development of new types of reference sources. Consider how, for example, the appearance of the *Social Sciences Citation Index* has altered the pattern of reference service in the social sciences. This means that both Pepper's quality and texture, in either *what* we as reference librarians work with at our tasks or *how* we assist library users is characterized by "change" and "novelty." Developing programs for teaching research strategy within this milieu merely makes more difficult an already complicated task.

Metaphors and Librarianship

How can metaphors be applied to librarianship, primarily as a way of illustrating the relationship of reference works to specific bodies of literature?

Librarianship as metaphysics

Reference librarians work with abstract material called information, used here in its loosest, most inclusive sense. What is meant by information must be specified because of the important distinction that disciplines make between "information" and "knowledge."[39]

Information is not "something physical, like a bullet, or like the electrical impulses which run about in our nervous systems and computers," says H. Curtis Wright. For him, information is derived from thought and so "cannot be reduced to a mechanics of atoms." Instead, he says, "information consists of ideas which are created abstractly in the mind, and expressed concretely in the world." By means of the senses, we contemplate something physical and create cerebral meanings; when no sensation is involved, our meanings are created by "reflection." "Then our minds," Wright says, "also 'inform' the world by creating [for us] the concrete material forms."[40]

Wright argues that "librarianship [as opposed to science] is a knowledge system based on control of metaphysical meanings by means of physical conditions."[41] To Wright, science "which is also a knowledge system, is based on control of physical conditions by means of metaphysical meanings."

The implication of Wright's argument is that, because libraries are composed of abstract material contained in physical objects, librarianship must be metaphysical rather than scientific. Joseph Nitecki, in a solution to this dilemma, proposes that a theoretical framework for librarianship can be based on "metaphysical models."[42]

Knowledge as consensus

Before published research can be considered knowledge, it must be accepted by those actively engaged in research in a field of inquiry. Before the published results of research become knowledge, material is considered scientific information.

After publication comes the slow, erratic process of collectively assessing and integrating findings into the existing body of literature. As this process continues, the substantive content of the literature is also changing, so that through consensus, new findings displace those previously agreed on, creating a fluid literature.[43]

Referencing as persuasion

According to G. Nigel Gilbert, another form of achieving consensus occurs as authors justify statements or "knowledge claims" regarding findings in research reports. Such statements, Gilbert contends, are presented as persuasive arguments.[44] By citing other authors' works to support their own claims, says Gilbert, authors ensure that the procedures, theories, and data to justify their arguments are convincing to the scholars in that field. Thus, the authority is established on which the author's argument is founded. "At the time, in supporting his argument by referring to a particular knowledge claim, the author implies that he accepts the validity of that claim; put simply, a citation used to justify an argument

suggests that the author recognizes the cited claim as a contribution to knowledge."[45]

The way these claims gain acceptance among researchers in
a field of inquiry is, by implication, also a form of consensus.

Support for Gilbert's arguments comes from Ziman. "A scientific paper does not stand alone," Ziman says; it must be
"embedded in the 'literature' of the subject. Every argument
that is presented, [and] many of the facts that are adduced,
must be supported by documentation."[46]

The bibliographic citation as metaphor

References to specific research publications, or secondary
sources, are marked by a *bibliographic citation*. A "short-
hand" for a specific primary or secondary source, a bibliographic citation is a means of identifying, locating,[47] and representing the subject matter in a specific publication.[48]

The first two functions of a bibliographic citation seem
straightforward. The "identifying" or other information
needed for accurate location is a sign for the physical document
itself. The relationship between the document and its sign is
"metonymic," meaning that the two share physical characteristics.[49] A bibliographic citation, as a symbol for a concept,
functions as a metaphor for the cognitive content of a specific
publication. That is, the relationship between the cited document and the concept[50] it symbolizes is metaphoric.[51]

Another important function of citations is to make more
concrete that which is abstract.[52] Using metaphorical analogy,
abstract material is treated as if it is a physical entity. Thus,
by citing a physically existing document, the concept contained in this document achieves, metaphorically, physical
presence.

When concepts—products of the mind, or "mentifacts"—
are converted into material objects, they are given a "relative
permanence," according to Leach. Once turned into a sort of
permanent material form, Leach says, they can be subjected to
technical operations that, otherwise, are "beyond the capacity
of the mind acting by itself."[53]

Figure 3-1 illustrates how a bibliographic citation is a metaphor for a publication's concept. Notice, too, in the illustration that just as a bibliographic citation metaphorically represents a published article, an abstract of the same article also
can logically be a metaphorical representation of it.

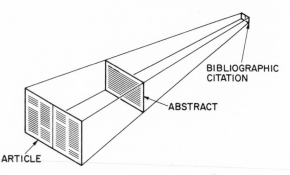

*Figure 3-1. Article projected through abstract to biblio-
graphic citation.*

Bibliographic structure

When authors cite the works of other authors in a written
text, they are in effect embedding their own work in the existing literature associated with a particular research topic. The
cited documents become symbols for the concepts they contain. A theory of citation practice must consider the symbolic
act of authors' associating particular ideas with particular
documents.[54] When one author cites the work of another, the
author creates a link between the two works.

Following traditional scholarly convention, an author's references (footnotes) are the "sources," that is, the foundations,
he or she draws on to give further meaning to a text. Small
argues that this view also can be reversed: When authors cite
specific "sources," they impart meaning to those sources.[55]

I argue for a similar view. Footnotes have a definite function. The assumption is that each literature network shares a
common feature. Each entry is explicitly or implicitly linked
to at least one entry in the network, most probably the key
source. Key sources are base studies that establish a focus of
concept or direction of inquiry. Subsequent investigators indicate their indebtedness to key sources or to surrogates of key
sources, such as review articles, by referring to them in published research, and in so doing help to develop a pattern as
literature on the topic is published.

In addition, relationships among footnotes are reciprocal.
Every entry in this network is both a source and a recipient of
influence in relation to other studies in the network.[56] That
is, if Jones cites Smith, this information can be related in two
ways. One is to emphasize Jones as the source of a citation to

Smith: Jones → Smith; the other is to emphasize Smith as the recipient of a citation from Jones: Jones ← Smith.[57] Viewed in this way, referencing is "a labeling process"; by citing a document, an author creates its meaning, which "is a process of symbol making."[58]

The bibliographic structure of a body of literature is fixed; contributions to it enter the published records of research in the chronological sequence in which they appear.[59] Figure 3-2 depicts a metaphorical model for the bibliographic structure of the concept of ethnic stereotypes. The nodes represent research published on the topic. At the bottom of the chart, one node is identified with the name of Katz and Braly, the "key source."[60]

Substantive structure

Implied in the concept of bibliographic structure is the idea that it forms the framework to support the substantive or cognitive content of that body of literature. Substantive structure means the shape that is assumed by the cumulation of the content of each contribution in a research field as a consensus is achieved. Substantive structure is, therefore, the fluid component of scientific literature.

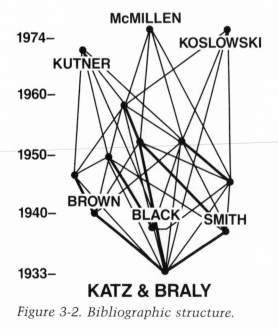

Figure 3-2. Bibliographic structure.

Since the idea of substantive structure is necessarily a problem of conceptualizing subject matter concretely, it is logical to depict it metaphorically (see Fig. 3-3). Conceptualizing subject matter concretely is easier when we recognize that, along with new configurations of the substantive content of a literature, we form both a synchronic and a diachronic structure. Synchronic structure refers to the body of substantive content of a literature that, at a particular moment, through consensus is considered valid. In Pepper's contextualist root-metaphor, "quality" corresponds roughly to the synchronic aspects of a body of literature, "texture" to its diachronic aspects. Figures 3-3, 3-8, 3-9, and 3-10 illustrate the synchronic structure of a specific literature. Diachronic structure, as shown in Fig. 3-2, encompasses all the contributions to a body of literature.

Basically, Fig. 3-3 is the same as Fig. 3-2.[61] Through consensus, valid portions of each contribution are absorbed into the substantive structure of that topic's literature. The "bites" and "warts" on the circle that indicate the key source of Katz and Braly in Fig. 3-3 show how the process of consensus occurs; that is, the bites and warts show either retention or

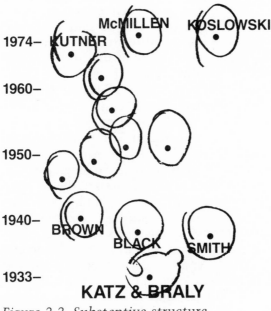

1974–
1960–
1950–
1940–
1933–

McMILLEN KOSLOWSKI
KUTNER
BROWN
BLACK SMITH
KATZ & BRALY

Figure 3-3. Substantive structure.

elimination of substantive material. A bite indicates the diminished importance of a particular contribution when a later contribution criticizes it. A wart indicates the increased importance of that same contribution when another contribution praises it. This process does not focus entirely on the key source; throughout the network, the process of retaining and eliminating substantive material, through consensus, occurs as a natural process.

Reference Works as Intermediary Sources

To help students develop effective research strategies, it is necessary to give them an idea of how either bibliographic or substantive information, or combinations of the two, is obtained. Superficially, this sounds straightforward, although experience suggests that such is not the case when teaching people how to develop effective library research strategies.

As stated earlier, literature of disciplined inquiry comprises two main structural components: substantive structure and bibliographic structure. In retrieval, searchers seek either substantive or bibliographic portions of these structures, or some combination, associated with a given field of investigation.

In inquiry, the ultimate goal is to gain access to the substantive portions of a topic's literature. However, this component is fused to the bibliographic structure of the literature, and so neither can be avoided.

If the needed amounts of either bibliographic or substantive portions are to be retrieved efficiently, the topic's literature must be reduced or distilled to manageable size, with minimum distortion of its content. The instruments to accomplish this task are traditionally known as reference works. However, because their function is to provide access to varying amounts or different combinations of the two components of the literature, reference works should be considered *intermediary sources.*[62] That is, basically reference works function as intermediate forms or stages of a literature. The term "intermediary sources" puts the function of reference works more firmly into the epistemological foundations of the literature—both the substantive and the bibliographic elements—with which they are associated.

Thus, the relationship of reference works to a literature is metaphoric. As intermediate forms or stages of the literature to which they are related, reference works are instruments that can be said to treat metaphorically the bibliographic and/or substantive components of a literature.

Reference works, seen as intermediary sources, provide special forms, in a compressed or distilled format, of the substantive and bibliographic portions of the bodies of literature they represent. As a means of gaining access to a body of literature, intermediary sources, in other words, can be consulted in a step-by-step procedure.

The tripartite matrix

To demonstrate how reference works function as intermediary sources, we can treat them as one component of a three-part, or tripartite, matrix, the other two components being the bibliographic and substantive elements. This matrix helps researchers visualize how intermediary sources are related to a specific body of literature. First, we must understand that, although we have been discussing the bibliographic and substantive components of literature in terms of their structures, for practical purposes—that is, preparing students to work in the library—it is better at this point to think about bibliographic and substantive information. Second, an understanding of the function of the key source, the base study to which subsequent studies of a particular topic of inquiry are linked, is central to the idea of the tripartite matrix.[63]

To develop the tripartite matrix, substantive and bibliographic information as components of literature are placed at opposite ends of a continuum (see Fig. 3-4). Intermediary sources, as the third component, are superimposed on the continuum (see Fig. 3-5).

In this context, reference works, as intermediary sources, create a matrix of five categories (Fig. 3-5). Sources in each division expose either substantive portions, bibliographical portions, or different combinations of the two as they apply to particular literature networks.

Three-dimensional perspectives of the tripartite matrix

The bibliographic and substantive components of literature should be seen as integrated. After all, they are separated only for analytical purposes. Once they have been integrated, they

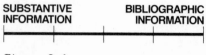

Figure 3-4.

can be shown in three-dimensional perspective. That is, imagine that Figs. 3-2 and 3-3 are brought together to form a
single figure, and this figure is then shifted slightly to an
oblique angle, as shown in Fig. 3-6. The bibliographic structure is indicated by the few lines running from later articles
back to the key source article. The substantive structure,
however, cannot be shown.[64]

Now that we have a three-dimensional perspective of a literature network, it is possible to show, also in three dimension, the
relationship of the various reference works that deal with a body
of literature. Moreover, it is also possible to justify that reference works are intermediary sources to the literature they represent. That is, reference works as intermediary sources present
intermediate stages of larger bodies of literature.

The substantive structure, in particular, emerges in greater
evidence in the "article" or textual parts. The textual parts
would fall in categories in the center and to the left of the
continuum in Fig. 3-5. For example, Fig. 3-7 shows how a
dictionary article can be visualized as a very compact, synthesized form of a topic's literature.

Although compact, the article is a statement of what,
through consensus, represents the valid portions of knowledge
on the topic.

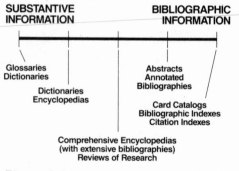

Figure 3-5.

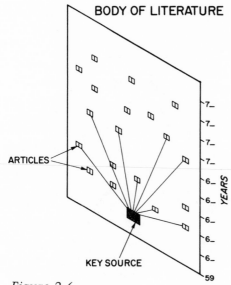

BODY OF LITERATURE

ARTICLES

KEY SOURCE

YEARS

Figure 3-6.

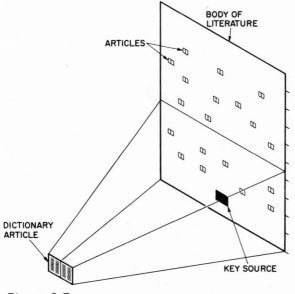

BODY OF
LITERATURE

ARTICLES

DICTIONARY
ARTICLE

KEY SOURCE

Figure 3-7.

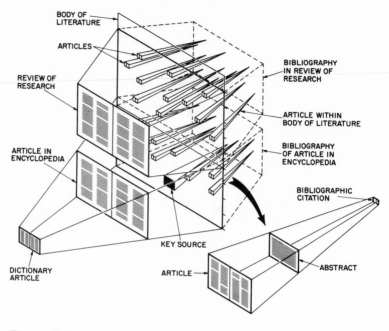

Figure 3-8.

Figure 3-8 shows how to visualize what relations encyclopedia articles and reviews of research have to the bodies of literature they represent. In general, these are located in the middle category of Fig. 3-5. Encyclopedia articles and reviews of research are shown to treat the substantive aspects of a topic's literature in a synthesized form and to present portions of the bibliographic structure in an analytical form.

For emphasis, the form in Fig. 3-1 is added to the bottom of Fig. 3-8. This helps to clarify the proposal that the encyclopedia article and review of research can perform an important bibliographic function.

Different characteristics of consensus are shown in Fig. 3-8. In the encyclopedia article, for example, we expect to find more theoretical concerns about the topic. In the review of research, which is more recent, usually more concern is given to empirical findings about the subject.

A side view is shown in Fig. 3-9. It confirms the ideas from Figs. 3-6, 3-7, and 3-8.

Figure 3-10 presents a slightly different version of Fig. 3-8.

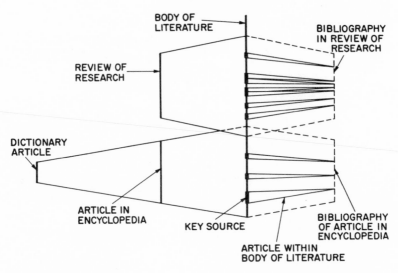

Figure 3-9.

In Fig. 3-8, the review of the research article comprises a synthesis (that is, the article itself) and a bibliography. If we remove the outlines of the review article but retain the bibliographic portion, as in Fig. 3-10, we have a bibliography on a particular topic. (The bibliography falls in a category at the extreme right of the continuum in Fig. 3-5.)

Left out up to now is any consideration of abstracts and annotated bibliographies. Although it is possible to design an illustration for these materials, it does not seem necessary. First, the illustration would become cluttered. Second, it is implicit in Fig. 3-8 that, by slicing through the articles—say for example, where the arrowhead for "Article Within Body of Literature" information is located—a collection of abstracts of individual articles would be symbolically represented.

The use of broken lines to depict bibliographies on Figs. 3-8, 3-9, and 3-10 is intentional and appropriate. Whatever we say about how bibliographies are special forms of literature, just as we say the same thing about encyclopedia articles and reviews of research, bibliographies do their task in a unique way. They give us a fragmented, shadowlike view of the literature they represent. Also, frequently, bibliographies, especially larger ones, deal with publications in a manner that

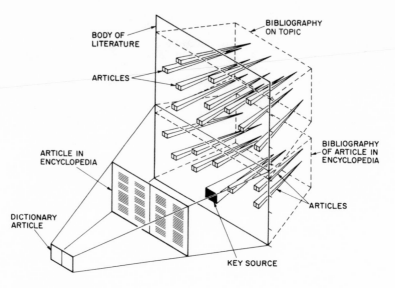

Figure 3-10.

makes it difficult to discover the entire body of studies that deal with a narrow topic.[65]

Playing out the analogy's implications

One approach to teaching students the types of information presented by reference works, and also to giving them ideas about how to develop research strategies, is to use actual examples. The examples I have developed are labeled "Structured Inquiry" handouts. They deal with the concepts of "ethnic stereotypes" and "kinship" (shown in Appendixes A and B of *New Perspectives*). Using material from a selection of reference works, these handouts are designed to illustrate the various forms given to the substantive and bibliographic components of a topic's literature. Materials selected from reference works are presented in a step-by-step, structured sequence.

The handouts demonstrate how the student can advance systematically from reference work to reference work and move from a point where little is known about a particular topic to a point where the desired level of understanding can be achieved. Put simply, in the sequence of illustrations of how reference works treat a topic's literature, the examples progress from simplified versions, similar to what is shown in

Fig. 3-7, to more complex forms, similar to those in Figs. 3-8, 3-9, and 3-10.

The object is to persuade students that reference works present, in effect, intermediate forms or stages of the literature for the research topics they actually represent. To Freides, this operation is an example of "tuning in" on a topic's literature.[66] Freides's analogy is particularly appropriate. It is also an example of Snow's idea about "playing out the analogy's implications."[67]

Conclusion

Critics of the metaphor approach to instruction argue that its use frequently leads to overgeneralization. The approach can be criticized "because other persons, when told of the metaphor, are likely to focus on irrelevant aspects until the theoretician's insight is explained to them."[68]

Other reservations about or weaknesses of this system are that it requires working directly with classroom instructors, prepared materials, such as library-produced research guides or structured inquiry handouts, and extensive presentation.

However, educators have long known the power of metaphors as teaching and learning devices. To summarize, C. S. Lewis, in recognition of metaphor as a tool of thought, identified master metaphors and pupil metaphors. In *World Hypotheses*, Pepper specifies six different levels of root-metaphors. His fifth root-metaphor, contextualism, has been widely applied because it can account for the exchange of order and disorder, change and novelty, quality and texture. This discussion argues that a contextualist root-metaphor has promise as a foundation for a theory of library reference work, under which is subsumed a theory of research strategy.

Among the epistemological components of a knowledge system, it is necessary to define primary sources, secondary sources, and key sources. Influential publications (key sources) give conceptual focus to subsequent inquiry on a research topic. Substantive information and bibliographic information, both with underlying structural characteristics, are the primary goals of library research. If viewed in certain perspectives, these characteristics of scientific literature networks (that is, the literature of disciplined inquiry) have both cognitive and heuristic features. Depicted metaphorically, the abstract structural characteristics of literature networks become a focus for both teaching and inquiry. In particular, their structural characteristics can be presented more concretely by symbolically representing them as models.

Arguments in support of a metaphorical treatment of library materials begin with the library's fundamental unit, the bibliographical citation. In disciplined inquiry, citations become metaphorical symbols for the publications for which they are signs. As a consensus develops in a knowledge field, bibliographic citations become labels that identify portions of a topic's substantive literature. Reference works are, basically, metaphors for the literature of the topics they represent. When their functions are analyzed, reference works designed for organizing and retrieving the literature of disciplined inquiry fall into five categories.

To illustrate the functions of reference works, the two primary components of knowledge, bibliographic structure and substantive structure, are placed on opposite ends of a continuum. The third component, reference works, is superimposed on the continuum, and a tripartite matrix is formed. For emphasis, the illustrations are presented in three-dimensional, isometric projections. Placing sources in each of the five categories on the continuum allows one to delineate bibliographic information, substantive information, or some combination of both.

Despite inconsistencies, the tripartite matrix is a master metaphor for whatever specific structure of organized literature we want it to represent. Pepper, in his ideas about "quality" and "texture" in the contextualist root-metaphor, presents some helpful considerations about how we should frame our ideas about metaphors. He confirms that we need not be concerned about the seeming "order" or "disorder" we must attach to the "particular situations" or "conditions" confronting us when we explain the concepts that underlie the matrix. Indeed, one cannot help but speculate that perhaps Pepper had our knowledge system in mind when he developed his own ideas about the contextualist root-metaphor.

By conceptualizing the functions of reference works and related materials in this manner, we have an instructional model for teaching research strategies. It is a generalized model, since any literature, either complex or emergent, will display inconsistencies among its reference materials. We must be conscious of these anomalies in our reference materials when we teach students to develop research strategies.

Acknowledgments

I am indebted to several colleagues, outside librarianship, for reading and commenting on this chapter. For his sympathetic criticism, I am particularly grateful to Vladimir Milicic. According to Professor Milicic, while my discussions of the theoretical literature and suggested applications of metaphor are sound, metaphor is an umbrella term, under which fall several narrower meanings. For definitions, readers can consult Kenneth Burke, *A Grammar of Motives* (Berkeley: University of California Press, 1969), pp. 503–517, for the article "Four Master Tropes," a discussion of metaphor, metonymy, synecdoche, and irony; C. Hugh Holman, *A Handbook to Literature*, 3rd ed. (Indianapolis: Bobbs-Merrill, 1972); and Alex Preminger, ed., *Princeton Encyclopedia of Poetry and Poetics*, enl. ed. (Princeton, N.J.: Princeton University Press, 1974). A British psychologist, Miller Mair, presents a good, brief review of theoretical statements about metaphors by a variety of writers. See his paper, "Metaphors for Living," in *Nebraska Symposium on Motivation, 1976*, ed. by Alvin W. Landfield (Lincoln: University of Nebraska Press, 1977), pp. 243–290. For a comprehensive source, see Warren A. Shibles, *Metaphor: An Annotated Bibliography and History* (Whitewater, Wis.: Language Press, 1971).

Notes

1. Joseph Z. Nitecki, "Metaphors of Librarianship: A Suggestion for a Metaphysical Model," *Journal of Library History* 14 (Winter 1979): 21.

2. Edmund Leach, *Culture and Communication: The Logic by Which Symbols Are Connected* (Cambridge: Cambridge University Press, 1976), p. 37.

3. E. H. Hutten, "The Role of Models in Physics," *British Journal of the Philosophy of Science* 4 (1953–1954): 289.

4. Raymond G. McInnis, *New Perspectives for Reference Service in Academic Libraries* (Westport, Conn.: Greenwood, 1978). Hereafter, this book is called *New Perspectives*.

5. *Cognitive* broadly refers to those things associated with "knowing" about something; Jack C. Plano and Robert E. Riggs, *Dictionary of Political Analysis* (Hillsdale, Ill.: Dryden, 1973), p. 57. *Heuristic* follows cognitive in a natural, or logical, sense. Heuristic device refers to activity associated with something that encourages or supports further investigation of a topic; Plano and Riggs, p. 37.

6. Thomas S. Kuhn, *The Structure of Scientific Revolutions*, 2nd ed. (Chicago: University of Chicago Press, 1970); Michael Polanyi, *Personal Knowledge* (Chicago: University of Chicago Press, 1969); and Eugene Garfield, "Primordial Concepts, Citation Indexing, and Historio-Bibliography," *Journal of Library History* 2 (1967): 235–249.

7. See John Ziman, *Public Knowledge* (Cambridge: Cambridge University Press, 1968), pp. 102–106. Literature in the philosophy of science, in the sociology of knowledge, and in phenomenology holds much promise for providing greater theoretical foundations for librarianship.

8. Nitecki, "Metaphors of Librarianship."

9. William Morris and Mary Morris, *Harper Dictionary of Contemporary Usage* (New York: Harper and Row, 1975), p. 400.

10. Kuhn, *The Structure of Scientific Revolutions*, p. VIII.

11. E. A. Gellner, "Model (Theoretical Model)," in *A Dictionary of the Social Sciences*, ed. by Julius Gould and William L. Kolb (New York: Free Press, 1964), p. 435.

12. Abraham Kaplan, *The Conduct of Inquiry* (Scranton, Pa.: Chandler, 1964), p. 265; Richard E. Snow, "Theory Construction for Research on Teaching," in *Second Handbook of Research on Teaching*, ed. by Robert M. W. Travers (Chicago: Rand McNally, 1973), p. 79. Following M. B. Turner, Snow argues that "models, analogues, and scientific metaphors [that is, paradigms] play an all but indispensable role in theoretical invention," p. 82. Similarly, Stephen C. Pepper notes in "Metaphor in Philosophy," in *Dictionary of the History of Ideas*, ed. by Philip P. Weiner (New York: Scribner's, 1973), p. 201, the stronger view of Thomas Kuhn: Kuhn "regards models and paradigms (virtually in the role of root-metaphors) as central explanatory instruments in science." On p. 201, Pepper notes, too, that Max Black in *Models and Metaphors* (Ithaca, N.Y.: Cornell University Press, 1962), "regards metaphors and models as explanatory devices, whether in the special sciences or in comprehensive metaphysics."

13. George Lakoff and Mark Johnson, *Metaphors We Live By* (Chicago: University of Chicago Press, 1980), p. 3.

14. Ibid.

15. See, for example, the discussions of the learning theories of Robert W. Gagné, Jerome S. Bruner, Jean Piaget, and David P. Ausubel—all essentially based on notions of metaphor—in Lee S. Shulman and Pinchas Tamer, "Research on Teaching in the Natural Sciences," in *Second Handbook on Teaching*, pp. 1098–1148; Theodore R. Sarbin, "Contextualism: A World View for Modern Psychology," in *Nebraska Symposium on Motivation*, ed. by Alvin W. Landfield, 1976 (Lincoln: University of Nebraska Press, 1977), pp. 1–41 (especially pp. 6–7); and Charles M. Reigeluth, *Meaning and Instruction: Relating What Is Being Learned to What a Student Knows* (Syracuse: School of Education, Syracuse University, 1980), ED 195-263. Reigeluth reviews the contributions to learning theory of the educational psychologist David P. Ausubel. An attempt toward explaining how Ausubel's learning theories apply to an individual's increasing command of a topic's subject matter is in Chapter 11, "The Psychological Structure of Knowledge," McInnis, *New Perspectives*.

16. Leona E. Tyler, "More Stately Mansions—Psychology Extends Its Boundaries," *Annual Review of Psychology* 32 (1981): 1–20.

17. Snow, "Theory Construction," p. 87.

18. C. S. Lewis, *Rehabilitation and Other Essays* (London: Oxford University Press, 1939), pp. 140–141. A statement by the culture critic Herbert Read reinforces Lewis's thoughts about metaphor. To Read, "Metaphor is the synthesis of several complex units into one commanding image; it is the expression of a complex idea, not by analysis, nor by direct statement, but by sudden perception of an objective relation." Read is cited by Robert Nisbet, *Sociology as an Art Form* (London: Oxford University Press, 1976), p. 33.

19. Sarbin, "Contextualism," p. 4.

20. Ibid.

21. Stephen C. Pepper, *World Hypotheses* (Berkeley: University of California Press, 1942), p. 91.

22. Snow, "Theory Construction," p. 89.

23. For example, attention is given below to the handouts I use with students in psychology, sociology, and anthropology. The examples, the treatments given in the literature of the concepts "ethnic stereotypes" and "kinship" in typical reference works, are designed to illustrate how, step by step, these sources provide from simple, generalized formulations to increasingly complex arrangements of the substantive and bibliographic literature of these concepts.

24. Sarbin, "Contextualism," p. 2.

25. Tyler, "More Stately Mansions," pp. 16–17.

26. Sarbin, "Contextualism," p. 6.

27. Ibid., p. 14.

28. Ludwig von Bertalanffy, *General Systems Theory* (New York: Braziller, 1968), p. 14. Nitecki, "Metaphors of Librarianship," p. 23, notes discussions of applications of general systems theory to librarianship. The general systems theory approach "implies holism" and assumes "that sets of related events can be treated collectively, as systems manifesting functions and properties on the specific level of the whole." This statement is from Ervin Laszlo, ed., *The Relevance of General Systems Theory* (New York: Braziller, 1972), p. 6, as cited by Nitecki, p. 23. See also Nitecki's "An Idea of Librarianship: An Outline for a Root-Metaphor Theory in Library Science," *Journal of Library History* 16 (Winter 1981): 106–120. Space does not allow further discussion, but, to me, the evidence in favor of applying the contextualist root-metaphor to librarianship rather than general systems theory is much more compelling.

29. Sarbin, "Contextualism," p. 6.

30. Tyler, "More Stately Mansions," p. 17.

31. Ibid.

32. Sarbin, "Contextualism," p. 6.

33. This notion is developed more elaborately in Chapter 13, "Reference Works as Artificial Constructs," in McInnis, *New Perspectives.*

34. Pepper, *World Hypotheses*, p. 234. Italics in original.

35. Ibid., p. 235.

36. Ibid., p. 236.

37. Ibid., p. 238.

38. See Ziman, *Public Knowledge*, pp. 102–106.

39. Along with citing what others say about the difference between information and knowledge, I myself have struggled toward definitions of these concepts. See McInnis, *New Perspectives*, pp. 61–68.

40. H. Curtis Wright, "The Wrong Way to Go," *Journal of the American Society for Information Science* 30 (March 1979): 69, 73.

41. Ibid., p. 74.

42. Nitecki, "Metaphors of Librarianship."

43. Along with the chapter "Knowledge as Consensus," in McInnis, *New Perspectives*, consensus is discussed by Henry G. Small, "Cited Documents as Concept Symbols," *Social Studies of Science* 3 (1978): 327–340; Michael Mulkay, "Consensus in Science," *Social Science Information* 17 (1978): 107–122; Michael Mulkay, *Science and the Sociology of Knowledge* (London: Allen and Unwin, 1979); and Ziman, *Public Knowledge*.

44. G. Nigel Gilbert, "The Transformation of Research Findings into Scientific Knowledge," *Social Studies of Science* 6 (1976): 282.

45. Ibid., p. 287.

46. Ziman, *Public Knowledge*, p. 58.

47. By locating is meant indicating where a publication is located in the literature.

48. Attributing these symbolic functions to bibliographical citations is not new. Along with the discussions of these notions in McInnis, *New Perspectives*, see Small, "Cited Documents as Concept Symbols." S. E. Cozzens summarizes the theories about citation practice in "Taking the Measure of Science," in *New Directions in the Sociology of Science*, ed. by S. P. Restivo (International Society for the Sociology of Knowledge Newsletter, March 1981).

49. For this notion, Small acknowledges his debt to Leach, *Culture and Communication*.

50. In this context, concept is not used according to its abstract or theoretical formulation. Instead, following Small, concept includes "experimental findings, methodologies, types of data, metaphysical notions, theoretical statements or equations—or, in general when dealing with citations, any statement which may be taken as characterizing or describing the cited document." Small, "Cited Documents as Concept Symbols," p. 329.

51. As librarians, at least unconsciously, we are aware of what is meant here. In his article, "Cited Documents as Concept Symbols," Small draws on empirical evidence taken from a survey of scientific papers to illustrate how bibliographical citations become metaphors for the material they contain. To me, there is no problem in visualizing this same behavior applied throughout the spectrum of systematic inquiry. Among examples given by Small on pp. 331–332 are Cited Document, R. F. Stewart et al., "Coherent X-ray scattering for the hydrogen atom in the hydrogen molecule," *Journal of Chemical Physics* 42 (May 1, 1965): 3175; Citation Context: "The scattering factor for the hydrogen atom was that given by Stewart et al. (1965):"; Citation Document symbolic of: Hydrogen scattering factor.

52. Small, "Cited Documents as Concept Symbols," p. 329.
53. Leach, *Culture and Communication.*
54. Small, "Cited Documents as Concept Symbols," p. 329.
55. Small explains: By citing the work of other authors, "the author is imparting meaning to his 'sources.' " As an example, Small uses Lowry's method of protein determination. By citing Lowry's paper, an author is "not only telling the reader where he can find a description of the method," but is also stating what Lowry's paper is about, that is, a method of protein determination. "Referencing viewed in this way is a labelling process. The language pointed to by the footnote number labels or characterizes the document cited—or, in other words, constitutes the author's interpretation of the cited work. In citing a document, an author is creating its meaning," which Small argues, "is a process of symbol making." Small, "Cited Documents as Concept Symbols," p. 328.
56. McInnis, *New Perspectives*, p. 92. Of course, certain qualifications need to be acknowledged here. Since authors cite other works for a variety of reasons, according to the value or purpose attached to each as justification to the argument presented, citations vary in their importance. For an extensive discussion of the variety of types of citations, supported by empirical evidence, see Theodora Hodges, *Citation Indexing: Its Potential for Bibliographical Control* (Ph.D. diss., University of California at Berkeley, 1978).
57. McInnis, *New Perspectives*, p. 92.
58. Small, "Cited Documents as Concept Symbols," p. 328.
59. McInnis, *New Perspectives*, discusses several attempts toward depicting bibliographical structures, notably those of Garfield and Skelton, and those developed by McGregor and McInnis. Figure 3-2 is a departure from the first bibliographical structures that McGregor and McInnis developed. Using black and white ovals, we developed a set of two charts that depicted the two-way relationships discussed above. Together, through symbolic notation, each set of ovals clustered around dots on each chart (symbolizing actual publications) illustrated several different kinds of information. Primarily to save time and to gain flexibility for a variety of instructional situations, these original charts are used less frequently. Instead, using two overhead projectors and multiple-layered transparencies, I present the concept of bibliographical structure by progressive disclosure.
60. The term "key source" is crudely written on the chart as part of the progressive disclosure used in presenting to students the bibliographical structure for the literature of ethnic stereotypes. Each additional transparency placed on the screen adds to the detail of the illustration. As each transparency is added, students get a rough idea of how a body of literature develops and of its increasing complexity.
61. In Fig. 3-3, the crude circle around each node is intentional. In presentation, as the nodes are circled, students are told that, while each of these publications (in this case, social psychology) may appear very logical, wrapped up in beautifully reasoned packages, when published they are looked at as being tentative. See Ziman, *Public Knowledge*, for an extensive discussion.
62. The following is a brief description of Chapters 13, 14, and 15 of *New Perspectives*. Above it is argued that the literature of disciplined or syste-

matic inquiry comprises two main structural components: substantive structure and bibliographical structure. In retrieval, researchers seek either substantive or bibliographical portions of these structures, or some combination.

63. This discussion sketches briefly ideas that are developed in more detail in McInnis, *New Perspectives*, especially Chapter 15. My *Research Guide for Psychology* (Westport, Conn.: Greenwood, 1982) and other research guides to be published in Greenwood's Reference Sources in the Social Sciences and Humanities series have an organizational scheme that includes substantive, substantive-bibliographic, and bibliographic arrangement of reference materials.

64. Although it is possible, using overhead projectors and transparencies, to draw in some of the "balloons" used to illustrate the abstract substantive structure in Fig. 3-3, merely by referring to that figure, individuals can understand readily that Fig. 3-6 incorporates substantive material.

65. These statements about bibliographies should not be taken as an indication of personal reservation about bibliographies. Rather, it recognizes that, realistically, bibliographies often do not organize the literature for a specific topic in quite the way an individual needs it.

66. Thelma Freides, *Literature and Bibliography of the Social Sciences* (Los Angeles: Melville Publishing Co., 1973).

67. See Snow, "Theory Construction," p. 89.

68. Snow, "Theory Construction," p. 89.

4

Information Problem-Solving: A Developmental Approach to Library Instruction

CONSTANCE A. MELLON

The profession of librarianship has long been with us, but the librarian as teacher is a relatively new role to the field. Only since the 1970s has library use instruction received increased attention from the academic community. All too often, however, instruction has focused on the discrete components of library use. Students are trained to use such tools as the card catalog, indexes and abstracts, encyclopedias, dictionaries, and almanacs. Search strategy, if mentioned at all, is done so only cursorily. Retrieval problems are rarely, if ever, discussed. Although certainly more effective than none at all, this type of instruction does little to produce an independent and capable library user. It is time for those engaged in library instruction to become aware of the growing body of literature on learning theory and to incorporate what is known about how people think and learn into the design of user instruction.

From the theoretical base on thinking and learning, two pro-

This chapter is adapted from a paper presented at the ACRL conference, Minneapolis, Minn., September 1981.

cesses in particular—problem-solving and developmental theory—seem to have immediate application to the design of more effective library instruction. Problem-solving is used extensively in business and industry and has been adapted to various other fields, including education. Since problem-solving processes can be effectively applied to the library research process from the basic short answer search to the more complex research project, they can provide a logical and unifying theme for multilevel library instruction programs. Developmental theory, the second process, offers to the designer of instruction programs a guideline as to where in a student's education various search strategies should best be introduced.

This chapter describes the basic problem-solving process and its application to library instruction, explains the cognitive developmental theory, which can inform the use of problem-solving at various levels of a library instruction program, and gives examples of its use in the instruction program of one specific academic library.

Basic Problem-Solving Processes

Problem-solving processes evolved from systems analysis, the theoretical base of computer software design. Systems analysis is generally shown in flowcharts or block diagrams, the basic one being the input-process-output model (Fig. 4-1A).

This basic systems model can be applied to problem-solving. It will then consist of three components (Fig. 4-1B).

Using the systems model of problem-solving in Fig. 4-1B to look at information needs, a basic model might be developed as shown in Fig. 4-1C.

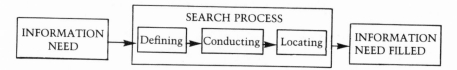

This is systems analysis at its simplest. The methodology requires that the "system with which one is concerned is broken into increasingly smaller subsystems until one arrives at the system's basic components."[1] In terms of problem-solving, the problem, or input, is first analyzed to determine need. Need can be considered as the difference between what currently exists and what is desired. Process, then, includes all those activities that must be performed in order to move from the existing situation (problem) to the desired situation. The solution is the outcome of that process and will create the desired situation.

Roger Kaufman provides an expanded version of the basic problem-solving model in his book *Identifying and Solving Problems: A Systems Approach* (see Fig. 4-2).[2] Kaufman explains that each component of the process is in turn broken down into smaller tasks, which, when accomplished, complete the larger task described in that component. For example, Kaufman's first component, which is Identify Problems Based on Needs, has been broken down into nine tasks (see Fig. 4-3).[3]

This process of breaking down a problem or situation into its component parts characterizes the systems analysis approach.

Another characteristic of systems analysis is feedback. Although the block diagrams that are used to represent systems are depicted in a linear fashion, the systems themselves are rarely linear. For example, when determining the process needed to move from the existing to the desired situation, the analyst may find that the existing situation has not been correctly analyzed. This information should then be fed back into the input component in order to cause adjustments as necessary. Or perhaps the output of the process is unsatisfactory in creating the desired situation. In this case, either input

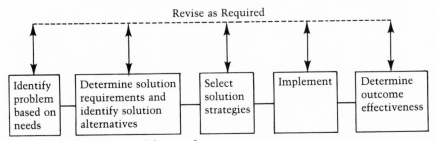

Figure 4-2. Problem-solving process.

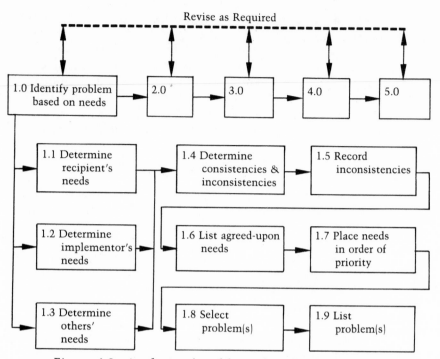

Figure 4-3. Analysis of problem identification.

or process must be reviewed, based on the nature of the output failure. This method of allowing for new information gained at each step in the process is called *feedback*. It can be depicted on the basic block diagram in Fig. 4-4. Notice the provision for feedback, labeled "Revise as Required," in Kaufman's problem-solving model (Fig. 4-2).[4]

In designing library instruction programs based on the problem-solving method, emphasize the process of moving from an information need to fulfilling that information need. The process, or search strategy, by which the need is satisfied is derived from identifying relevant library tools, then breaking down their use and application into the components neces-

Figure 4-4.

sary for mastery. In developing the process, however, remember that actual search strategy is rarely ever linear and that it is not helpful to students to teach it as if it were. The concept of feedback, or returning to preceding steps in the process as necessary, must therefore be built into the process.

Information Problem-Solving and Intellectual Development

Although it is both useful and appropriate to design library instruction programs based on the systematic, problem-solving methods outlined above, the student's level of cognitive development must be considered when determining the specific application of these methods. Among the developmental theories currently receiving attention at the college level is William Perry's theory of intellectual and ethical development.[5] This theory provides an excellent basis for determining what kinds of problem-solving processes to present to specific groups of students and when they can be used most effectively. Perry, a Harvard psychologist, has identified the stages of intellectual and ethical development of students during the college years as dualism, multiplicity, relativism, and commitment.

In the *dualism* stage, students view the world in terms of right or wrong, and therefore expect that there is a "right" answer to every question. They believe in "authority"—in college, represented by the instructor who knows what things are right and what things are wrong. Therefore, the job of the instructor is to pass this information on to students. Instructors who claim that there is more than one way to solve a problem, or more than one perspective on a situation, are seen as deliberately withholding the "right" information, and thus as playing games with students. Education at this stage of development is seen as a process of feeding in knowledge and producing answers. Students are externally oriented learners, compliant and responsive to authority. They see a world of little or no uncertainty, and a characteristic question of students at this stage is, What is the right answer?[6]

Research has shown that most students enter college in the dualistic stage of development.[7] Therefore, freshman composition students can usually be considered as operating at this level. Library instruction designed for this type of student should, for the most part, be simple, straightforward, and easily understood. Dualistic students have little patience with alternative search strategies, with wide varieties of reference materials all designed to answer the same type of question, and with the complexities of information retrieval. Although mention should be made of other, more complex, sources and techniques and students should be encouraged to ask questions or to seek further information from reference librarians, only the basic problem-solving processes should be presented at this stage.

As dualistic students are exposed to increased numbers of authorities who hold equally credible but conflicting views, they should become aware that the right/wrong view of the world is insufficient. They then move into the second developmental stage, *multiplicity.* Students in the multiplistic stage believe that there is a part of the world about which nothing can definitely be known. Although part of the world still remains right or wrong to them, it now becomes legitimate for there to be more than one perspective on a problem. Since students feel that there are parts of the world it is legitimate to be uncertain about, a characteristic phrase at this stage is "everyone has a right to his or her opinion."

Since research suggests that many students complete their undergraduate education in the multiplistic stage of development, it is reasonable to assume that many students in advanced disciplinary classes that incorporate library instruction are at this stage.[8] These students will be receptive to more complex problem-solving strategies and to the use of more advanced bibliographic tools such as abstracts. Furthermore, they will probably be more curious about the difficulties or inconsistencies in library use and less satisfied with viewing it as a simple, linear process. It is useful at this stage to mention that search strategy is a very individual thing and that the aim of a library instruction program is to produce an independent library user who has developed a successful problem-solving search strategy.

In the third stage, *relativism,* students become aware that there are few areas in which things can be known absolutely and thus recognize the necessity of supporting information to back up opinions. They accept the need for perception, analysis, and evaluation in forming judgments. Relativistic students are able to apply information from one area to the solution of problems in another area. This is the stage of abstract reasoning, the type of thinking most college instructors have as an ideal for their students, but which, the followers of Perry claim, many undergraduates never reach.[9] Since students in the relativism stage gather data before forming opinions and making decisions, the characteristic phrase of this stage of development is "it all depends."

Graduate students are often in the relativistic stage of intellectual development. With these students we can effectively discuss such complex retrieval concepts as evaluating various tools in relation to information need and defining alternative search strategies. Relativistic students are also curious about the similarities and differences among libraries they might have encountered and are interested in how the things they learn about information retrieval in one library can be applied to the search for information in other libraries. They are more willing to accept the responsibility for defining their own search for information and often display a curiosity about why things are arranged as they are in libraries and what techniques are best for filling information needs.

The final stage in Perry's developmental model is *commitment*, the outgrowth of accepting a world in which nothing is certain. Students come to realize the logical necessity to take a stand, to make choices upon which to act in a relative world. Commitment is characterized by the phrase "this is right for me."

Since relativism and commitment seem to be stages that blend one into the other, relativistic students are constantly evaluating parts of their relative world, then committing themselves to specific attitudes or actions that seem right at a particular time in their lives. It is the only way in which balance can be achieved in a world of shifting values. Therefore, relativistic students ready for commitment should be able to determine a personal approach to library problem-solving. Thus, experiences in selecting among alternative research strategies and in deciding on sources relevant and appropriate to their interests and needs should assist the students in evolving their personal search strategy and in determining its utility in actual library practice.

Intellectual development theory can provide an excellent conceptual framework for the application of learning constructs such as problem-solving to a collegewide program of library instruction. Although problem-solving provides the unifying theme for such a program, understanding the stages of intellectual development through which students pass and when they generally occur during the college years can help predict the most effective sequence for instruction. In applying cognitive development theory to instruction, however, remember that students are individuals and, therefore, do not all develop at exactly the same rate. Students at the stage of dualism may be among the graduate classes; the freshman composition class may include several relativistic students. Thus, guidelines provided by cognitive development theory are approximate, not absolute.

The PLUS Program: Applying the Theories

The University of Tennessee at Chattanooga, with support from the Lyndhurst Foundation, has developed a program of library use instruction based on the problem-solving methods and cognitive development theory discussed above. UTC's Program of Library Use Strategies (PLUS) introduces the problem-solving process at the basic level of instruction, the freshman composition classes. The concept is then consistently expanded and reinforced on disciplinary levels, both undergraduate and graduate. Complexities of retrieval and alternative strategies to meet differing information needs are included on more advanced levels. Fundamental to the application of these theories is the recognition of the academic library as a complex information system. Students are told that unless they understand this system and give careful thought to defining their information needs, chances are that they will be frustrated as they attempt to fill these needs.

At the freshman level of instruction, emphasis is placed on the difference between the academic library and other libraries, such as the public library and the school library, which students have used. As Evan Farber points out: "I have come to think that perhaps the biggest problem in giving college library instruction is correcting library skills learned in high

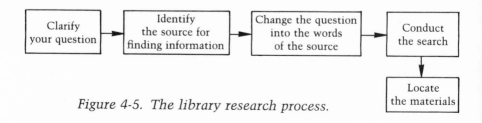

Figure 4-5. The library research process.

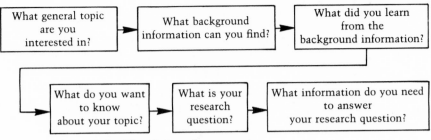

Figure 4-6. Clarifying the question.

school."[10] On the other hand, it is explained that by under-standing the system and planning approaches to satisfy infor-mation needs, the use of the library can be both effective and rewarding.

Problem-solving designs for the PLUS program are devel-oped as needed by the coordinator of library instruction, who works with faculty and reference librarians and provides an interface between the two. For the freshman composition se-quence, a continuing interaction with the director of composi-tion provides data that will eventually be integrated into the structure of all sections of this course. The sequence includes a number of simplified problem-solving processes, such as the ones for the library research process (Fig. 4-5),[11] for clarifying the question (Fig. 4-6),[12] for demonstrating how the library research process works (Figs. 4-7, 4-8, 4-9)[13] and for using peri-odical indexes (Fig. 4-10).[14]

The introduction of specific library tools is preceded by an explanation that incorporates the use of the tool into an ap-propriate process for filling an information need or for clarify-ing a part of the general process of library research. Each se-quence includes specific experiences with supervised practice using the tool under discussion. The instruction librarian and the classroom instructor cooperate in supervising the stu-dent's initial contact with these tools.

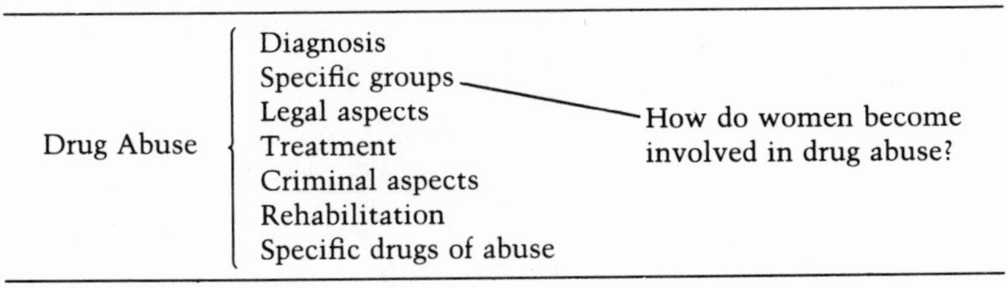

Drug Abuse
- Diagnosis
- Specific groups
- Legal aspects
- Treatment
- Criminal aspects
- Rehabilitation
- Specific drugs of abuse

→ How do women become involved in drug abuse?

Figure 4-7. Clarifying the question: an example.

IDENTIFY THE SOURCE

Readers' Guide to Periodical Literature
News magazines
The "popular" approach

Social Sciences Index
Scholarly approach

New York Times Index
Current aspects
News events

Figure 4-8. Identifying the source: an example.

A similar design technique is being used for the more advanced disciplinary levels. Faculty members requesting library instruction are interviewed on the library needs of their students for successful completion of course requirements and on searching techniques in their disciplines. Then, with the help of a reference librarian, processes for the use of appropriate research tools are determined. For example, a sequence of five classes was designed to meet the needs of a course on resources for the field of criminal justice. The general search process for statutory law (Fig. 4-11)[15] and the specific process for using the *Tennessee Code Annotated* (Fig. 4-12)[16] form a portion of that sequence.

Specific needs of faculty can be met using the problem-solving approach to library instruction. For example, working in cooperation with a faculty member in UTC's Department of Music, the library instruction coordinator was able to develop a three-part model that combined the needs of the faculty

How do women become involved in drug abuse?

Readers' Guide to Periodical Literature
Drug abuse
Drug addicts
Drugs and women

Social Sciences Index
Drug abuse
Drug addicts
Drugs and women
Drug abuse in pregnancy

New York Times Index
Drug addiction, abuse, and traffic

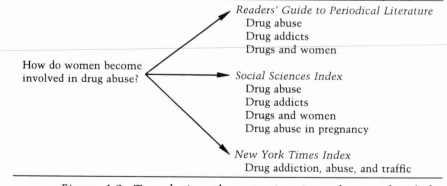

Figure 4-9. Translating the question into the words of the source: an example.

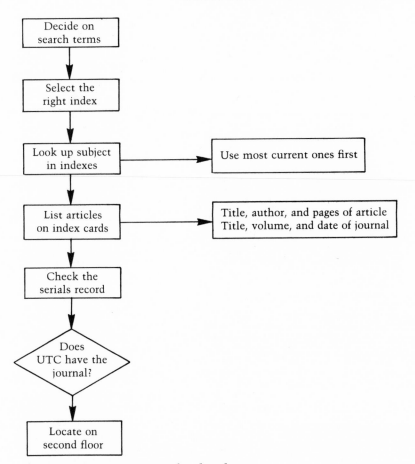

Figure 4-10. Using periodical indexes.

member, the needs of music research students, and the problem-solving approach to library instruction. These components were then expanded into the Systematic Inquiry Model shown in Fig. 4-13.[17]

Consulting between the library instruction coordinator and the faculty member was used to devise this model. In several meetings it was discovered that the faculty member was most concerned with student motivation and wished to construct an approach to research that would allow students to select areas of interest relevant to their professional lives. In addition, she wanted each student's research project to be presented to other class members in an interesting and meaningful way.

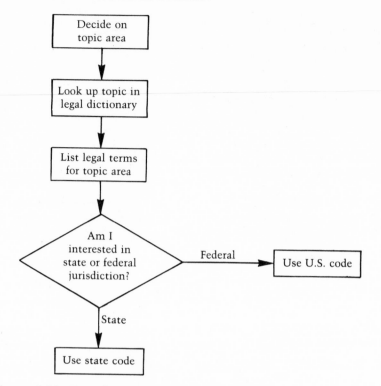

Figure 4-11. Search process for statutory law.

To develop a model to meet these needs, the faculty member and the library instruction coordinator spent several brainstorming sessions tracing in detail each task that had to be accomplished before the student could present the project. For example, before the information could be presented, it had to be located; before it could be located, it had to be defined. Within each of these components were a series of smaller tasks that had to be accomplished before the larger task represented by the component was complete. Through the interaction of the faculty member, with her content knowledge, and the library instruction coordinator, with her knowledge of the library research processes, this model was devised. It has provided a useful base from which to build a number of the problem-solving processes used throughout UTC's PLUS program.

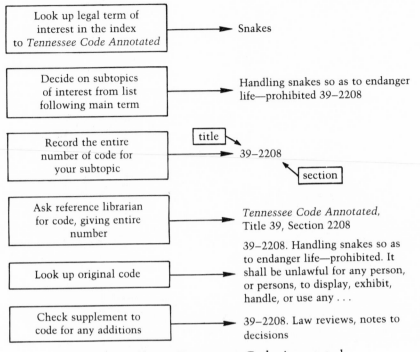

Figure 4-12. Using Tennessee Code Annotated.

Conclusion

With greater attention and concern focused on instruction activities in libraries, it becomes increasingly important to provide the most effective instruction possible. In order to do this, instruction librarians need to consider the application of various theories of learning and development to user instruction. Problem-solving and developmental theory seem to have immediate application to this type of instruction. The use of problem-solving processes and developmental sequencing provides for more than effective library instruction. It supports intellectual development and abstract reasoning abilities in participating college students. In this way, library instruction reinforces the major goal of higher education, the intellectual and academic growth of the student.

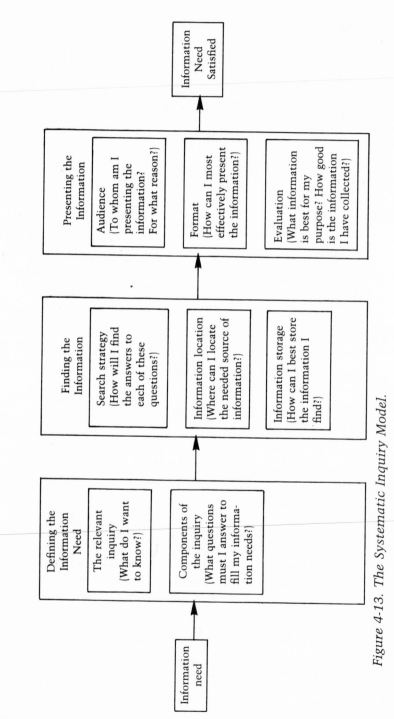

Figure 4-13. The Systematic Inquiry Model.

Notes

1. Stanley Young and Charles E. Summer, Jr., *Management: A Systems Analysis* (Glenview, Ill.: Scott, Foresman, 1966), p. 19.

2. Roger Kaufman, *Identifying and Solving Problems: A Systems Approach* (La Jolla, Calif.: University Associates, 1976).

3. Ibid., p. 67.

4. Ibid., p. 65.

5. William G. Perry, *Intellectual and Ethical Development in the College Years: A Scheme* (Cambridge, Mass.: Harvard University Press, 1970).

6. Constance A. Mellon and Edmund Sass, "Perry and Piaget: Theoretical Framework for Effective College Course Development," *Educational Technology* 21 (May 1981), pp. 29–33.

7. Clyde A. Parker, "Improving Instruction in Higher Education: Meeting Individual Needs of Students" (Proposal submitted to the Fund for the Improvement of Postsecondary Education, 1978).

8. Carol Widick, "An Evaluation of Developmental Instruction in a University Setting" (Ph.D. diss., University of Minnesota, 1975).

9. Ibid.

10. Evan Ira Farber, "Library Instruction Throughout the Curriculum: Earlham College Program," in *Educating the Library User*, ed. by John Lubans, Jr. (New York: Bowker, 1974), p. 150.

11. Constance A. Mellon, *Program of Library Use Strategies* (Chattanooga, Tenn.: University of Tennessee at Chattanooga, 1980).

12. Ibid.

13. Ibid.

14. Ibid.

15. Ibid.

16. Ibid.

17. Ibid.

5
Applying Educational Theory to Workbook Instruction

PATRICIA A. BERGE and JUDITH PRYOR

Since the early 1970s, workbooks have become a popular method of instruction for user education in libraries at every level, from elementary school to college. Although they are a relatively new tool in libraries, workbooks began to be used as a general method of instruction in the early 1920s. They developed from the long-time tradition of using laboratory manuals in high school and college science classes and exercise sheets in elementary and high schools in all subjects.[1]

History of a Teaching Tool

W. P. Johnson, the former president of the Webster Publishing Company, took credit for being the first commercial publisher of workbooks. He said he got the idea during time spent as a textbook representative in the field. While visiting classrooms, Johnson noted that materials for drill work were laboriously written on the board and copied by students. Since students did more than one assignment each day and not all students needed the same assignments, the result was a great loss of teachers' and students' time. Johnson asked an English teacher to write a text for high school students that would provide ready-made assignments. The book was published in 1923. The name "workbook" came later and has since been applied to seatwork books, practice books, drill books, activity books, or any books containing consumable materials.[2]

Initially, school administrators were opposed to spending money on a method considered a fad and in a format that students would eventually discard after completing. Although professionals in the field of teacher education were generally against the idea of using workbooks, the popularity grew.[3] In the 1930s and 1940s, during and after the depression, class sizes in public schools were on the increase, and teachers began looking for effective, time-saving ways to teach more students at once. Besides saving preparation time, workbooks made it possible for some students to work on their own with well-prepared supplementary materials, while the teacher worked directly with other students in recitation. By 1948 the sale of workbooks accounted for about 25 percent of the instruction budget in public school systems.[4]

Use of workbooks in the classroom expanded rapidly, but research to their effectiveness as an instruction tool came more slowly. By 1935 there was only one published study on the use of workbooks. A. W. Hurd did extensive experiments involving the use of workbooks in high school physics classes. The first two experiments attempted to compare the lecture method of instruction with a supervised-study method. The supervised-study groups used workbooks as their primary method of instruction. The results of these experiments proved inconclusive. Hurd later planned experiments in which the use of workbooks was the only variable in instruction. The results of eight experiments showed consistent differences favoring groups using workbooks. Four experiments showed consistent differences favoring groups not using workbooks, and two experiments showed little differences between groups. Hurd concluded from these experiments with workbooks in high school physics classes that although workbooks are helpful to some teachers in increasing measured achievement, they were not a panacea for instruction, and they were most useful in directing the attention of students to specific items of knowledge, techniques, and applications.[5] He further concluded that workbooks help students become more independent "by showing them tasks the accomplishment of which will help them in the achievement of the larger objectives of education and by indicating the nature of the specific steps to be taken in the accomplishment of these tasks."[6]

In a 1938 review of research on workbooks, Robert W. Jacks stated that results were inconclusive when workbooks had been compared with other methods of teaching. Jacks attributed the findings to the high number of variables that had to be controlled, since the level at which these variables are successfully controlled can greatly affect the results of experiments. Nevertheless, Jacks stated that workbooks were an efficient method of instruction for both instructors and students. Workbooks, said Jacks, allow for individual student differences and enable students to proceed at their own pace. Instructors can follow closely students' progress and readily identify areas where individuals or groups are having difficulties.[7]

Despite controversy over the merits of the workbook as a teaching tool, and perhaps because the research on both sides of the issue has been inconclusive, workbooks continue to be a familiar and extensively used teaching tool in most subject areas and at all grade levels. It is not surprising, therefore, that they have also been widely used to teach library skills to elementary, secondary, and college students.

The first use of workbooks in library instruction is credited to Miriam Dudley, who adapted the workbook method for use in teaching library skills to minority students at UCLA in 1969. Dudley soon became aware that most college students lack the necessary skills to use a college library successfully, and the workbook program was expanded for use with all incoming freshmen (more than 3,500 a year).[8] After Dudley's pioneering efforts, workbooks began to be used by a number of academic libraries. According to a list compiled in 1979 by LOEX (Library Orientation/Instruction Exchange), the National Clearinghouse for Academic Library Use Instruction, 90 libraries were using some form of workbook in their instruction programs. Most of these workbooks were based on the Dudley model.[9]

The debate over the value of workbooks as a teaching tool has troubled librarians as it has other educators. Evaluation of teaching methods in library instruction, however, has been limited, as evidenced by the lack of reported findings in the literature of library instruction. The earlier research that failed to demonstrate any one method of instruction as definitely superior appears to be supported by the few studies that have evaluated teaching methods in library instruction. In 1971, Thomas Kirk found virtually no difference in a comparison of two methods of library instruction involving two groups of biology students. One group received instruction in library use by lecture-demonstration; the other was instructed through guided exercises (a form of programmed learning). When evaluated, the two groups did not differ significantly either in scores on objective exams or in attitude toward the instruction. Kirk concluded that neither method was superior. However, the guided exercises continued to be used because, although the initial time spent in preparing the lecture method and the exercises were the same, the exercises could be used in succeeding years with only minor revision. Further, students could learn at their own pace, and students needing instruction in only one aspect could do just that part of the assignment.[10]

Shelley Phipps and Ruth Dickstein in 1979 reported the results of an experimental program conducted at the University of Arizona in 1976.[11] The study compared two groups of students enrolled in a composition course. Students in 12 sections received library instruction by means of a library skills workbook (modeled after the Dudley workbook). The students in 8 control sections of the same course received no library instruction other than what they may normally have been exposed to in other courses. The same objective test of multiple-choice and true-false items was used to pretest and posttest the students in all 20 sections in the study. Although both groups showed improvement on the posttest, the experimental group showed significantly greater improvement. To the authors' knowledge, this is the only workbook evaluation reported in library instruction literature that attempts to measure changes in student knowledge about the library, although there are studies that measure change in student attitude. The findings of this study are most useful for documenting the value of formal library instruction versus no formal instruction. However, because no other method of instruction was tested, the findings have little meaning when comparing workbooks with other teaching methods.

Since the superiority of any one method of instruction has not been proved, and would seem unlikely to be, attention should be directed to examining the strengths and weaknesses of individual teaching methods. In recent years librarians have taken an increased interest in the underlying educational philosophies regarding learning and teaching and how these philosophies affect library instruction programs and methods. Analyzing the effectiveness of any teaching method requires an understanding of how learning takes place.

Learning Theories

The study of learning has occupied psychologists for more than a century, and many viewpoints have been proposed. Two major and widely differing schools of thought have prevailed—association learning and cognitive learning. Association theorists, also known as behaviorists, view learning as the result of the learner making associations between stimuli and observable responses. Cognitive theorists, or Gestaltists, define learning as the result of the learner adjusting previously acquired perceptions in order to understand or grasp new relationships.

Association theorists base their theories of learning on observable environment and behavior, rejecting as unscientific those theories based on unobservable mental exercises such as thinking or concept formation. Early association theorists—Edward Lee Thorndike, Ivan Pavlov, and others—believed that behavior was totally dependent on the stimulus-response sequence, stimulus being the environment acting on the learner, and response being the learner's behavior in reaction to the stimulus. The learner's ability to make the appropriate association between the stimulus and the response based on the consequence of the response is defined as learning. Simply stated, if a positive consequence is produced by a particular response to a stimulus, the rate of the same response being given to that stimulus will increase. A negative consequence will alter or eliminate any further response to the stimulus. Learning has then occurred.

Today's foremost spokesperson for association theory is B. F. Skinner, who has taken the theories of these early associationists a step further by emphasizing the response-stimulus association as well as the stimulus-response. Unlike previous theorists, Skinner believes that the learner can emit a response that is not covertly related to an observable stimulus, thus initiating the stimulus-response interaction. Skinner has labeled this "initiating" response "operant behavior." As explained by Finley Carpenter, operant behavior theory has three main points: (1) What a person does often has consequences that alter his behavior, (2) the consequences arise in the environment, and (3) the environment operates on a contingency basis; that is, it yields rewards only after certain acts are performed."[12]

Reinforcement (roughly equivalent to rewards) is a key element in Skinner's theory of learning. Skinner's studies have shown that variations in frequency and temporal proximity of reinforcement to the response affect the length of time needed to condition the appropriate response and the strength of the conditioned response. Basically, the schedules of reinforcement can be divided into two groups: continuous and intermittent. Continuous reinforcement occurs when every response consistently elicits a reward. This pattern of reinforcement encourages rapid learning of appropriate responses. However, Skinner's studies indicate that continuous reinforcement tends to develop a low frustration threshold in the learner.

The second group of schedules, intermittent reinforcement, applies to patterns of rewards that occur intermittently, rather than every time the appropriate response is given. Different patterns of intermittent schedules determine whether the reinforcement occurs at regular or irregular intervals and whether reinforcement is triggered by a series of responses, or by elapsed time between reinforcements. Intermittent reinforcement is less useful for rapid acquisition of skills than for strength and durability of the learning. Learners in this schedule develop more perseverance and remember the stimulus-response association longer.[13]

Skinner defines knowledge as the buildup of the learner's stock or repertoire of stimulus-response associations.[14] Teaching a subject is dependent on breaking it into very small steps and reinforcing the learner when each step is completed. Dividing the learning task into small but increasingly more difficult steps increases the frequency of responses to which reinforcement is patterned. Humans being what they are, Skinner has advocated the use of teaching machines as the most effective method of providing consistent reinforcement, whether continuous or intermittent, to the learner's responses.[15]

Skinner's theories of learning have had great impact on educational theory and on the techniques teachers have used in their classrooms, especially during the 1950s and 1960s. However, Skinner's influence has diminished in recent years as other theories have become more prominent. Nevertheless, Skinner's imprint is still visible in many teaching methods. Forms of teaching such as programmed instruction and behavior modification can be directly attributed to his theories.

On the other end of the learning theory spectrum are the cognitive theorists. They view learning as the ability to perform internal cognitive processes such as thinking, formulating concepts, perceiving, or problem-solving. Early cognitive theorists such as Max Wertheimer and Wolfgang Köhler saw learning as a psychological experience to be studied as an organized whole.

One of today's most prominent cognitive theorists is Jerome Bruner. He verbalizes cognitive learning principles through a theory of instruction, his goal being to prescribe the most effective method for a subject to be taught.[16] The theory of instruction proposed by Bruner has four major principles: predisposition toward learning, or motivation; structure of the body of knowledge; most effective sequence of presentation; and the nature of rewards and punishments, or reinforcement.

Like the associationists, Bruner believes that physical, social, and personal reinforcers play an enormous part in the learner's motivation to learn. However, Bruner is more concerned with intrinsic motivation, which he sees as sustaining the will to learn far better than external reinforcers. Intrinsic motivation includes such elements as a basic curiosity, the drive to achieve competence, or, as Bruner puts it, "interest in what we get good at,"[17] and reciprocity, or the need to work cooperatively with others. The teacher's role is one of facilitator, providing the type of instruction that activates, maintains, and gives direction to the learner's exploration of alternatives.

The second principle in Bruner's theory of instruction is one he considers fundamental to learning—teaching the structure of a subject. Three basic cognitive functions support this claim. First, knowing concepts simplifies a subject and makes it more understandable. Bruner feels that "any idea or problem or body of knowledge can be presented in a form simple enough so that any particular learner can understand it in a recognizable form."[18] Second, human memory retains structured concepts and facts tied to this structure longer and more readily than detailed information that is not tied to a structure.[19] Third, an understanding of the basic concepts that make up the structure of a subject is what the learner draws on to aid in solving new problems or in comprehending new subjects. This transfer of concepts allows previous learning to facilitate future learning.

This leads to Bruner's third principle of instruction—sequence. The learner will have less difficulty mastering a subject when the material is presented through an effective sequence. The appropriate sequence depends on a variety of factors concerning the intellectual development or previous experiences of the learner and the nature and complexity of the subject being taught. Every subject lends itself to certain sequences that are prone to enable the learner to understand the basic concepts and ideas.[20]

Bruner's fourth principle concerns reinforcement, and closely agrees with association theories. Learning requires correctly timed reinforcement. Reinforcement that comes too soon can be confusing or meaningless. Delayed reinforcement will often be too late to aid the learner in subsequent learning. However, although association theorists recognize only extrinsic reinforcers, cognitive theorists place great emphasis on intrinsic rewards, such as the challenge of solving a problem, the satisfaction in mastering a subject, or the excitement of discovery.[21]

Examination of Skinner's and Bruner's theories provides insight into two widely different forms of learning, both of which have much to offer educators. Other learning theories have been proposed by psychologists and educators alike. Many of these attempt to bridge the gap between association and cognitive learning theories. Jean Piaget has had enormous influence on current learning theories through the development of his four stages of cognitive growth. Within these stages, Piaget describes two types of learning: P learning, which occurs when physical things act on the learner (association), and LM learning, which occurs when the learner acts on physical things (cognitive). Piaget stresses the learner's active participation as the key factor in cognitive growth.[22]

Learning theories and workbooks

As mentioned earlier, the theoretical value of workbooks as a method of teaching library skills has never been closely examined. Most of the literature has focused primarily on the practical aspects of developing and/or implementing workbooks in an instruction program. Analysis of workbooks in terms of learning theories can be conducted from two perspectives: first, from the functional or operational characteristics that are common to the genre, and second, from the type of organizational scheme used to present the substantive information.

Several functional characteristics are common to most workbooks: The material is divided into relatively short, concise chapters, progressing from basic to more complex topics; each chapter is usually devoted to one general idea or concept; and all workbooks have exercises or assignments as a follow-up to each chapter. All three of these characteristics could, on the surface, have been seen as elements in Skinnerian theories of learning—small, sequentially arranged segments, each culminating in a series of stimulus-response-reinforcement interactions. Library skills workbooks often have been described loosely as programmed instruction. However, on closer analysis, these characteristics actually typify both association and cognitive theories to some extent. Both theories recognize the importance of dividing a subject to be learned into manageable units. The difference lies in the size of units and the pattern of reinforcement to learning. True programmed instruction breaks the material into very small units or frames, which take the learner step by step to a specific outcome. Actually, only a few library workbooks strictly follow this method.[23] A classic example of programmed text for teaching library skills was produced in the 1960s by the library staff at Georgia State University.[24] Each chapter, or "section," of this workbook is divided into two parts. The first, labeled "information and facts," organizes the information into frames or small bits. Following is an example of one frame.

IV-3
Subject headings for specific periods of history are arranged *chronologically* by the subdivision.
Examples:
    U.S.—HISTORY—COLONIAL PERIOD
    U.S.—HISTORY—REVOLUTION
    U.S.—HISTORY—WAR OF 1812
    U.S.—HISTORY—CIVIL WAR

Part two, questions, is made up of frames of exercises that directly relate to the information covered in part one. The answer to each exercise is given in the right-hand column.

The student doing the exercises uncovers each answer as each frame is completed, receiving immediate reinforcement. Following is an example of an exercise frame.

> IV-18
> Arrange the following headings in the correct order:
> (a) GEORGIA—HISTORY—REVOLUTION   Ans. (b), (a),
> (b) GEORGIA—HISTORY—COLONIAL PERIOD   (d), (c)
> (c) GEORGIA—HISTORY—CIVIL WAR   (See IV-3)
> (d) GEORGIA—HISTORY—WAR OF 1812

The entire workbook is made up of hundreds of frames of information and corresponding exercises. The step-by-step approach of programmed instruction is designed to reduce the number of errors made by the student. As a result, the learner receives instant feedback and almost constantly experiences success. This exemplifies Skinner's schedule of continuous reinforcement. Although small steps and repetition of information are the basis of programmed instruction, they can also be a hazard. Occasionally, inexperienced or overzealous programmers may go overboard and produce materials that are tedious and boring. Skinner warns against this by emphasizing that programming is a challenging yet difficult procedure, which must not become a means in itself, but must always place the learner's needs first.

Most library skills workbooks do not follow the strict frame-by-frame presentations of information found in true programmed instruction. The usual format presents information in chapters in standard textbook style. Cognitive concepts of the subject are covered, as well as skills needed to apply the concepts. In nearly all basic library skills workbooks, the text of each chapter discusses the principles of a particular type of reference source (a framework to be discussed in detail later) and provides specific information on skills needed to make use of that type of source. For example, in most basic level workbooks, the chapter on indexes describes what indexes are, when and why they should be used, and identifies specific examples of indexes. This chapter also provides factual information on how to decode an index citation and how to interpret entries in the serials listing. Presenting information in this manner within each chapter relates closely to Bruner's theory. The unit of learning is small; yet overall concepts are introduced to which the factual type of information is tied.

The exercises generally used in these workbooks require the student actually to use the example sources discussed in the chapter to solve hypothetical problems. These exercises do not have the "rote drill" flavor of programmed instruction, but many still view them as a form of drill. Bruner, Piaget, and others feel that "doing" is often crucial to achieving understanding and mastery of a subject and that "drill" need not necessarily mean "rote." The key, according to Bruner, is to identify the most effective method of exercise for teaching any given subject that provides some degree of challenge for the student and does not emphasize the trivial.[25]

The latter qualities are those most difficult to achieve and those in which most library skills workbooks are least successful. Unlike true programmed instruction materials, the answers to the exercises are not immediately provided; thus, there is a delay before the learner receives reinforcement. When the reinforcement is received, it is generally as a reward for the successful completion of a series of exercises. This pattern can be classified in Skinner's intermittent schedule of reinforcement, which should produce stronger, more durable learning. The danger here lies in the delay between the "doing" (response) and the reinforcement. Skinner clearly prefers immediate reinforcement, and Bruner suggests that too long a delay may render the reinforcement useless to the learner.

The second perspective from which workbooks can be examined is the organization of the substantive information. This perspective correlates with Bruner's concept of structure. Many librarians have been giving a great deal of attention to the structures or frameworks in which library skills can be taught. In 1975 Elizabeth Frick divided the structure of information into four levels of awareness: specific reference sources, types of reference sources, the way in which these sources represent the nature of the discipline, and information structure in society.[26] Thelma Freides and Raymond McInnis view scholarly literature as having two structures—substantive and bibliographic—which parallel each other.[27] Recently, Pamela Kobelski and Mary Reichel identified seven frameworks that can be used to provide a context in which the specifics of library sources can be related. The seven frameworks are type of reference tool, systematic literature searching, form of publication, primary/secondary sources, publication sequence, citation patterns, and index structures.[28] It is the context that the conceptual frameworks provide that allows the learner to retain the concepts and apply them to other situations.

Workbooks designed to teach library skills in academic libraries have generally been organized around three of the conceptual frameworks identified by Kobelski and Reichel—type of reference tool, form of publication, and systematic literature searching. A combination of type of reference tool and form of publication is used in most library workbooks at the basic skills level. Type-of-reference-tool framework groups reference sources "by their format and the type of information they provide"; form-of-publication framework groups sources by the format in which they are published.[29] This organization allows students to build on the knowledge they may already possess by reviewing familiar sources while at the same time learning the characteristics of the type and, finally, becoming aware of additional examples of the type. Students usually come to college knowing about a few specific sources. They normally cannot describe the characteristics of particular sources and may not realize that many other works have the same purpose as the ones they know.

The workbook developed by Miriam Dudley follows this organization. The book is divided into 20 chapters, covering encyclopedias, dictionaries, almanacs, book review indexes, plot summaries, atlases, periodical indexes, and newspaper indexes.[30] Each chapter contains a concise discussion of the type of source, lists several annotated examples, and concludes with exercises that require students actually to use the sources discussed in the chapters. The exercises are individualized so that each student has a different question to answer about each source. This combination of frameworks enables students to transfer the concept of types to other research situations. A student who knows that *Social Sciences Index* is an example of a type of source will realize that other indexes should be available for other disciplines or subjects.[31]

The second framework used in workbooks is a combination of type of source and systematic literature search. As defined by Kirk, "search strategy is a conceptual framework for logically organizing use of the library and for explaining the organization of recorded literature."[32] Many forms of search strategies are used in library instruction. Freides and Carl M. White suggest an organization that leads students from general "substantive" sources to "bibliographic tools."[33] Students often wish to research topics about which they have little or no knowledge; this search strategy allows them to learn about their topics, narrow them, and more effectively select and use reference sources as they gain knowledge. Freides suggests that students writing a term paper should begin with a general overview of the subject. They might consult a guide to the literature to locate such a book. The general source will help students define and narrow the topic. Next, students will want to consult a more detailed discussion of their topic. This might be in the form of handbooks or annual reviews. Bibliographies and indexes would then be used to locate recent and very specific material on the topics.[34]

The workbooks developed at the University of Wisconsin at Parkside are organized with this strategy in mind and are used with undergraduate students just beginning work in their major fields.[35] Each chapter describes a type of source and lists important examples. Students are then asked to complete exercises using the sources discussed. The questions pose specific study or research problems and are designed to emphasize points made in the text about the general utility of a type of source. The final chapter discusses a systematic approach for using the sources to find information for a term paper. The assignment for that chapter asks students to select a topic in their major field and prepare a bibliography of 12 to 15 items. They must also keep a "journal" or "log" describing their search process in detail. The flowcharts used to explain the research strategy were modified from Kirk[36] (see Fig. 5-1 for example).

Another approach that involves search strategies has been used at the University of Toledo. The search process is similar to a model articulated by James Benson and Ruth K. Maloney.[37] In this model "there exists two 'givens'—a system and query. Any organized presentation of information is a system; any request for information is a query. Both the query and the system can be defined by specific characteristics. A successful search is achieved when congruity is achieved between the characteristics of the query and those of the information system being searched."[38] The workbook developed by Paul G. Cappuzzello and Sharon J. Rogers "specifically attempts to teach this process of searching for information and uses exercises with particular sources as illustrations of the search process."[39]

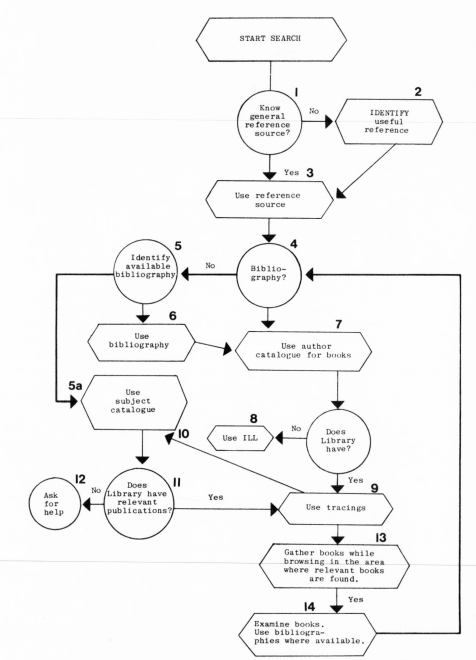

Figure 5-1. *Search strategy flowchart for books. Used with permission from Judith Pryor, Patricia A. Berge, and James Gruber,* Materials & Methods for Sociology Research *(New York: Neal-Schuman Publishers, Inc., 1980).*

Three types of search strategies are presented: the tracings approach to the card catalog, the translation approach to the card catalog, and the translation approach to periodicals indexes. The workbook emphasizes the role of language in the search process. Students complete assignments that help them translate language they know into language used in the source they are using. Knowing the indexing language allows students to query the system (reference books, periodical indexes, encyclopedias, and so on). Becoming self-sufficient in the library requires the ability to manipulate symbols, of which language is one example.[40] The workbook was used in a teacher education program and introduced students to educational tools as well as to basic library sources. Following is an example.

UNIT 10.
Subject Encyclopedias
and Subject Dictionaries*

Learning objectives

You will be able to:

1. identify subject encyclopedias in subject catalog, using the *Library of Congress Subject Headings* to determine the appropriate form subdivision for "encyclopedias."

2. determine the coverage and arrangement of a subject encyclopedia.

3. use the *Encyclopedia of Education, Encyclopedia of Educational Research,* or *International Encyclopedia of the Social Sciences* to identify background information on a particular research topic.

4. list natural language relevant to a particular research topic, based upon prior knowledge gained through reading, exposure to news media and discussion.

5. translate natural language into the indexing language used in a subject encyclopedia.

6. use subject encyclopedia to identify terminology associated with a particular research topic.

7. identify relevant citations to books in bibliographies attached to subject encyclopedia articles.

8. define the role of subject dictionaries in the search process.

9. identify subject dictionaries using the subject catalog.

10. use subject dictionaries to define the meaning of a word in the context of a given subject encyclopedia article.

*From Paul G. Cappuzzello and Sharon J. Rogers, *Information Gathering Skills for Pre-Service Teachers* (Toledo, Ohio: University of Toledo Libraries, 1979). Used with permission.

Introduction

By moving directly from articles in a general encyclopedia to the card catalog, a researcher ignores two important intermediate resources: subject encyclopedias and subject dictionaries.

Purpose and coverage
of subject encyclopedias

Subject encyclopedias include both single-volume works and multi-volume sets devoted to music, art, education, philosophy, religion, social sciences, or science and technology, just to name a few. Subject encyclopedias contain articles written by recognized scholars. These articles are more detailed and exhaustive than articles appearing in general encyclopedias and include bibliographies that tend to be more extensive.

You can use subject encyclopedias in several ways:
1. To find an overview of a subject about which you know very little.

Unit 10: Subject encyclopedias
and subject dictionaries
Information-gathering worksheet

Name_____

Course & section_____

1. Does Carlson Library have a specialized subject encyclopedia on
_____?

    a. Write down the call number, author (if available), and title below:

    b. Carefully describe each of the steps you followed to locate the encyclopedia in 1.a.

c. Locate the encyclopedia. What does the encyclopedia cover? How is it arranged?

2. Why would you use subject encyclopedias in searching for information?

3. Imagine that you are working with a group that is doing a class presentation on _____.

   Step 1: List five natural language terms or phrases that might be used to describe your topic. (Remember that you can (a) list key terms and phrases taken directly from the topic statement, and (b) combine key words and phrases from the topic statement to form new phrases.)

   Step 2: Use your natural language to find the *most relevant* encyclopedia article on your topic in the *Encyclopedia of Education*. Look up your natural language in the index volume of *Encyclopedia of Education*. List only the index terms or phrases that relate to your topic, with volume and page number references for each.

   <u>Index Terms and Phrases</u>   <u>Volume and Page Numbers</u>

   Step 3: Select the most relevant encyclopedia article on your topic located in Step 2. Write down the indexing term or phrase and the volume and page(s) where the article is located.

Step 4: Read carefully the encyclopedia article you have selected. From your reading of the encyclopedia article, list at least three specialized words and/or phrases that are used to discuss your topic. The terms and/or phrases that you select should facilitate your search for more information in either the subject catalog or a specialized periodical index. Therefore, pick terms and phrases most likely to be used as subject headings in the subject catalog or a specialized periodical index.

Look up any one of the specialized words or phrases (indicate which one by circling the word or phrase in the above answer) in the *Dictionary of Education*. On what page did you find the term?

Page_____.

Conclusion

Workbooks have become a popular and accepted method of teaching library skills because they offer several practical advantages to both students and librarians. They allow students to learn at their own rate. It is possible for students to get immediate feedback, especially when using a programmed workbook. Individualized help is available at all times from reference librarians. Workbooks are inexpensive and may even be self-supporting. The method makes students active learners since they must actually use the materials discussed in the text. Instructors find it a flexible method of instruction that can be used in a variety of educational settings and is especially effective in large libraries. The workbook helps make efficient use of staff time, since most instruction is done at the reference desk, which must be staffed anyway. Once written, the materials are easily revised and updated.

Workbooks as a method of instruction incorporate various aspects of widely diverse learning theories. However, workbooks never have been and never will be a panacea for library instruction. Bruner, Skinner, and Piaget all emphasize the importance of the teacher in the learning process. No printed material can provide all the guidance, stimulus, and reinforcement that the learner needs. No matter how expertly a workbook is written, it is basically a static element in the learning process. The instructor must facilitate the dynamic aspects of learning, and the success or failure of a teaching method ultimately depends on the instructor's ability to fill this role.

Notes

1. C. R. Maxwell, "The Workbook: A Recent Development," *School Board Journal* 88 (March 1934): 16, 44, 46.

2. W. P. Johnson, "Then Came the Workbook," *Journal of Education* 131 (February 1948): 64–66.

3. Ibid., p. 66.

4. Ibid.

5. A. W. Hurd, "The Workbook as an Instructional Aid," *The School Review* 39 (October 1931): 608–616.

6. Ibid., p. 616.

7. Robert W. Jacks, "The Status of the Workbook in Classroom Instruction," *Educational Method* 18 (October 1938): 105–109.

8. Miriam Dudley, "The Self-Paced Library Skills Program at UCLA's College Library," in *Educating the Library User*, ed. by John Lubans, Jr. (New York: Bowker, 1974), pp. 330–335; and Miriam Sue Dudley, *Chicano Library Program* (Los Angeles: University of California Library, 1970), p. 1.

9. Carolyn Kirkendall, *Academic Library Skills Workbook Listing* (Ypsilanti, Mich.: Project LOEX, 1979).

10. Thomas Kirk, "A Comparison of Two Methods of Library Instruction for Students in Introductory Biology," *College and Research Libraries* 32 (November 1971): 465–474.

11. Shelley Phipps and Ruth Dickstein, "The Library Skills Program at the University of Arizona: Testing, Evaluation & Critique," *Journal of Academic Librarianship* 5 (September 1979): 205–214.

12. Finley Carpenter, *The Skinner Primer: Behind Freedom and Dignity* (New York: Free Press, 1974), p. 15.

13. Ibid., pp. 27–32.

14. This is a condensed and simplified definition. For a full understanding of Skinner's theories, consult Carpenter, *Skinner Primer*, or B. F. Skinner, *The Technology of Teaching* (New York: Appleton-Century-Crofts, 1972).

15. Skinner, *Technology of Teaching*, p. 21.

16. Jerome Bruner, *Toward a Theory of Instruction* (Cambridge, Mass.: Belknap Press, 1960), p. 40.

17. Ibid., p. 18.

18. Ibid., p. 44.

19. David P. Ausubel, *Educational Psychology: A Cognitive View* (New York: Holt Rinehart and Winston, 1968) pp. 108–109.

20. Jerome Bruner, *The Process of Education* (Cambridge, Mass.: Harvard University Press, 1960), p. 82.

21. Ibid., p. 50.

22. Jean Piaget, *Science of Education and the Psychology of the Child* (New York: Viking, 1970).

23. The Kirkendall listing of library skills workbooks identifies three institutions that have specified using a programmed instruction format. One commercially published programmed instruction workbook for library skills is Richard R. Strawn, *Topics, Terms, and Research Techniques: Self-Instruction in Using Library Catalogs* (Metuchen, N.J.: Scarecrow, 1980).

24. William P. Pullen, *A Programmed Text on the Use of the Library for Georgia State University Students* (Atlanta: Georgia State College Library, 1966). (This text currently is not being used at Georgia State College.) Used with permission of the Pullen Library, Georgia State University, Atlanta.

25. Bruner, *Process,* pp. 29–30.

26. Elizabeth Frick, "Information Structure and Bibliographic Instruction," *Journal of Academic Librarianship* 1 (September 1975): pp. 12–14.

27. Raymond McInnis, *New Perspectives for Reference Service in Academic Libraries* (Westport, Conn.: Greenwood Press, 1978); and Thelma Freides, *Literature and Bibliography of the Social Sciences* (Los Angeles: Melville, 1973).

28. Pamela Kobelski and Mary Reichel, "Conceptual Frameworks for Bibliographic Instruction," *Journal of Academic Librarianship* 7 (May 1981): 73–77.

29. Ibid., pp. 74–75.

30. Miriam Dudley, *Workbook in Library Skills: A Self-Directed Course in the Use of UCLA's College Library* (Los Angeles: University of California, Los Angeles, College Library, 1973).

31. Frick, "Information Structure," p. 12.

32. Kirk, "A Comparison of Two Methods," p. 90.

33. Freides, *Literature and Bibliography*; and Carl M. White, *Sources of Information in the Social Sciences* (Chicago: American Library Association, 1973).

34. Ibid., p. 264.

35. Workbooks for history, political science, sociology, and business have been published by The Library Works, a division of Neal-Schuman Publishers, Inc.

36. Thomas G. Kirk, "Problems in Library Instruction in Four-Year Colleges," in *Educating the Library User,* ed. by John Lubans, Jr. (New York: Bowker, 1974), pp. 83–103.

37. James Benson and Ruth K. Maloney, "Principles and Searching," *RQ* 14 (Summer 1975): 316–320.

38. Ibid.

39. Paul G. Cappuzzello and Sharon J. Rogers, *Information Gathering Skills for Pre-Service Teachers* (Toledo, Ohio: University of Toledo Libraries, 1979). (This text currently is not being used at the University of Toledo.) Used with permission.

40. Telephone interview with Paul G. Cappuzzello, January 28, 1982.

6
Guided Design: Teaching Library Research as Problem-Solving

CERISE OBERMAN and REBECCA A. LINTON

Through the 1970s to the present, instruction librarians have struggled with a variety of methods for teaching effective library research skills. In an attempt to meet these needs, emphasis has fallen not on abstract concept-based processes, but on concrete skill-based processes of tool usage. This is unfortunate, for research is not a series of predetermined procedures; rather it is open-ended, involving problem-solving and creative thinking. As such, with its emphasis on decision-making skills, Guided Design can be an effective teaching model for library research methodology.

Library Research as a Problem-Solving Task

Library research is a problem-solving task requiring knowledge of tools and bibliographic structure as well as an ability to construct a strategy for locating information. More often than not, however, library instruction has emphasized tool usage and, more recently, bibliographic structure.[1] But it is the intellectual process underlying successful research that should be stressed in bibliographic education.

A problem-solving task arises "whenever a problem-solver desires some outcome or state of affairs that he does not immediately know how to attain." Furthermore, "imperfect knowledge about how to proceed is at the core of the genuinely problematic."[2] Many students, especially undergraduates, regard library research with a sense of helplessness. Too often they settle for information gathered from scattered efforts. This inability to attain desired results stems in large measure from "imperfect knowledge." Not only does problem-solving strive for "perfect knowledge," but effective problem-solving involves a systematic approach.

A number of educational theorists have discussed the problem-solving process in ways that pertain to library research. Dolores Silva identified four steps in the problem-solving process: (1) An image of the problem is determined, (2) a general plan that is most likely to "bridge the gap between the data and the unknown is devised," (3) the plan is executed, and (4) the solution is reviewed.[3] Richard Gross and Frederick McDonald offer a slightly different analysis, concluding that problem-solving has three steps: (1) an orienting process, (2) an elaborative or analytical process, and (3) a critical process.[4] Both studies agree that problem-solving involves a series of distinct steps.

The three steps of Gross and McDonald, when applied to library research, become more than just a "systematic approach." They emerge as underlying principles for the library research process itself. In fact, a direct correlation can be made between the three elements of problem-solving and the three underlying concepts of research: needs analysis, linkage, and evaluation.

Needs analysis, like orienting, clarifies the problem. In research, needs analysis determines the shape and scope of the problem. Its goal is the identification of variables in order to formulate a well-defined research problem. This identification involves three general categories: scope, perspective, and discipline. Scope outlines the temporal and geographical limits of the problem. Perspective delineates the person or group with which the problem deals and the viewpoint from which the problem will be addressed. Discipline defines the fields of study on which the problem will focus. Identification of these components delineates the research problem, which helps the researcher achieve direction and cohesion.[5]

Linkage, like the analytical process of Gross and McDonald, allows for formulation of the approach to the problem. In research problems, linkage bridges the gap between substantive knowledge and bibliographic structure. Understanding the relationship that one piece of research has to another is a necessary step in the research process. As Eugene Garfield notes, there is a "building-block development of [all] human knowledge," which is eventually represented in an increasingly cross-linked "network."[6] It is this network that the researcher must penetrate in order to locate key sources.

Perhaps the most significant step in the process of library research problem-solving, *evaluation,* like the critical process, tests results. In library research, evaluation involves reviewing and examining tools and their selection. At the same time, it can be the most difficult. Since evaluation is a subjective process, it is not the process itself that must be clarified, but rather the process of establishing criteria against which evaluative judgments can be made. The formulation of criteria, whether to evaluate sources (documents, books, articles, and such) or tools (indexes, bibliographies, statistics, and so on), should consist of such elements as accuracy, currency, depth of information, and level of information. Perspective is also a key evaluative element. In this case, perspective is concerned with the recognition of viewpoints that may color the analysis of an argument.

Basic to problem-solving is the ability to identify the essentials of a problem, recall previously learned principles, and assimilate them. "When problem-solving is achieved," says educational theorist Robert Gagné, "something is also learned, in the sense that the individual's capability is more or less permanently changed."[7] But the recognition and mastery of concepts will not necessarily make the student an effective library researcher/problem-solver. Problem-solving demands a framework that will stimulate it as a process. Guided Design provides such a framework.

Guided Design as a Decision-Making Model

Guided Design is an educational model developed by Charles Wales and Robert Stager in the late 1960s.[8] It was originally intended for engineering students who needed experience in solving open-ended problems. Wales and Stager were aware of the need to construct a problem-solving model in order to teach subject matter and to develop decision-making skills.

Psychologist Abraham Maslow's "hierarchy of needs" is the beginning point for the theory of Guided Design. Wales divides Maslow's "self-actualization" level into three parts: knowledge (principles, concepts, and facts), sensitivity/sensibility (values clarification), and decision-making (a means for problem-solving). He argues that "knowledge" is the predominant goal of classroom teaching, that sensitivity/sensibility receives some sporadic attention, and that decision-making is virtually ignored.[9] Since Wales believes that "self-actualization . . . should be of greatest concern to educators,"[10] his attention to decision-making is understandable.

In order to construct a model that would address his three components of "self-actualization," Wales delineates five "psychological principles."[11] For him, these principles represent effective teaching as well as providing the necessary interaction between student and teacher.[12]

1. Guide. A teacher should guide students' learning of a task by providing specific objectives, close supervision, and appropriate evaluation.

2. Practice. Students should be involved in the process of answering both single-answer and open-ended problems in either independent or supervised atmospheres.

3. Evaluate. Students should have direct interaction at every opportunity, preferably written, from teachers through the use of specific feedback information sheets.

4. Maturate. Reinforcement through feedback serves as a source that produces motivation and, therefore, maturation. Maturation is also encouraged when the student realizes that learned concepts and principles have direct application in a larger context.

5. Individualize. Through a variety of learning materials and through group work with peer tutors, individualization of learning allows students to learn at their own pace.

The actual Guided Design model is drawn from the problem-solving models of educational theorists such as John Dewey, Benjamin S. Bloom, J. P. Guildford, and Gagné.[13] From these models, Wales devises a system of decision-making steps incorporating his psychological principles of teaching. The four overall goals of his Guided Design system are (1) subject matter achievement, (2) skill in open-ended problem-solving, (3) development of social concerns and values, and (4) ability to model the professional decision-maker.[14]

The Presentation of Guided Design

Guided Design consists of structured teaching/learning models developed around Wales's decision-making steps (see Table 6-1). Each Guided Design model, regardless of its subject content, is constructed in the same format.

The actual Guided Design begins with the presentation of a situation, or setting, which usually portrays a fictitious group of students who are faced with a research problem. Working in groups, the students go through a series of instruction/feedback decision-making sequences. Each step contains an "instruction," providing an opportunity for students to participate in one of the decision-making operations. After completing an instruction, groups are given written feedback statements. In addition to providing possible answers, feedback allows the group to check its progress and becomes a basis for additional discussion. The feedback statement suggests the correct decision-making step and introduces new ideas or materials that will help in subsequent steps.

Throughout this process, the instructor acts as a facilitator, encouraging groups, when appropriate, to discuss, to think in a different vein, or to return to the original question. The interaction between the instructor and members of the group is crucial to the success of Guided Design.

The Guided Design Approach to Library Instruction

Guided Design provides for the teaching of the three basic elements of library research—needs analysis, linkage, and evaluation—as well as for the teaching of information sources. It is also a model that can be adapted either to the teaching of the research process as a whole or to any of its individual components. It provides a decision-making framework that can be transferred from one problem situation to another. However, Wales's "Steps in Decision Making" must be modified to meet the needs of library instruction (see Table 6-1).

Table 6-1 Steps in Decision-Making

Wales's Steps in Decision-Making*	Steps in Decision-Making for Library Instruction
Gather Information. This step is listed first because it is usually a component of each step in the decision-making process. It involves a search for pertinent information from the person's own background, books, printed matter, media, other people, experts and experimental work.	*Gather Information.* This step and its use are the same as in Wales's model, i.e., gathering pertinent information needed to solve a library research problem.
A. *Identify the Problem* Someone may ask you to solve a problem or you may discover it by yourself. In either case you must learn to look beyond the symptoms of the problem to find out what is wrong.	A. *Identify the Scope of the Problem* In order to solve a library research problem, you must examine the problem thoroughly to ascertain the scope of the problem. This includes temporal and geographical dimensions.
B. *State the Basic Objective or Goal* The Basic Objective focuses your thoughts on the real problem to be solved. It should be a statement which is broad enough so no reasonable possible solution is eliminated.	B. *Analyze the Scope of the Problem* What factors, i.e., interest group or perspective, arise from the temporal and geographical dimensions of the problem? What disciplines are involved?
C. *State the Constraints, Assumptions and Facts* Constraints are factors which limit the outcome of the project and cannot be changed to simplify the problem and make it solvable. Facts are statements of things that are known.	C. *State Constraints of the Scope* Determine what factors both internal and external to the problem limit its scope. Internal factors include such things as whether or not the information necessary for solving the problem exists. External factors include such things as the time available for carrying out the research.
D. *Generate Possible Solutions* This is the time for creative thinking. Don't prejudge ideas as they are generated; get all the different thoughts you can.	D. *Generate Possible Solutions* Decide what information sources will provide the information needed to answer each part of the research problem.
E. *Evaluate and Make a Decision* Determine which possible solution is most likely to solve the problem.	E. *Refine Solutions* Determine which sources provide the information needed to answer each component of the research problem.
F. *Analysis* Separate the chosen possible solutions into meaningful elements. Determine and gather the information you need to develop each element.	F. *Analysis* Evaluate each source in terms of its accuracy, currency, depth-of-information, level of knowledge, etc. and its relevance to the research problem.

Table 6-1 (cont.)

Wales's Steps in Decision-Making*	Steps in Decision-Making for Library Instruction
G. *Synthesis* Combine the elements to create a detailed solution.	G. *Synthesis* Rate the evaluated sources against the specific information needs to determine which source will best answer each need.
H. *Evaluate the Solution* Does it satisfy the basic objective: is it feasible, practical, economical, safe, legal, and moral?	H. *Formulate the Search* Devise a strategy for consulting the tools chosen to answer the various information needs of the research problem.
I. *Report the Results and Make Recommendations* Prepare a report that describes what you have done and decided. Think about the information needs of the person who will read the report. Don't write what isn't necessary.	I. *Search* Consult appropriate sources and gather information.
J. *Complete the Research Report* Using the information which has been gathered, answer the components of the research problem, and complete the project.	J. *Complete the Research Project* Using the information which has been gathered, answer the components of the research problem, and complete the project.

*From Charles E. Wales and Robert A. Stager, *Guided Design* (Morgantown: West Virginia University, 1977). By permission of Charles E. Wales and Robert A. Stager.

The modifications of the decision-making steps for library instruction cover the three basic elements of library research from a problem-solving base: needs analysis, linkage, and evaluation. The first four steps—Identify the Scope of the Problem, Analyze the Scope of the Problem, State the Constraints of the Scope, and Generate Possible Solutions—all deal with needs analysis. The concept of linkage between substantive knowledge and bibliographic structure is covered in Refine Solutions and Synthesis. Evaluation, the third element of library research, is dealt with in both Analysis and Synthesis. The remaining steps, Formulate the Search, Search, and Complete the Research Project, are execution steps.

A Guided Design

The Guided Design that follows in part, and is reproduced in full at the end of the chapter, illustrates the adaptation of Wales's decision-making steps to library instruction.[15] It was developed for use as part of a 90-minute library instruction seminar for graduate students in public administration. The objectives are to introduce the concepts of primary and secondary sources and to acquaint students with specific sources.

Students are, first, in The Setting (below) given a description of a research problem situation, including who is doing the research, the topic of the research, and the desired product.

The setting

The students were assembled in the senator's reception room anxiously waiting to be briefed on their internship project. The internship program, a new component in the public administration graduate program, promised to be exciting and educational. Working as staff assistants to Senator Dipper would provide substantial experience in public administration.

All four students, Rachel McDonald, Jim Paper, Ginger Turner, and Leonard Brach, were speculating on their assignment when the door opened and Sam Weston, staff assistant to the senator, asked the group to join him in the conference room.

After formal introductions, Sam began to explain the project they wanted the interns to begin working on. "As you know, the senator is up for reelection in November, and he is preparing his campaign platform. He needs to have several major issues that have local impact explored thoroughly. He would like you to research the issue of nuclear waste transportation in South Carolina and prepare a thorough, documented report, including your recommendations as to his stance on this matter." Sam continued, "The actual research is up to you entirely. Make sure you consult primary as well as secondary sources for your information. You have two weeks to complete this first project. I am available for consultation at any point, but I must excuse myself now, I have another appointment."

After the problem has been presented, the first set of instructions is given. Through the continuing narrative, these instructions, underlined at the end of the narrative sections, correspond to steps in the decision-making process; in this case, the first step—Identify the Scope of the Problem.

Instruction A

> *The students were rather stunned; they had anticipated a bit more direction than that. After looking at one another questioningly for a few moments, Rachel finally broke the silence. "Well, this sounds like a challenging project, and I'm excited about working on it, but does anyone have any idea where we begin?"*
>
> *"I suppose we ought to go to the library," Jim replied. "Surely the information we need will be there."*
>
> *"The library does sound like the right place to start, but how do we find the information we need once we get there?" Leonard asked.*
>
> *Ginger broke in at this point. "I think you're both on the right track. The key to our problem is in the information we need. We have to prepare a report for the senator on the issue of nuclear waste transportation. Before we can begin gathering our information, we need to figure out exactly what information we will need to write a thorough report."*
>
> *"I'm not sure what you mean," Leonard said.*
>
> *Rachel responded, "I think Ginger wants us to compose some questions that we need to investigate."*
>
> *"Like what areas in South Carolina are affected?" Leonard asked.*
>
> *"Exactly," Ginger said.*
>
> *They all agreed that <u>making a list of questions they need to answer</u> would be a good place to begin.*

Next, students look at such factors as time frame, geographic considerations, and definitions of terms operative in the problem. This step of the narrative, Analyze the Scope of the Problem, concentrates on the perspective of the problem. In determining this, students suggest possible interest groups, the disciplines covered, and how these relate to the temporal and geographic limitations/possibilities of the problem. Other additional constraints include the availability of information, the time available to the researcher for gathering information, and the types of sources that must be consulted. The last point lays the groundwork for teaching the distinctions between primary and secondary sources.

Instruction B

"Okay," Jim said, "we know that our goal is to write a thorough report on the issue of nuclear waste transportation in South Carolina, and we know what kinds of information we need to write it. But how much information do we need, and how much can we gather, assimilate, and incorporate into a report in two weeks?"

"Jim has a good point," Ginger replied. "We know we only have two weeks in which to write the report, and we can assume that the senator wants us to take an unbiased approach in our research."

"It seems that we need to be careful; we don't want to try to collect information from every state on this issue," Rachel commented.

"On the other hand," Leonard interrupted, "we cannot solely concentrate on South Carolina. The rest of the country is also facing similar problems. We might learn a great deal from what they are doing."

"Why don't we use our list of questions to make a chart that would help us decide if we need local, state, or national data for our answers," Rachel urged.

Using the following chart, the group <u>indicated what geographic emphasis, if any, they wanted to place on the answers to their questions.</u>

	Local	State	National
Population			
Transportation routes			
Laws			
Hazards			
Needs			
Lobby groups			
Other			

Once the scope of the problem has been defined, students can Generate Possible Solutions, from the instructions in the next three steps of the narrative.

Instruction C

> "I'm beginning to feel much better about this project every minute," Rachel said. "At least now we know what kinds of information we'll need. That should give us some direction."
>
> "I agree," Leonard said. "Now all we have to do is figure out how to find all this information we've decided we need!"
>
> "I'm not sure that's <u>all</u> we have left to do, but it does seem to be the most logical step to take next," Jim replied.
>
> "Well, we've all had some experience in using libraries," Ginger added. "So why don't we pool our knowledge again and come up with <u>a list of possible sources for our information.</u>"
>
> "Great idea," Rachel agreed. "Obviously, we can start with books. What else?"

Instruction D

> "These types of sources are all useful, and we certainly will need to consult them to gather the information we need," Rachel offered.
>
> "I don't want to throw a kink in the works, but I'm not sure what Mr. Weston was talking about when he said we would have to consult both primary and secondary sources. I'm not sure if I know the difference between the two," Leonard said.
>
> "I don't want to look too dumb," Rachel said. "<u>Let's draft our own definitions</u>, and then I'll run over to the library and ask a friend of mine, Sydney Lion, who is a librarian, what she thinks of them."

Instruction E

> The group felt more confident about their abilities once they compared their definitions with Sydney's.
>
> Rachel interrupted the general self-adoration. "Sydney suggested that we <u>take</u> our list of source materials we compiled

and identify them as either primary sources or secondary sources. This way we will make sure to include primary sources, and it may be useful to know in terms of accessing the materials."

The group drew up a chart, shown below.

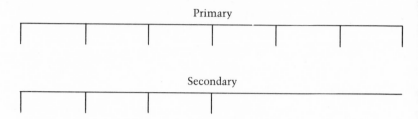

Students are asked to link the type of information need with either primary and/or secondary sources in the next step of the narrative. They can then evaluate the usefulness of each source in relation to specific information needs. Thus, students can generate criteria for evaluation, such as accuracy, currency, or level of information. Once sources have been evaluated, those that will best answer each need can be determined.

The final aspect of the needs analysis/linkage/evaluation process is devising a search strategy for consulting the pertinent sources. Students should be introduced to specific tools they will need to consult in order to retrieve the required information sources. For example, a brief presentation of tools can be made if time permits. Or students can be given an annotated bibliography of tools, describing functions and uses. With the knowledge of which tools to use to access the various information sources, they can devise their own strategy. This search strategy is based on the bibliographic structure of the discipline they have uncovered.

Instruction F

The group examined the chart carefully. They decided that the next logical step would be to examine their original list of information needs and decide which sources—primary or secondary—would most likely satisfy that need.

Once again, they drew a chart, shown on the facing page.

	Primary	Secondary
Definition of nuclear waste		
Possible hazards resulting from transportation of nuclear wastes		
Laws governing nuclear waste transportation		
Transportation routes		
Population of areas affected		
Lobby group stands		
Comparison with other states		
Alternative transportation methods		
Others		

The final steps of the library research decision-making process are Search and Complete the Research Project. In these steps students consult sources and gather information needed, using, first, the search strategy they have devised, and, second, the information they have gathered to complete their research project.

Instruction G

The group looked over the chart and decided that they were almost ready to begin their research. They knew what information they needed and what types of sources would have that information. But they were not sure how to identify the specific sources that would contain the exact information they needed. They knew they would need to use the card catalog to find books. But how were they going to find magazine and journal articles, or specific laws, agency reports, or census materials? They felt sure that there were tools that would enable them to locate the specific sources they needed. So they decided to see Sydney again and ask her how they could find the specific sources they needed.

Adapting Guided Design to Particular Instruction Needs

One of the values of the Guided Design model is its versatility. In addition to the Guided Design for public administration just presented, Guided Designs can and have been developed that are not discipline-oriented and that are aimed at teaching a specific type of information source, rather than at the entire research process. The decision-making steps incorporated in a Guided Design can be chosen and modified to meet the objectives and requirements of a particular research problem. The factors that must be considered in developing a library instruction Guided Design are the same ones that must always be considered.

In developing any Guided Design, it is necessary to build both on the objectives intrinsic to the process and on the specific objectives of a particular instructional situation. The initial step is to determine objectives that should be paired with the appropriate decision-making steps. For example, in a Guided Design developed to teach students about the use of encyclopedias, the objectives might include a number of goals: (1) to teach the role encyclopedias play in the research process, (2) to provide criteria for evaluating encyclopedias, and (3) to introduce the differences between general and subject encyclopedias. All the decision-making steps can be used to accomplish these goals.

Although the objectives of the instructional situation are the prime factor in the development of a Guided Design, another important factor is the time allowed for implementation. Is it to be used in a one-hour session, or is there more than one hour or one session allotted for it? It is often possible to combine steps or objectives if time is limited. Or, if more than one class session is available, it might be desirable to plan a Guided Design to incorporate work outside the classroom.

The level of the students must also be considered. How much information they can be expected to bring to the Guided Design will affect the content of the feedback instructions and the decision-making steps used to achieve the desired objectives.

Whether it is to be used for a specific assignment or course, or for general library use instruction, this will affect the problem situation around which a Guided Design is created. However, since Guided Design teaches library research as an open-ended process, it is actually easier to make the instruction example relevant to students' needs than it is in more traditional forms of instruction.

Transference of the Decision-Making Framework

Because the decision-making framework of Guided Design teaches library research as an open-ended, problem-solving task, students learn skills they can recognize as being transferable from one library research problem to another. Rogers emphasizes the importance of the transference of knowledge in library instruction when she suggests that:

Students must be encouraged to view information gathering activities as open tasks by giving them information to convince them that the activities they work on in a particular learning experience will be applicable on future occasions and in different situations.[16]

The Guided Design process gives students the decision-making skills that will enable them to adapt what they have learned to each individual situation.

The use of Guided Design in library instruction is in its infancy, and no concrete data supports the conclusion that students are indeed transferring decision-making skills. However, evidence collected from the use of Guided Design in other disciplines suggests that this transference is occurring. For example, David Lawrence has used Guided Design in his political science course at Westmont College and has found that the analytical and problem-solving skills learned by students carry over to other situations.[17] Wales has found that graduates of his program at West Virginia University have higher grade point averages than those who have not been exposed to Guided Design.[18]

Guided Design is perhaps most valuable in that it forces the teacher to rethink the presentation of subject matter. For us, that involved recasting the library research process and searching for the conceptual core of a dynamic search process. The underlying principles of needs analysis, linkage, and evaluation remain the same, but strategies for solving library problems vary. Thus, this approach recognizes both the importance of satisfying an immediate research need and the importance of providing students with a structure for meeting longer range research goals.

Guided Design provides an alternative for the library instruction movement by articulating research principles, by emphasizing the need for students to be creative problem-solvers, and by presenting library research as a complex and intricate process that involves intellectual concepts and decision-making. It is a means for instructing students in both subject content and thinking processes. If we are successful in merging the concrete aspects of searching with the more abstract principles of thinking and are able to provide students with a framework in which they can systematically approach a problem, then we are, to quote Wales, "help[ing] the student learn to solve open-ended problems, to think for him[her]self, thinking logically, [and to] gather and organize information, make decisions, communicate ideas and use the intellectual modes: analysis, synthesis, and evaluation."[19]

Appendix: Guided Design Model

The setting

The students were assembled in the senator's reception room anxiously waiting to be briefed on their internship project. The internship program, a new component in the public administration graduate program, promised to be exciting and educational. Working as staff assistants to Senator Dipper would provide substantial experience in public administration.

All four students, Rachel McDonald, Jim Paper, Ginger Turner, and Leonard Brach, were speculating on their assignment when the door opened and Sam Weston, staff assistant to the senator, asked the group to join him in the conference room.

After formal introductions, Sam began to explain the project they wanted the interns to begin working on. "As you know, the senator is up for reelection in November, and he is pre-

Note: This format, which is an instruction followed by a feedback, is presented on separate pages for classroom use. See p. 115 for presentation procedure.

paring his campaign platform. He needs to have several major issues that have local impact explored thoroughly. He would like you to research the issue of nuclear waste transportation in South Carolina and prepare a thorough, documented report, including your recommendations as to his stance on this matter." Sam continued, "The actual research is up to you entirely. Make sure you consult primary as well as secondary sources for your information. You have two weeks to complete this first project. I am available for consultation at any point, but I must excuse myself now, I have another appointment."

Instruction A

The students were rather stunned; they had anticipated a bit more direction than that. After looking at one another questioningly for a few moments, Rachel finally broke the silence. "Well, this sounds like a challenging project, and I'm excited about working on it, but does anyone have any idea where we begin?"

"I suppose we ought to go to the library," Jim replied. "Surely the information we need will be there."

"The library does sound like the right place to start, but how do we find the information we need once we get there?" Leonard asked.

Ginger broke in at this point. "I think you're both on the right track. The key to our problem is in the information we need. We have to prepare a report for the senator on the issue of nuclear waste transportation. Before we can begin gathering our information, we need to figure out exactly what information we will need to write a thorough report."

"I'm not sure what you mean," Leonard said.

Rachel responded, "I think Ginger wants us to compose some questions that we need to investigate."

"Like what areas in South Carolina are affected?" Leonard asked.

"Exactly," Ginger said.

They all agreed that <u>making a list of questions they need to answer</u> would be a good place to begin.

Feedback A

> What is nuclear waste?
>
> What is the population in the areas that would be affected?
>
> Where are the transportation routes?
>
> What are the laws governing hazardous waste transportation?
>
> What are the possible hazards that might result from transportation of nuclear wastes?
>
> What are the alternative transportation methods?
>
> What is the need for transportation of nuclear wastes?
>
> What are the lobby group stands on this issue?

Instruction B

> "Okay," Jim said, "we know that our goal is to write a thorough report on the issue of nuclear waste transportation in South Carolina, and we know what kinds of information we need to write it. But how much information do we need, and how much can we gather, assimilate, and incorporate into a report in two weeks?"
>
> "Jim has a good point," Ginger replied. "We know we only have two weeks in which to write the report, and we can assume that the senator wants us to take an unbiased approach in our research."
>
> "It seems that we need to be careful; we don't want to try to collect information from every state on this issue," Rachel commented.
>
> "On the other hand," Leonard interrupted, "we cannot solely concentrate on South Carolina. The rest of the country is also facing similar problems. We might learn a great deal from what they are doing."
>
> "Why don't we use our list of questions to make a chart that would help us decide if we need local, state, or national data for our answers," Rachel urged.
>
> Using the chart on the facing page, the group indicated what geographic emphasis, if any, they wanted to place on the answers to their questions. The X's indicate geographic emphasis that the group considered important.

	Local	State	National
Population			
Transportation routes			
Laws			
Hazards			
Needs			
Lobby groups			
Other			

Feedback B

	Local	State	National
Population	X		
Transportation routes	X		
Laws	X	X	X
Hazards	X		
Needs			
Lobby groups			
Other		X	X

Instruction C

"I'm beginning to feel much better about this project every minute," Rachel said. "At least now we know what kinds of information we'll need. That should give us some direction."

"I agree," Leonard said. "Now all we have to do is figure out how to find all this information we've decided we need!"

"I'm not sure that's <u>all</u> we have left to do, but it does seem to be the most logical step to take next," Jim replied.

"Well, we've all had some experience in using libraries," Ginger added. "So why don't we pool our knowledge again and come up with a <u>list of possible sources for our information.</u>"

"Great idea," Rachel agreed. "Obviously, we can start with books. What else?"

Feedback C

> Books
>
> Statistical materials
>
> Laws
>
> Congressional reports
>
> Newspaper articles
>
> Magazine articles
>
> Journal articles
>
> Census materials
>
> Agency reports

Instruction D

> *"These types of sources are all useful, and we certainly will need to consult them to gather the information we need," Rachel offered.*
>
> *"I don't want to throw a kink in the works, but I'm not sure what Mr. Weston was talking about when he said we would have to consult both primary and secondary sources. I'm not sure if I know the difference between the two," Leonard said.*
>
> *"I don't want to look too dumb," Rachel said. "Let's draft our own definitions, and then I'll run over to the library and ask a friend of mine, Sydney Lion, who is a librarian, what she thinks of them."*

Feedback D

> Sydney read over the definitions that the group had written. She thought they looked fairly reasonable, and she made a few additions, which she gave to Rachel.
>
> Primary source materials: original material that has not been interpreted, condensed, or evaluated by a second party, for example, statistics, laws, congressional reports.
>
> Secondary source materials: books, articles, or unpublished materials in the compilation of which information in primary sources has been modified and used.

Instruction E

> *The group felt more confident about their abilities once they compared their definitions with Sydney's.*

Rachel interrupted the general self-adoration. "Sydney suggested that we <u>take</u> our list of source materials we compiled and identify them as either primary sources or secondary sources. This way we will make sure to include primary sources, and it may be useful to know in terms of accessing the materials."

The group drew up a chart, shown below.

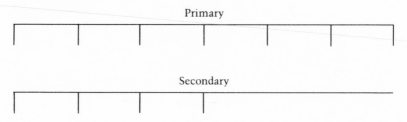

Feedback E

Leonard took the chart to Sydney for her comments. Sydney explained that dividing source materials into primary and secondary categories can be very tricky sometimes. For instance, newspaper articles, which are considered secondary materials, can often become primary materials in a historical context. Given this particular project, the chart looked like this:

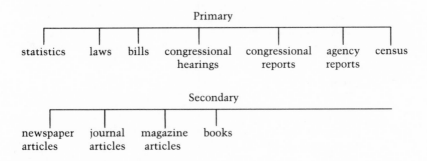

Instruction F

The group studied the chart carefully. They decided that the next logical step would be to examine their original list of information needs and decide which sources—primary or secondary—would most likely satisfy that need.

Once again they drew a chart, as shown on the following page.

	Primary	Secondary
Definition of nuclear waste		
Possible hazards resulting from transportation of nuclear wastes		
Laws governing nuclear waste transportation		
Transportation routes		
Population of areas affected		
Lobby group stands		
Comparison with other states		
Alternative transportation methods		
Others		

Feedback F

	Primary	Secondary
Definition of nuclear waste		X
Possible hazards resulting from transportation of nuclear wastes	X (cong. hearings)	X (articles, books)
Laws governing nuclear waste transportation	X	
Transportation routes	X	
Population of areas affected	X (census reports)	
Lobby group stands	X (publications)	X (articles)
Comparison with other states	X (laws)	X (articles)
Alternative transportation methods	X (agency reports)	X (articles)
Others		

Instruction G

The group looked over the chart and decided that they were almost ready to begin their research. They knew what information they needed and what types of sources would have that information. But they were not sure how to identify the specific sources that would contain the exact information they needed. They knew they would need to use the card catalog to find books. But how were they going to find magazine and journal articles, or specific laws, agency reports, or census materials? They felt sure that there were tools that would enable them to locate the specific sources they needed. So they decided to see Sydney again and ask her how they could find the specific sources they needed.

Notes

1. There have been a number of methods introduced and used that focus on the use of bibliographic structure as a framework for instruction. See Pamela Kobelski and Mary Reichel, "Conceptual Frameworks for Bibliographic Instruction," *Journal of Academic Librarianship* 7 (May 1981): 73–77 for a discussion of such techniques. A few techniques in library instruction have flirted with the idea of teaching the mental processes involved in the search process: flowcharting, systematic searching, structuring of disciplines. However, each of these techniques stopped short of actually incorporating decision-making or problem-solving steps.

2. A. Newell, J. C. Shaw, and H. A. Simon, "Report on a General Problem-Solving Program," in *Readings in Mathematical Psychology*, vol. 2, ed. by R. D. Luce, R. R. Bush, and E. Galanter (New York: John Wiley, 1965), p. 4.

3. Dolores Silva, "A Search Paradigm for the Description of Problem-Solving Processes," *Educational Technology* 13 (August 1973): 38–39.

4. Richard E. Gross and Frederick J. McDonald, "Classroom Methods: III, The Problem-Solving Approach," *Phi Delta Kappan* 39 (March 1958): 260.

5. For a more detailed explanation of needs analyses, see Cerise Oberman-Soroka, "Question Analysis, Piaget, and the Learning Cycle" (Paper presented at the 2nd Annual Conference on Reasoning and Piaget, Denver, Colorado, March 1981).

6. Eugene Garfield, "Primordial Concepts, Citation Indexing, and Historio-Bibliography," *The Journal of Library History* 2 (July 1967): 239.

7. Robert M. Gagné, *The Conditions of Learning* (New York: Holt, 1965), p. 157.

8. Charles Wales and Robert Stager developed Guided Design at West Virginia University, where it has been adopted as the instructional model for the engineering curriculum.

9. Emphasis on knowledge rather than decision-making seems to stem from, and is reinforced by, the views of both researchers and teachers. This results from a belief that students are not capable of achieving complex educational objectives. See Tamar Levin, "Instruction Which Enables Students to Develop Higher Mental Processes," in *Evaluation in Education*, vol. 3 (Elmsford, N.Y.: Pergamon Press, 1979), pp. 173–176.

10. Charles E. Wales, "Should Curriculum Planning Start with Subject Matter?" *Journal of Educational Technology Systems* 4 (1975): 24.

11. Charles E. Wales, "Improve Your Teaching Tomorrow with Teaching-Learning Psychology," *Engineering Education* 66 (February 1976): 390.

12. Ibid. Wales suggests that his "psychological principles" for teaching be adopted by teachers regardless of whether they use Guided Design.

13. For a detailed explanation of the adaption of the problem-solving methods of Dewey, Bloom, Guildford, and Gagné to Guided Design, see "The Theoretical Rationale for Guided Design" in Charles E. Wales and Robert A. Stager, *Guided Design* (Morgantown: West Virginia University, 1977), pp. 136–149.

14. Ibid., p. 149.

15. Developed and copyrighted by Cerise Oberman and Rebecca Linton.

16. Sharon Rogers, "Class-Related Bibliographic Instruction: A Philosophical Defense," in *Proceedings from the 2nd Southeastern Conference on Approaches to Bibliographic Instruction*, ed. by Cerise Oberman-Soroka (Charleston, S.C.: College of Charleston Library Associates, 1980), p. 29.

17. David Lawrence, "Guided Design in the Basic American Government Course," *Teaching Political Science* 7 (April 1980): 324.

18. Charles Wales, "Data on New Educational Strategy: Guided Design," *Phi Delta Kappan* 59 (December 1978): 314. For additional discussion on the success of Guided Design, particularly as it relates to group problem-solving, see R. C. Hess, "Guided Design, User Attitudes, & Group Problem-Solving Research," in *Proceedings of a National Conference on Teaching Decision-Making: Guided Design, 1980, May 28, 29, 30* (Morgantown: West Virginia University, 1980), pp. 16.1–16.5.

19. Wales and Stager, *Guided Design*, p. 1.2.

7

Teaching Library Researching in the Humanities and the Sciences: A Contextual Approach

TOPSY N. SMALLEY and STEPHEN H. PLUM

In the development of library instruction programs, the tendency has been to conceive of desirable learning outcomes in fairly broad terms. The assumed goal is that instruction will impart a level of skill and knowledge sufficient to enable a student to interact, successfully and independently, with the library and its resources. The components necessary to achieve that goal include acquiring specific skills and a general understanding about the organization of the library.

Along with this approach there has been an inclination on the part of librarians to design bibliographic instruction programs that reflect three basic, presupposed constructs: (1) a framework for imparting skill and knowledge, which is centered on the tools themselves, (2) a prototypical model for successful interactions with library information systems, which is widely applicable to all disciplines, and (3) a learner who, once exposed to the tools and the model, is able to integrate cognitively these learning experiences for all other information searches.

These three presuppositions have served important purposes. They have provided an initial, common framework for bibliographic instruction efforts. They have promoted opportunities for exchange and adoption of ideas from one setting to another. They have reinforced a shared sense of purpose and contribution to the instructional process. Yet, important as they are in themselves, they imply further possibilities for growth, exploration, and refinement. Relatively little discussion, for example, has been devoted to basic differences among processes of research in various disciplines and how these affect instruction and learning outcomes.

In this chapter, we investigate some elements of these processes that differentiate the humanities from the sciences.[1] Our examination focuses on differences in the structures of the literatures in these areas, distinctive features of scholarship that characterize and shape these literatures, and distinctions between reference and access tools serving these disciplines. Two interactive themes govern our investigation: first, that structural differences between the literatures significantly affect strategies for teaching library researching, and, second, that effective teaching is characterized by developing student capabilities to transfer learning to new situations.

Why Explore the Structures of the Humanities and the Sciences?

Sorting out the distinguishing features and structural differences of humanities, as opposed to science, research may be intrinsically interesting, but may, on first glance, seem somewhat removed from bibliographic instruction. For most librarians, training has consisted of piecemeal, type-of-tool learning, even in subject bibliography courses, and insights connecting skills of access to an understanding of disciplinary research needs have usually been experienced in pragmatic, situational contexts.

We need to be more constructively thoughtful about these connections for the following reasons. First is the necessity to formulate teaching approaches that facilitate the transfer of learning. Contemporary research in cognitive learning theory shows that meaningful learning takes place within the context of conceptual structure and that the processes of effective inquiry originate within such a structure. (Cognitive learning theories as they apply to our teaching are discussed later in the chapter.) If we are to teach in ways that will foster independent inquiry, we ourselves need to be clear about the concepts that shape our teaching. Second, our students are interested in becoming effective inquirers, not librarians. The structures of the literatures of various disciplines reflect distinctive research processes, and the products of those processes can be reached at the library. Effective inquiry, as well as the effective use of library resources, requires an understanding of the processes of scholarship.

Neither of these reasons is novel. Other librarians have emphasized the importance of conceptual frameworks for bibliographic instruction,[2] or have advocated teaching students search strategies that involve understanding scholarly research.[3] Our own point of departure hinges on substance and context. Others have been interested in conceptual frameworks and research processes, but their focus has primarily been on library systems. Their proposed teaching structures, then, have centered on concepts that either elucidate bibliographic organization, or support the use of various library search strategies, or both. Although neglecting neither of these, our approach has been to drive the center of concern back an additional step, to a framework of concepts about the structures of the disciplines and their research processes. These contexts, we assume, generate the distinctive qualities of information systems and strategies for bibliographic inquiry.

Disciplines and Research Processes

The humanist and the scientist use different sorts of research methods and study different types of objects. They record their achievements via distinctive literatures, and access to those documents involves distinctive strategies of inquiry. The methodologies of the humanist are shaped for interpretative validity; those of the scientist seek experimental validity. The humanities professional studies the products of human imagination; the scientist studies the natural world. The literature of the humanities is primarily monographic and enduring; the literature of the sciences is based largely in periodicals and is characterized by currency. Useful search strategies in the humanities can be discursive and intuitive; those in the sciences are typically focused and direct.

For both the humanist and the scientist, inquiry originates in distinctive conceptual structures governed by what it means to understand in that area of knowledge.[4] These different conceptual structures influence processes of researching and processes of reporting research. As Frederick B. Thompson noted,[5] conceptual organization determines the nature of the information transmitted; that is, the ways of understanding generate the meanings shared in reports of research.

The humanities

For the humanities professional, understanding flows from close examination of particularities: a poem, a painting, a musical score. The aim of humanists is elucidation in a way that carries interpretative validity. They attempt to penetrate both the particularity and the whole of which it is a part. The humanist's thinking is at once focused and holistic, with the objective being to understand individual creative work within a meaningful and illuminative context.

The humanist studies products of human creativity, each reflecting complexities of personality, social experience, and form of expression. The context chosen by the humanities scholar may center on the individual artist, the artist as part of a given social environment, the artist as expressive within a particular form of creativity, or a combination. To understand in the humanities is to apply and interrelate knowledge on these various levels. However composed, the research fabric of the context reflects the scholar's judgment that it provides meaningful and authentic elucidation.

Humanities scholars concern themselves with expressive content, with connotative and symbolic associations. In large part, the meaning of the expressive content is subjected to interpretation along discipline-determined lines. Yet the humanist is also an individual, a unique personality, a specialist on forms of expression, and he or she becomes a part of the process of understanding. Objects of study in the humanities are, in Jung's sense, symbols; they have multiple meanings and are incapable of exhaustive explanation.[6] The humanist personally encounters the object under study, and in this encounter he or she is autonomous and the involvement is unique.

In scholarly writing, the humanist combines a discipline-determined conceptual framework with personal, unique perceptions. This combination is crucial. Presumably, in choosing and applying interpretative context, the humanist uses the conceptualizations, the criteria for judgment, and the logic of inquiry that prevail in the field. Within this, the humanist applies knowledge about the artist, the artist's social environment, and the specific form of expression. The humanist is also the instrument in these studies, and what he or she understands is determined both by discipline frameworks and by qualities of personal encounter. The language used by the humanist to convey his or her understanding reflects this union of intellect and personality and is both descriptive and emotive. The meaning that is captured and shared is a reorganization of both intellectual and highly individual experience.

In the end, the humanist's product is evaluated on grounds of interpretative validity. The arguments used, the evidence marshaled, and the context chosen are judged relative to the expressive content of the original material. The authenticity of the humanist's use of personal response is also evaluated. The emotive encounter is measured as to whether it is faithful to symbolic possibilities inherent in the original, and whether precise insights constitute illuminative communication to others. The meaningful organization imposed by the humanist becomes the information that is transmitted.

The sciences

For the scientist, on the other hand, the structure of understanding flows not so much from close examination of particularities, as from close examination of regularities. The scientist's aim is to understand relationships assumed to be patterned. Interest in any particularity is bounded by the extent to which it represents a generality. The scientist's objective is to elucidate some piece of the pattern in ways that carry experimental validity and in ways that will reproduce results. To understand in science is to understand individual instances as explanatory parts of generalities.

Underlying scientific research is the assumption that an independent world, governed by ordered relationships, exists and, further, that systematic, objective investigation yields successively approximate, and increasingly valid, explanations. Validity is ensured by two fundamental, interrelated conditions. First, a set of precepts, known as the scientific method, governs scientific investigation. These precepts, a combination of conventions about performing inquiry, assure objectivity and reproducibility of findings. Second, science is a public enterprise. A scientist's results are openly shared and accessible to confirmation.

Scientific investigation takes place within a theoretical context. Theories propose substantial propositions about lawful relationships among establishable facts. In posing patterns to explain relationships, theories also suggest relationships to be investigated. By offering a structure in which experimentally known variables can be explained, the theories disclose ways of exploring that which is as yet unknown and unexplained.

Reality is enormously complex, and scientific understanding about it is incomplete. As Harold I. Brown has pointed out, the structure of reality undermines the structure of scientific theories.[7] Theories and their laws simply offer propositional constructs, and these explain only ranges of facts. Scientific investigation tests the scope and limits of hypotheses about specific outcomes consonant with expectations derived from theory. When hypothesis testing produces evidence predicted by theory, theory is said to be supported.

Theory plays a significant role in guiding expected observations and in forming interpretations applied to evidence. The occurrence of scientific revolutions, in Thomas S. Kuhn's sense,[8] is generally explained as a consequence of the interaction of these several factors, that is, that theories are constructs providing connections between laws that explain particular ranges of facts; that the complexities of reality resist comprehensive, theoretical explanation; and that scientific investigation occurs under conditions delimited by a matrix of theoretical and methodological assumptions (in Kuhn's language, a paradigm). Given these circumstances, competing theories are probable, as are scientific results unaccounted for by theory. Science strives for validity in understanding reality. A preponderance of anomalous evidence will eventually compel a shift in theory, or in paradigm—in essence, a shift in modes of exploration and in ways of understanding.

The scientist's work takes place within a community of researchers who subject it to judgment on two grounds: the soundness of its method and the extent to which it contributes to valid and useful understanding. Experimentally and theoretically sound approaches are preconditions to science; they assure reproducibility, as well as close correspondence of the investigation with the realities examined. The scientist's work is judged by how significantly it contributes to cumulated knowledge.

Thinking, judging, and understanding in the sciences involve internalizing complex methodological and theoretical principles and applying cumulated knowledge through new inquiry to further that knowledge. The scientist's work is discipline-determined, and the methods, the theoretical assumptions, and the types of questions pursued are those that science has judged worthy. The objects of study in science are, in C. G. Jung's sense, signs as opposed to symbols.[9] Within the context of the research, they point to identifiable, singular meanings. As a consequence, the language of science is designative and objective. In contrast to the humanist, the scientist's work is structured to discount individuality and to ensure, as far as possible, the neutrality of the investigator. The strictures of methodology intend the suppression of the scientist to be a variable, to the exposure of relationships correspondent to reality. Meaningfulness in science is derived solely from the dictates of experimental validity. The organization imposed by the rigors of the scientific process becomes the information transmitted.

The Literatures and the Research Tools

The distinctive features of the types of knowledge and understanding that characterize the disciplines of the humanities and the sciences have significant effects on their literatures and, consequently, on the use of their bibliographic access tools. Disciplines are dynamic structures of inquiry, and their literatures reflect the processes that generate them. Libraries acquire, organize, and provide routes of access to these literatures with the intention of facilitating further inquiry. Functionally, libraries are the intersections between the products of research processes and their means of access.

The humanities

The structural features of humanistic literatures exemplify the researcher's concern with dual aspects of scholarly enterprise: understanding within context and interpretative validity. The monograph is the predominant vehicle for scholarly communication precisely because its format allows the scope required for in-depth exploration of context and for exacting presentation of method and argument. The contextual structure is often exhaustively traced, both conceptually in narrative and bibliographically in references. The humanist is likely to have drawn upon diverse resources to arrive at the meanings to support his or her understanding. The course of the investigation must be documented, both to clarify the foundation on which elucidation is based and to expose it to evaluative scrutiny. Citations in the humanities represent significant conceptual connections that are meaningfully interrelated in the text.

The methodologies used by the humanist—identifying significant problematics and applying the logic of inquiry to their understanding and explanation—follow no prescribed norm. There is no generally accepted structure, in Kuhn's sense, that governs the humanistic research process. Rather, the approaches reflect discursive and eclectic adoptions, often creatively implemented. Meaningful communication requires a carefully presented reconstruction of the methods used. The monograph serves this need to explicate both context and approach, as well as the need for a communication format that allows for extensive presentation of argument. Estimates are that from two-thirds to three-quarters of the humanities literature is in book form and that about half the citations in the humanities literature are to books.[10]

The scholarly journal article plays another, not entirely separate, role. The humanist uses the journal article to convey theoretical insights, or to share understandings gleaned from exploration of a narrowly focused topic. But meaningful communication requires thoughtful reconstruction of conceptual patterns, which typically are individualistic. Consequently, a series of journal articles by a scholar may, when taken together, constitute a unique intellectual contribution, and collections of reprinted articles published as monographs are not uncommon in the humanities.

The products of humanistic understanding do not, at least in the usual sense, replace one another; contributions to understanding maintain value over time. Studies have shown that the half-life of the humanities literature is substantially greater than that of the literature of the sciences.[11]

The humanistic scholarly enterprise is individualistic, and the majority of publications in the humanities are by single authors.[12] Joint or multiple authorship may occur when larger projects are undertaken. The edited monograph, common in the humanities, is not so much a product of multiple authorship as it is a collection of intact, notable essays on a particular topic.

The products of scholarly communication in the humanities—in structure, content, and subject matter—reflect the scholar's concern with contextual meaning in order to understand particularities. Subject heading assignment to monographs, as well as the content and coverage of handbooks, bibliographic access tools, and other reference sources, can be illuminated when examined from a dual point of view. First, the humanist's writing flows from a distinctive research process and mirrors the substantive components of that process. Second, the routes of information access that serve the humanist have developed to promote these scholarly pursuits and themselves exemplify its basic elements.

Library of Congress subject headings applied to monographs in the humanities illustrate humanistic attention to levels of understanding within context. The humanist is interested in creative works that reflect social and personal experiences characteristic of certain time periods and national traditions. Subject headings available for humanistic searches correspond to these interests and provide access by personal name (for example, WAGNER, RICHARD, 1813–1883); personal name accompanied by the name of the creative work (WAGNER, RICHARD, 1813–1883. TRISTAN UND ISOLDE); name of the movement with which the artist is identified (ROMANTICISM; ROMANTICISM IN MUSIC); period in which the artist worked (MUSIC—HISTORY AND CRITICISM—19TH CENTURY); national tradition (MUSIC, GERMAN); and genre or type of work (OPERA). In a large-scale study of patterns of Library of Congress subject headings assigned to monographic records, Edward T. O'Neill and Rao Aluri note a statistically significant relationship between number of subject headings assigned and LC class, finding that personal names predominate in the classes that cover the humanistic disciplines.[13]

Handbooks and other reference sources in the humanities also illustrate concern with levels of analysis, providing summaries of generally accepted knowledge about persons, their creative works, national traditions, characteristics of time periods, movements, and genres. These summary-type works facilitate the humanist's research by explicating context and by carefully referencing sources.

The approach to literature searching is itself a significant and creative component of the humanistic research process. The humanistic scholar requires opportunities for open and discursive interactions with resources. Often organized by levels of analysis (for example, national traditions, persons, genres), the major bibliographies typically provide extensive coverage, offering the scholar wide ranges of possibilities. Productive encounters with bibliographic tools are highly dependent on recognition of connotations, which acquire meaning as they relate to the humanist's spheres of knowledge and interest, and bibliographic searching is a process rarely delegated. Bibliographic access tools in the humanities may appear to be loosely arranged aggregations;[14] yet, given the nature of the humanistic research process, it is difficult to imagine them otherwise.[15]

Humanistic scholarship entails applying knowledge in the pursuit of insight and involves impressing personalistic organization within context. The structural components constituting humanistic scholarship determine not only the nature of the literatures produced by that process, but also the nature of the bibliographic and other reference tools that promote it.

The sciences

The structural features of the literatures of science likewise reflect the components of the research processes. Considered as a whole, they symbolize the scientist's concern with investigating the context of theory in order to promote collective, cumulative understanding.

The major vehicle of scholarly communication in science is the research report. If one independent and patterned reality is assumed, original contributions to knowledge can only be made once. The cumulative nature of scientific knowledge requires both immediacy in sharing results and a means for establishing priority in discovery. The primary research report fulfills these dual requirements.[16]

The major component of the scientific literature is the journal article, and an estimated 80 percent of the research literature of science is in this format.[17] The journal article is the scientist's highly structured, peer-reviewed account of a research endeavor. It is a reorganized report of the investigation, written to reveal theoretical context, methodology, and implications of findings. Unlike the humanist, who pursues contex-

tual realms of symbols with potentially inexhaustible meanings, the scientist is concerned with one world of signs and
singular meanings. Likewise, paradigms governing the scientist's investigation are, at any one time, well established, given
conditions. The paradigm and its application require explication, but not, as for the humanist, thorough justification. The
research report is descriptive and compact and is constructed
to facilitate its contribution to the scientific community.

The growth of scientific knowledge is cumulative. Scientists build on the work of others and, by their own contributions, seek to forward the state of understanding. Cumulative
growth of scientific understanding necessitates consensus formation and the integrative absorption of knowledge. The rest
of scientific literature provides the means by which the primary research report can be integrated into the general fund of
knowledge.

The first stage of this process is the research review, the
vehicle for selecting, critically evaluating, and intellectually
integrating new research in a specialized area. The review
brings together and organizes the significant elements of what
would otherwise be disparate research efforts. Through substantive synthesis and compaction, the review simultaneously affords integrative, bibliographic access to the original
research documents and may itself act as a catalytic agent for
new investigations.

Interesting parallels can be drawn between the role played
by the book review in humanistic disciplines and the function
of the scientific review article. The purpose of each is to inform a specific community of scholars about new and significant contributions to the primary literature. Each evaluates
the research effort and draws conclusions about the merits of
the professional contribution. The significant differences,
however, are attributable to the characteristics that mark the
humanities and the sciences as distinct areas of knowledge.
Because no overriding, commonly acknowledged paradigm exists for the research process in the humanities, the scholarly
book review usually devotes significant attention to consider-
ing the adequacy of the humanist's interpretations. Although
the book reviewer renders a professional judgment, his or her
own intellectual approach may be quite different from the
writer's; in such cases, it is not unusual for an author to be
allowed a forum for response. In the sciences, on the other
hand, paradigms are generally accepted parameters of the re-

search process. The review considers single research reports only in relationship to others. Significance is judged by assessing the contribution made to current scientific understanding.

Given the cumulative nature of the sciences, the most useful literature is the most recent, a fact confirmed by half-life studies.[18] The success of citation indexing systems in the sciences demonstrates the cumulative properties of scientific research and attests to the citations themselves being discrete indicators of substantive contributions. As scientists working in similar specialties build on common ground, bibliographic cocitation and coupling patterns identify active research fronts.

Scientific research is frequently a cooperative endeavor, and multiple authorships are common. Unlike the humanist, the scientist is not seen as a variable in the conduct of research or its report. The usual use of initials for first names in scientific publication points up this impersonalization.

The substantive integration required to advance scientific knowledge also explains the importance of the abstracting tool. As a document surrogate, the abstract transmits all essential information. Grouping abstracts in the tool by categories that correspond to research specialties aids integration for the user.

Discrete facts in science have meaning only as integral parts of cumulative knowledge. Information in scientific handbooks is arranged by divisions of knowledge paralleling the research areas of the discipline. Since access to the most recent material is important, major handbooks in the sciences are revised regularly, often annually.

The scientific monograph summarizes and integrates well-established knowledge and is usually a textbook or a treatise. The O'Neill and Aluri study of Library of Congress subject headings by LC class demonstrates that headings assigned to books in science are, by and large, topical.[19]

Scientific terminology can change rapidly, reflecting new research interests, discoveries, or applications of knowledge. Formal subject heading analysis, and the use of precoordinated subject authority systems, may work well enough when applied to the tertiary literature (for example, the scientific monograph), but be unsuccessful in providing subject access to primary research literature. Although evolutionary, scientific terminology is nonetheless designative, postcoordinate indexing systems are functionally sufficient and thus common.

When using a bibliographic tool, the scientific searcher usually has a preconceived notion of the object of the search. Like laboratory work, bibliographic research is directed toward particular ends, and, as in the laboratory, much of the work of the search process can be delegated.

The structural components of the scientific research process determine the literature that flows from it. Scientists seek to develop substantial knowledge within theoretical frameworks about relationships among variables in the real world. The scientific process orders the transfer of information to the scientific community. There it is integrated into the cumulative fund of knowledge and made intellectually accessible. The structures of the bibliographic tools that provide access to the scientific literature parallel the research processes intrinsic to the scientific enterprise.

Teaching Library Use

Our contextual approach to bibliographic instruction in the humanities and the sciences is derived from concern with formulating a teaching structure that promotes transfer of learning on the part of the student. For both the humanist and the scientist, inquiry originates in conceptual structure; for the student, the same is true. If we are to teach students effective manipulation of pertinent information systems, we must impart conceptual understanding of research processes, of the literatures that record and communicate scholarship, and of the principles governing information retrieval.

It is frequently argued that successful library use teaching is timed to coincide with student need for library resources. Coordinating instruction with actual library use does capitalize on immediate, rather than potential, incentive. Underlying this tenet, however, is a less defensible assumption, that arranging instruction to coincide with heightened student motivation will itself provide the conceptual structure necessary for effective learning.

Basing instruction on cognitive structure

Contemporary research in various areas of instructional psychology has emphasized the importance of cognitive structures, or frameworks, in the learning process.[20] A related development has been the recognition that although teaching obviously is directed to promote learning, the learning process itself must be better understood. The combined effect has been to focus attention on the interdependence of teaching and learning theories, on the cognitive conditions requisite to learning, and on the operative requirements for facilitating transfer of learning.[21]

Although cognitive learning theorists disagree on many points, they also have common ground. First, cognitive structure is hierarchically organized and is a crucial variable in the learning process. Second, meaningful learning requires the presence of relatable, corresponding concepts. Third, transfer depends on the learning of concepts at generic, or generalizable, levels. And, fourth, the way in which material is taught can significantly affect desired learning outcomes.

Learning effective library use obviously involves the acquisition of skills, and much effort has been devoted to teaching students the use of specific access tools. Whether legitimate substance supports teaching beyond this level has long been debated. There are convincing arguments that there is not. Some maintain, for example, that in contrast to subject disciplines, library use instruction has no cohesive body of knowledge to convey and that skills development in the use of tools is the proper center of the teaching effort. A second problem carries this issue an additional step. If the focus is on imparting skills of access, then instruction sessions in upper-level courses should expose students to specific, advanced tools. This combination—concern with skills acquisition, incorporating the teaching of types of tools—has been a mainstay of bibliographic instruction programs. Instructional objectives and tests of library use competence often reflect considerable attention to developing students' skill-level proficiency in using specific research tools.[22]

Although legitimate arguments support the general outlines of this approach, a substantial case can be made to the contrary. Peter H. Martorella summarizes a crucial result of contemporary work in instructional psychology in pointing out that it is clearly unwarranted to assume that concepts can be learned from systematic exposure to facts;[23] meaningful learning takes place within context. Considerable evidence indicates that learning is an interactive process between hierarchically organized cognitive structure and newly presented instructional material. Indeed, patterns of mental structures in students powerfully influence what is learned.[24] To orient teaching toward skills acquisition and acquaintance with specific tools is to discount consideration of the learner's conceptual, organizational principles. Segregating what is taught into discrete, homogeneous units centered on instances of tool use leaves the student little alternative but to mechanically absorb information by rote.

In our teaching, we slight neither the imparting of skills nor the presenting of specific types of tools and their use. Both underlie effective learning in the use of libraries. We try, however, to frame our teaching and the learning experiences we construct on conceptual principles. These are derived from our understanding of the basic structural components that organize the research process, its corresponding literature, and the conduct of inquiry in the humanities and the sciences. Our aim is to promote assimilated, cognitive learning and to facilitate the development of student capabilities to generalize and transfer knowledge.

Library researching in the humanities

There are significant parallels between characteristics of humanistic research and processes that structure productive inquiry for the student of the humanities. These include the importance of context, the importance of the individual researcher, and the essential role of interpreting and evaluating sources.

The basics of meaningful cognitive structure can build on concepts already present in the learner, if only intuitively. Paul H. Hirst has observed that the purpose of teaching a subject is to have the student begin to think in a way distinctive to that particular subject and to do so with some style and imagination.[25] Thus, the student begins to think historically, philosophically, or, in the case of literature, critically. Through normal course work, students have been exposed to disciplined study in the humanities. Encouraging student contributions, we construct with them an overall conceptual model of humanities research that incorporates their personally meaningful experiences. The goal is to create a condition for learning in which new material can be assimilated by being substantively related to what the learner already knows. The process makes the learning elements salient and provides for their integration into a generalized, substantive pattern. On this basis, the relationships between the research process and the structure of a specific body of literature can be delineated.

Inquiry in the library is itself a way of knowing, a process of encountering and learning. It is important that the context for this inquiry be well defined. Philip H. Phenix makes the point that the substantive materials used in teaching should be selected so as to be paradigmatic or representative of the ways of knowing.[26] Only if students grasp the major components of what it means to the scholar to do research in a discipline, only if they understand the relationship between the research process and its written products, only if students perceive the distinctive structural features of the library access tools for these disciplines will they have available a cognitive structure for organizing productive search strategies.

Meaningful assimilation learning requires both reception learning and guided discovery approaches.[27] The broad outlines of the research process, and the literature produced by that process, are the subject of an opening lecture and discussion. As Robert M. Gagné points out, however, stability in concept learning is highly influenced by ability to make meaningful discriminations.[28] The learner, therefore, must be exposed to a range of situations to which the concepts apply. Studies have shown that practice with a variety of application-type problems produces learning that is transferable to a wide range of different situations.[29] Classroom experiences are, therefore, supplemented by worksheet assignments that guide the learner to apply the concepts and to make necessary discriminations. Worksheets allow students to identify and relate verbal concepts to concrete situations, thus providing operationalized meanings for otherwise abstract ideas.

An underlying premise that substantiates this approach is that learning is an interactive process, with the student bringing conceptions from the past experience to a learning situation. If cognitive structure in the student is to be developed, the student must participate in the process of applying, discriminating, and interpreting. As Jerome S. Bruner observed, an important cognitive interrelationship exists between doing and understanding; doing plays an important part in building understanding.[30]

To facilitate organization of newly presented material, we have experimented with heading student worksheets with narrative introductions or organizers as advocated by David P. Ausubel.[31] Presented in advance of the planned learning experience, the organizer elucidates the primary concepts that shape the worksheet. The organizer is neither a summary nor an overview, as either of these would simply repeat the major points presented in the learning material. Rather, the organizer functions as a cognitive tool, making explicit the superordinate principles and relating elements already in cognitive structure to those being newly presented.

The context that informs the class sessions and their accompanying worksheets is the delineation of the basic elements of the research process in the humanities. In the English literature library researching course, the introductory class is followed by two worksheet assignments that examine alternative ways to identify books on a particular topic. The many approaches to the primary research literature in the humanities are emphasized as are the advantages and disadvantages of each. The first of these two assignments introduces the student to functions and comparisons of background sources for literature, delineates the scope and limitations of the principal selective bibliographies, and compares other types of selective bibliographies such as bio-bibliographies. The second worksheet assignment has the student explore the card catalog as an access tool (emphasizing the availability of levels of subject headings paralleling levels of approach), the structure of the Library of Congress classification system for literature, access tools for locating book reviews, and use of the *National Union Catalog, Pre-1956 Imprints* for identification of editions, locations, and general inferences about social history and popular acceptance of original publications. In a supplement to this assignment, students consider the functions of bibliographic documentation of sources.

The third class and its assignment expose students to the scholarly journal article, uses of basic indexing tools for locating scholarly discussion on a specific topic, and personal selection of basic journal titles for continuous coverage of scholarly articles. The fourth class and accompanying worksheet explore in greater depth the literary work against its historical contexts—both as exemplified in the content of the work itself and in the time period in which it was created—through the use of handbooks, biographical works, and major histories. For the fifth and final assignment, students execute a personal inquiry into library materials on an assigned author and work and produce a selective, annotated bibliography of sources.

The learning materials presented in class and in the worksheets are aimed not so much at producing excellent performance on a single task (although this is certainly desirable) as they are at enabling the student, in Bruner's sense, to go beyond the information given and to assimilate new information into a learning set through developing meaningful generic coding systems. The student must, of course, be taught skills and techniques for using the tools, but these are treated in relation to their functions for inquiry within the discipline. Meaningful cognitive structure is accentuated by having students describe and justify steps taken and by having them keep research reports on major tools used.

Emphasis on basic features of the scholarly research process in the humanities helps to develop personal capabilities for productive inquiry. The conditions for transfer are founded on the contextual approach to the presentation of information, on the use of organizers and worksheets, and on thoughtful interaction with sources. Superordinate to these is the desire to teach the student an inquiry process consistent with ways of understanding in humanistic disciplines. Thus, students are encouraged to exercise intuitive thinking, to explore connotations of meaning, and to see themselves as instruments in the research process.

Library researching in the sciences

Substantive parallels also exist between the kinds of processes that characterize research in the sciences and those that shape effective inquiry for the student of the sciences. These include the cumulative nature of scientific understanding, the guiding force of theory, and the importance of consensus formation in presenting and interpreting experimental results.

The conceptual structures for understanding the scientific research process and its literature are conveyed to the student much as they are in the humanities course. The goal is to encourage students to build on their current state of knowledge and relate this to a generalizable framework of generic level concepts.

Library inquiry in science corresponds to the generalized pattern of inquiry in science itself. Bibliographic searching in the sciences is directed toward specific, well-defined ends. Strategies most useful for literature searching in the sciences are analogous to those used for hypothesis testing. Given a stable research paradigm, the information need is tested against the available literature. In much the same way that the scientist confronts an experimental task with the operative framework that there is one real world, so also is there one real world of recorded information. If the information required has been the subject of research, a properly conducted search should be able to locate it.

A far greater emphasis is placed on the manipulation of access tools in the sciences course than in the humanities course. Just as mastery of laboratory instruments is necessary to scientific investigation, so also is mastery of access tools necessary to investigate the literature of science. No science teacher would instruct students in skills of instrument use as a goal in and of itself, but would rather consider command of instrumentation as supportive to objectives of conceptual learning. Similarly, our instruction in the use of scientific access tools seeks to develop student expertise supportive of broader learning objectives.

Scientific knowledge does not consist of discrete units of facts, but rather, sets of facts that acquire meaning through successive integration. Productive inquiry to solve specific informational needs requires an understanding of the cumulative nature of the scientific enterprise. Building on information conveyed in the opening lecture and discussion about the scientific research process and its literature products, students work in small groups on a guided exercise. They are given a group of materials, each of which represents a distinctive level of communication of scientific knowledge—a conference report on research in progress, an original research article resulting from that investigation, the incorporation of that research report as a document surrogate in an abstracting service, its subsequent integration with similar research in a review article, and, finally, its acceptance as common knowledge in a textbook, and a handbook or encyclopedia. Each group of students reports to the class by writing brief answers to questions on the board and orally sharing what has been learned. The group reporting mechanism is useful as a teaching device since it encourages the reorganization of notions students already have about scientific communication and heightens distinctions among concepts.

The learning experience throughout the rest of the course is a search worksheet that presents a complex research problem, different for each student. The research problem is successively tested against the literature through use of various access tools. As in the humanities course, organizers are used with weekly assignments to facilitate generalizable levels of understanding. The presentation of each tool in class is followed by group exercises on sets of directed information searches, during which students can implement skills and interact with one another and the instructor to solve immediate problems.

One important learning objective is to help the student understand and interpret phases of scientific communication. The initial search assignment has the student confront the paradox of needing information already integrated into scientific knowledge, simultaneously requiring information about current research work in that area. The mechanism used is to have the student identify the most recent review article related to his or her research problem and then trace references from that review through current issues of *Science Citation Index*. Subsequent assignments call for use of scientific indexing and abstracting services. The final project is an exhaustive bibliography on the assigned research problem.

As in the humanities, definitive features of the investigative process in science parallel the development of student capabilities to conduct literature searching. Our efforts to create learning conditions that will support transfer hinge on the contextual approach to presentation of new information, the integration of learning experiences with an authentic search problem, and the use of organizers to facilitate learning. The superordinate teaching concept is to help students develop approaches to the search process that correspond to ways of understanding in science. Thus, the student is encouraged to conceptualize information problems in ways that can be directly tested against the literature and to recognize the roles played by scientific theory and research paradigms.

Some conceptual comparisons

The contextual approach to instruction suggests ways of teaching that are concerned with distinctive features of the research process, the structure of the literature, and the access systems in particular areas of knowledge. The following comparisons between techniques of instruction used in the two courses illustrate some of the conceptual differences inherent in humanities and scientific research and their meanings for teaching effective library inquiry.

In the humanities course, the final selective bibliography assignment occurs early in the course and is constructed around the major work of a well-known author designated by the instructor. Through a series of comparisons, the student ascertains the definitive edition of the work. To demonstrate to the student the role he or she personally plays in humanities research, the student is required to develop a thesis statement concerning a specific aspect of the assigned work. The statement serves as a criterion against which to judge relevance and allows for student creativity in the research process. By contrast, the information problem given the student in the sciences course is based on ongoing scientific research efforts and is detailed and explicit. The demand on the student in this case is to seek evidence to solve the problem, not to create it.

In the sciences course, students learn requisite skills through group work. A consensus must be formed within each group on interpretation and presentation of the investigation prompted by the exercise. Consensus formation concerning results pertains to library searching, rather than to experiment, but the process is analogous to that of science. By reporting to the class, students also experience the public nature of scientific research. In the humanities course, on the other hand, requisite skills are learned through individual work on weekly assignments, supplemented by class discussion of problems and successes. These discussions focus on evaluating an individual's work and reinforce the personal, interactive nature of the research process in the humanities.

Using the skills acquired in guided group exercises, the student in the sciences course solves the information problem leading to the final bibliography by using a search worksheet, a portion of which is completed, submitted, graded, and returned weekly. The search worksheet cumulates student research efforts and reflects the successive nature of scientific understanding. By the end of the course, the search worksheet constitutes the raw data that will enable the student to compile a final bibliography on the information problem. The bibliography is exhaustive and not annotated; its completeness is the major criterion on which the success of the search is judged.

In the humanities course, the student, while working on the weekly worksheets, is also working on the final project. The process is such that the student must discover the principles underlying each worksheet for the purposes of implementing them in the final bibliography. In this way, the principles are transferred from very structured situations, in which there are right and wrong answers, to a situation that provides very little guidance but requires mastery of both skills and principles to be successful. The student's own bibliographic project parallels the worksheets; all worksheets, for example, emphasize interpretation and evaluation of sources. The final annotated bibliography is a selective and evaluative product; the annotations and the quality of them allow the instructor to judge the success of the inquiry process.

Teaching of reference works, such as handbooks and manuals, also demonstrates features unique to these disciplines. In the humanities course, handbooks, biographical sources, and encyclopedias are always introduced through the framework of a specific search. Forming each worksheet around a unified search emphasizes the importance of context to humanities research, and a particular reference work is presented only as it contributes to the search. In the sciences course, focus on manipulation of access tools creates a group assignment in which a selected number of handbooks and encyclopedias are closely examined, and the examination is an end in itself. The two sets of learning experiences, therefore, are distinct and result from the fact that reference tools in the humanities reflect interaction of authors with subject matter, whereas authors of scientific reference works attempt to report impartially on observable regularities. In the sciences, a reference work that definitively covers a subject area can only be updated. In the humanities, the definition of coverage is much more equivocal and more dependent on the author's interpretative framework and experience: Two humanities reference works covering the same subject area can contribute equally on the basis of arrangement, purpose, and critical view.

The final bibliography in the sciences course is judged on accuracy and style of the citations and on completeness in addressing the research problem. This final bibliography measures the success of applying the set of methodological norms that were taught. In the humanities course, on the other hand, more emphasis is placed on the process of research itself. To observe growth in understanding, the student is required to submit a summary of the course of research. The summary is based on the student's research reports, which function as a research log, requiring evaluation of tools used and justification for consulting them. In the humanities course, the focus is on teaching approaches to thoughtful, critical searching, not norms.

The role of the individual in the research process creates different purposes for documentation in the humanities as opposed to the sciences. In the sciences course, three reasons are given for citing: (1) to demonstrate that the relevant literature has been thoroughly investigated and that the research cited is new and necessary, (2) to document how new research has built on that which preceded it, and (3) to enable others to locate cited reports. In addition to enabling researchers to locate sources, the purpose of documentation in humanistic research is to lend authority and credibility to the work and is, thus, a means to an end. In the humanities, citations can be used creatively, even artistically and with flair, whereas in the sciences their use is systematic. Although not always the case, the general trend in the humanities is to weave citations throughout the narrative, using them to lend credence, strength, and authority to the arguments. This contrasts with their use in the sciences to demonstrate awareness of the appropriate literature.

Citation use in the humanities, then, involves value judgments, and one can legitimately question whether citations have been used well. To illustrate this, one worksheet in the humanities course presents an essay using references to a standard work of Shakespearean criticism. Students respond to questions about the effectiveness of the citations, their necessity and frequency, and the use of paraphrases and quotations. In the sciences course, by contrast, the assignment introducing citations illustrates that citations in science are designative and that the only legitimate question is whether they are correct. Rather than evaluating usage, the student identifies and writes citations for a selection of books, parts of books, reviews, and journal articles. The assignment on citations in the humanities course requires judgment on the use of citations, as well as on form, whereas the assignment in the sciences course simply seeks the latter. Bibliographic instruction exercises in microbiology, English literature, and Shakespearean criticism used at the Benjamin F. Feinberg Library, State University College, Plattsburgh, New York, appear as an appendix to this chapter on pages 159–167.

Conclusion

Contemporary work in cognitive learning theory supports the notion that learning is very much an interactive process, with the student bringing and applying available organizational structures to the learning situation.[32] Cognitive structure is not only the major learning outcome, or dependent variable, of instruction, it is also the primary significant independent variable influencing the learner's capacity to acquire new knowledge.[33] In our contextual approach to teaching these courses, we have sought ways of working with conceptual structure present in the learner to accomplish desired learning outcomes. At the same time, we have sought to provide opportunities for students to develop personally meaningful intellectual capabilities within the context of an understanding of the research process and its products. The contextual approach offers a teaching framework within which bibliographic instruction could progress beyond the aims of instilling relatively isolated end states of learning to integration of that learning with cognitive structure supportive of personal capacity to perform productive library inquiry.

Acknowledgments

Our sincere thanks to John K. Clark, Head of Reference, Feinberg Library, Plattsburgh State University College, who, in initiating the sciences course, led the way, and whose constant support and sharing of ideas have been invaluable; and to Dr. Vladimir I. Munk, Department of Biological Sciences, and Dr. Bruce Butterfield, Department of English, also of Plattsburgh State, for providing us the opportunity to develop in the classroom some of the ideas they inspired.

Appendix

Benjamin F. Feinberg Library
State University College
Plattsburgh, New York

BIO307
Smalley/Munk

Name_____

BASIC REFERENCE TOOLS IN MICROBIOLOGY; CITATION FORMAT

Introduction
    The published literature of science records the knowledge that scientists gain
through their research efforts. The work of science is forwarded by the process of
publication. Through the published record, scientists share their results, subject
their work to public evaluation and verification, and contribute to the fund of knowledge available to other researchers.

    The various components of the scientific communication system function to incor-
porate the work of individual scientists into what is known about a subject. Information dissemination in science originates with direct, original reports of research,
their findings, and the scientist's own assessment of the implications of results.
In successive stages, the essential, contributive elements of the new knowledge in
these reports are subjected to judgment by others, integrated into recorded scientific
understanding, and made accessible to other researchers.

    The phases of scientific communication are represented by distinctive types of
publications. Each type has a specific purpose. Through a knowledge of the characteristics of each type, and its functions, the student is able to select and use specific
sources most appropriate to solving a given information problem.

    In a previous exercise, you explored examples of publications representing phases
of scientific communication, and examined their distinctive features. You traced a
scientific contribution in microbiology from its first report at a conference, its
later publication as a formal journal article, and its subsequent accessibility
through an abstracting service. You then followed the course of this contribution
through the stages of its integration into a review article, its incorporation into
a textbook discussion, and its eventual integration into a standard scientific reference work. Throughout this process, you observed that bibliographic citations are
unambiguous descriptions of publications written in a precise style. You also
observed how a single bibliographic citation comes to acquire a meaning which represents a particular contribution to knowledge.

    In this assignment, you examine in greater depth tools that are examples of that
last stage of the scientific communication system. You explore two standard reference
works in microbiology to discover how they function to transmit established knowledge,
and how sources of that knowledge are documented (Exercise I). You then practice
writing bibliographic citations for various types of scientific publications following
a prescribed style (Exercise II).

Exercise I: Handbooks in Microbiology[1]
    Reference works in science are tools. They assemble, organize, and make readily
accessible knowledge that has been judged by those in the scientific community to be
reliably established and thus standard. Information in reference works is presented
concisely, and is arranged to facilitate consultation.

    A handbook is a compendium of primary data assembled from diverse sources and
arranged in a format that is useful to practitioners in the field or speciality. As
with any complex tool, it is necessary to familiarize yourself with a reference work
prior to using it. Reference tools new to you should be carefully examined to
determine such things as the following:

1. What the function of the tool is, i.e., what it is designed to do;
2. What the scope of the work is, i.e., what subject matter is covered;
3. What arrangement is used within the tool to group the information;
4. What types of indexes, or other access devices, are provided within the
   tool;
5. What the introduction (to the work as a whole, or to its sections) indicates about how the tool is to be used, its limitations, its presentation
   of data;
6. How authorities for the information are documented;
7. How current the data are;
8. What appendices are included, and their value.

_____
[1]This exercise has been adapted from one originally developed by John K. Clark.

Advance Organizer

*presents most inclusive
concepts first*

*emphasizes research
context from which
publications flow and
how they support the
process of inquiry*

*indicates relevance of
new learning material*

*reinstates previous
learning experiences*

*recalls experience with
bibliographic citations
as precise, unambiguous
signifiers of substantive
research contributions*

*states the instructional
intent of this particular
assignment*

*Handbooks
Emphasizes role of con-
sensus formation in the
determination of gener-
ally accepted knowledge
that is found in hand-
books.*

*Reflecting the importance
of the guiding force of
theory in the sciences,
a set of theoretical
criteria is presented
against which all hand-
books can be measured.
The humanities assign-
ment does not assume or
present similar norms.*

Basic Reference Tools in Microbiology; Citation Format   -2-

This exercise exposes you to the use and function of two basic handbooks in microbiology. In section A of the exercise, you use the CRC Handbook of Microbiology;[2] in section B, you use Bergey's Manual of Determinative Bacteriology.[3]

A. Using the CRC Handbook of Microbiology (Ref.QR6.C2)

PROBLEM 1: In your work as an agricultural microbiologist, you are dealing with an outbreak of food-intoxication among cattle. You suspect the cause to be aflatoxin G_1, produced by the fungus *Aspergillus flavus*, which you believe has infected several corn storage facilities in your region. Locate the table(s) which provide useful data on this compound, and answer the following questions:

1. What is the chemical formula for aflatoxin G_1? _____

2. What is the optimum temperature (^{o}C) for production of the toxin in the substrate [corn]? _____

3. Dosage of aflatoxin G_1 that caused death in 50% of ducklings tested is reported to be two to almost three times that of aflatoxin B_1. What original papers could you read which might inform you further about these lethal dosages, and supply you with other data on the sources and effects of aflatoxin G_1?

_____
_____

PROBLEM 2: For your research work, you need to identify the amino acids that are associated with the growth of naturally occurring *Aspergillus flavus*.

1. Locate the appropriate table(s), and name the amino acids that are stimulatory to growth:

Those found stimulatory:	Those found to provide better than average stimulation:
_____	_____
_____	_____

2. What is the original paper that is the source for these data?
_____
_____

B. Using Bergey's Manual of Determinative Bacteriology (Ref.QR81.B47 1974)

PROBLEM 1: You are working as a food microbiologist in a creamery. There, it is your job to supervise the use of cultures of *Leuconostoc citrovorum* in the production of butter.

1. How does *L. citrovorum* differ from the type species in its growth requirements?
_____
_____

2. *L. citrovorum* acts to convert pyruvate to acetoin and diacetyl (diacetyl is used as a flavor component in butter). What article is given as a reference for this process?
_____
_____

PROBLEM 2: You have isolated a microorganism from a sulfide-containing marine mud sample and need to identify it taxonomically. The cells are spiral (helical) in shape, 5.5-7 μm long, 0.4-0.5 μm wide, with two subterminally inserted axial fibers; the organism is obligately anaerobic and gram negative.

1. Identify the species described: _____

_____
[2]A. I. Laskin and H. A. Lechevalier (ed.), Handbook of microbiology. 1974, CRC Press, Cleveland.

[3]R. E. Buchanan and N. E. Gibbons (ed.), Bergey's manual of determinative bacteriology, 8th ed. 1974, The Williams & Wilkins Co., Baltimore.

Using the CRC Handbook
A series of problems is proposed, each to be tested against reality, as found in the literature.

Using Bergey's Manual
Use of complex tools in science requires mastery of technique, but is pursued in relation to a specific research problem.

Basic Reference Tools in Microbiology; Citation Format   -3-

2. Describe how you used <u>Bergey's Manual</u> to identify this species:

_____
_____

C. Comparing Bergey's Manual and the CRC Handbook
    Through the process of comparing these handbooks for coverage of the same topic,
differences in orientation and use become more apparent. Locate the section in each
of the handbooks that describes the species of the genus <u>Spirillum</u>. You will note
that there are differences between the handbooks in comprehensiveness and type of
information provided. Reconsider the function and coverage of each of the handbooks.
Explain below the differences you have found, and justify your conclusions:

_____
_____

Exercise II: Writing Bibliographic Citations
    In scientific writing, bibliographic citations (such as those you worked with
in Exercise I) are used to reference publications as authority, precedent, or evidence.
A citation functions as a precise record of publication data; it must be accurate,
unambiguous, and unique. Attention to bibliographic detail is requisite to successful
scholarly communication.

    Unambiguous and unique citations are achieved by presenting required bibliographic
data in a format that follows a prescribed style. A standard style manual for biological publications is the <u>Council of Biology Editors Style Manual</u>[4] (often referred to
as the <u>CBE Style Manual</u>). The specific citation style used in this course is that of
the American Society for Microbiology (ASM). This style is, in large part, based on
the <u>CBE Style Manual</u>, and is spelled out once a year in the various ASM journals, e.g.,
the "Instructions to Authors" section of the January issues of the <u>Journal of Bacter-
iology</u>. This instruction sheet provides sufficient guidance in most cases, but the
student is referred to the <u>CBE Style Manual</u> for further elucidation of the principles
of scientific citation, and other matters of writing style.

    Attached are three sets of pages photocopied from various sorts of microbiology
publications. The publications from which these photocopies were made are on a worktable labelled "BIO307" in the Reference Alcove. In the spaces below, write correct
bibliographic citations for these three publications, following ASM style:

#1._____
   _____

#2._____
   _____

#3._____
   _____

[The three publications are: a review article from the <u>Annual Review of Microbiology</u>;
a journal article; a chapter in an edited book.]

Students are required to conceptually review and then verbalize the specific search techniques used.

*Comparing the Handbooks
The description in the CRC Handbook draws heavily upon Bergey's Manual, 1957 (7th ed.). In the sciences, a reference book that definitively covers a subject area can only be updated. The student must decide whether the CRC Handbook has accomplished this successfully. An understanding of the cumulative nature of scientific knowledge is reinforced.*

*Writing Bibliographic Citations
Citations in the sciences are designative, and the exercise, therefore, teaches form.*

_____
    [4]Council of Biology Editors, Council of Biology Editors style manual, 4th ed.
1978, American Institute of Biological Sciences, Arlington.

Benjamin F. Feinberg Library
State University College
Plattsburgh, New York

ENG391
Plum/Butterfield

Name_____

BASIC REFERENCE TOOLS IN ENGLISH LITERATURE

Introduction

Research in the humanities involves the discovery of relationships among the imaginative constructs created by individuals. The specific poem, painting, or sonata--reflections of unique minds--is the object of study. The humanist may attempt to discover meaning in the relationships between different works of an artist, between the collected works of an artist and the works of other artists of the same period or school, or between the artistic creation that has preceded or that follows the work under study.

Because the explication of relationships between artifacts of the imaginative world often entails lengthy background discussion, the products of scholarly work in English literature more frequently are published as books, rather than as journal articles. The literary scholar himself interacts with the object of study in establishing and articulating the relationships he probes, thus bringing a personal and unique perspective to understanding the work. There is little likelihood that another researcher will examine the same relationships in precisely the same way, or from the same perspective. The scholar is afforded time to reflect, time even to produce the definitive work over a period of years.

As a result of the frequency with which research appears as books in English literature, two tools are used to initiate research on a topic. The first, the selective bibliography, can include both books and journal articles, and either implicitly or explicitly evaluates the material. The second, the library's card catalog, is limited to listing books, and does not evaluate. This assignment approaches research through selective bibliographies to find the best books on a topic. Another assignment examines the card catalog. Several other strategies for identifying books complement the two basic approaches.

A selective bibliography organizes and lists citations to the books that are the accepted, standard works on a certain topic. The information presented in the bibliography may include descriptive annotations (brief descriptions of the contents of publications) or it may include evaluative annotations (succinct assessments of the worth of publications). In either case, the listing of a book in the selective bibliography indicates its worth and usefulness to research.

In this assignment, you use selective bibliographies to identify and to evaluate material that is relevant to a specified topic. Your search takes you through the following steps:

A. By using handbooks you become aware of the background information necessary to anticipate the relationships and themes that scholars could use to examine the specified topic.

B. You explore the New Cambridge Bibliography of English Literature[1] and discover why use of this tool is the best initial step to pursue information on the topic.

C. You examine bio-bibliographies, and bibliographies that are organized around nationality and genre, to identify the purposes of each type of tool.

D. Bibliographies on an individual often include both citations to books by that author and citations to books about the author. In this section you examine two individual bibliographies to determine why they are different from the bibliographies in section C, and to distinguish lists of books by your author from lists of books about him.

E. Finally, you use what you have learned in the preceding sections in the following two ways: to evaluate a particular book, and to determine the best book on a related, but different, topic.

Notice that some of this assignment takes place on the worktable in the Reference Alcove, labelled "ENG391."

_____
[1] George Watson, ed., The New Cambridge Bibliography of English Literature, 5 vols. (Cambridge: Cambridge Univ. Press, 1969-1977).

Advance Organizer

presents most inclusive concepts first

emphasizes how the research process affects the structure of the literature

indicates how access to the literature depends on its structure

stresses relevance of new learning material

introduces evaluative function of selective bibliographies

organizes this particular assignment so that the sections are seen as contributing to a unified whole

demonstrates the plurality of approaches to finding information

gives a readily apparent goal to the assignment

Basic Reference Tools in English Literature   -2-

TOPIC FOR THIS ASSIGNMENT

You are interested in studying <u>Troilus and Criseyde</u> by Geoffrey Chaucer, particularly the theme of courtly love in this work.

A. Finding Background Information

Most scholarly investigations in English literature are focused on an author. Paradoxically, in order to find information about a topic or author, the researcher in literature must already be aware of basic facts about that topic. When looking for, or when using, bibliographies, for example, the researcher must know the time period in which the author lived, the country of origin, the genre with which the author is primarily identified, and the language in which the author writes.

Use the <u>Reader's Encyclopedia</u> and the <u>Oxford Companion to English Literature</u>, both located on the worktable, to determine the following information about the topic:[2]

1. When did Chaucer live?_____
2. In what language did he write?_____
3. What is his country of origin?_____
4. With what genre is he primarily identified?_____
5. Compare the background information in the <u>Readers' Encyclopedia</u> with that found in the <u>Oxford Companion</u>, and briefly describe the differences.
_____
_____

B. Using the New Cambridge Bibliography of English Literature (NCBEL)

The <u>NCBEL</u> covers both works by an author and works about the author, and is selective, in spite of its inclusive appearance. The <u>NCBEL</u> is on the worktable.

1. Using the <u>NCBEL</u>, what <u>book</u>, in Feinberg Library, is the most recent bibliography about Chaucer?
   a. Author: _____
   b. Title: _____
   c. Place of publication: _____
   d. Publisher: _____
   e. Date of publication: _____
   f. Call number: _____

2. According to the <u>NCBEL</u>, what is the title of the source that could be used to update the information found in the bibliography identified in question #1, above?
_____

3. Is this source in the Library? _____

4. Identify one book, listed in the <u>NCBEL</u>, which discusses courtly love and <u>Troilus and Criseyde</u>, and which is in the Library:
   a. Author: _____
   b. Title: _____
   c. Place of publication: _____
   d. Publisher: _____
   e. Date of publication: _____
   f. Call number: _____

5. The Library has a copy of the following book: Kittredge, George Lyman. <u>Observations on the Language of Chaucer's Troilus</u>. 1891; rpt. New York: Russell and Russell, 1969. Is this book included in the <u>NCBEL</u>? _____

6. If yes, in what column number will it be found? _____

7. The Library has a copy of the following book: Rowe, Donald W. <u>O Love, O Charite! Contraries Harmonized in Chaucer's Troilus</u>. Carbondale: Southern Illinois Univ. Press, 1976. Why is this book not listed in the <u>NCBEL</u>? _____

8. Richard Altick states, "in most cases the <u>NCBEL</u> is the best place to begin research into a topic in English literature. . ."[3] Do you agree? Justify your answer.
_____
_____

_____
[2] William Rose Benet, <u>The Reader's Encyclopedia</u>, 2nd ed. (New York: Crowell, 1965); Sir Paul Harvey, ed., <u>The Oxford Companion to English Literature</u>, 4th ed., rev. (Oxford: Clarendon, 1967).

[3] Richard D. Altick, <u>The Art of Literary Research</u>, rev. ed. (New York: Norton, 1975), p. 152.

Topic
A single topic is pursued through all the different tools; in the parallel sciences assignment, a number of different problems are presented.

Background Information
Almost all the assignments have background information requirements. Handbooks are not presented as intrinsically important tools, but rather as the means to important ends. Background information, helpful for using bibliographies, can easily be used in other ways, e.g., for identifying bibliographies through the subject headings in the Subject Card Catalog.

NCBEL
Although this assignment emphasizes teaching approaches to thoughtful, critical searching, NCBEL is presented as a starting point for research. It then serves as a framework against which other approaches to research can be placed.

Basic Reference Tools in English Literature   -3-

C. Using Various Types of Selective Bibliographies

A publication that combines a list of citations with background information on the author in question is a fortunate find in literary research. Such a publication can be termed a "bio-bibliography," since it shares attributes of both biographies and bibliographies. Examine the following two examples of this type of work, found on the worktable:

Scott-Kilvert, Ian, gen. ed. British Writers. Vol. I: William Langland--The English Bible. New York: Scribner, 1979.
Vinson, James, ed. Poets. New York: St. Martin, 1979.

Read the background information presented in each book on the theme of love in Troilus and Criseyde.

1. Each of the two bio-bibliographies covers a different list of literary authors. Why is Chaucer included in each list?

_____
_____

2. What are the differences between the background information, presented in each bio-bibliography, on the theme of love in Troilus and Criseyde?

_____
_____

3. Compare the bibliographies on Chaucer in each book. Which book gives critical studies of Troilus and Criseyde? Why?

_____
_____

Also on the worktable are two selective bibliographies that share both national and genre characteristics:

Beale, Walter H. Old and Middle English Poetry to 1500: A Guide to Information Sources. Detroit: Gale, 1976.
Dyson, A. E., ed. English Poetry: Select Bibliographical Guides. Oxford: Oxford Univ. Press, 1971.

Examine these books, and locate the section on Chaucer in each. There you will find comments on the following book: Meech, Sanford B. Design in Chaucer's Troilus. Syracuse: Syracuse Univ. Press, 1959.

4. Which bibliography describes Meech's book? _____

5. Which bibliography evaluates Meech's book? _____

6. Which bibliography lists additional citations on courtly love and Troilus and Criseyde that are not listed in the section on Chaucer?

_____
_____

7. Which of the two bibliographies would be more valuable for your research on the topic? Why?

_____
_____

D. Using Bibliographies on Individual Authors

Although no bibliography can really be complete, bibliographies that are limited to a single author tend to be more complete, and hence less selective, than other types of bibliographies. Bibliographies on individual authors also tend to list both citations to works by the author, as well as citations to works about that author. Examine the following three bibliographies on the worktable:

Baugh, Albert C. Chaucer. New York: Appleton-Century-Crofts, 1968.
Griffith, Dudley David. Bibliography of Chaucer: 1908-1953. Seattle: University of Washington Press, 1955.
Hammond, Eleanor Prescott. Chaucer: A Bibliographical Manual. New York: Peter Smith, 1933.

1. Why would you use an individual bibliography, such as Baugh's Chaucer, instead of a national or genre bibliography, such as Dyson's English Poetry, presented in the preceding section?

_____
_____

Various Selective Bibliographies
Intent here is to instill in the student an appreciation of possible approaches to finding books on a topic.

Bibliographies reflect levels of understanding within context: the creative work within national traditions, time periods, and genres.

The student must create the definition of "valuable." The idea of the humanist's personal interaction with the search and with the product of the search is introduced.

Bibliographies on Individual Authors
These are examples of several humanities reference works, covering essentially the same subject area, yet equally contributive on the basis of arrangement, purpose, and critical view.

Basic Reference Tools in English Literature   -4-

2. Compare the bibliography by Hammond with that by Griffith. Which is more useful
   for research into criticism and background on Troilus and Criseyde?

_____

_____

E. Discussion

1. Drawing upon your work with bibliographies, comment on and evaluate the following
   edition of Troilus and Criseyde, found on the worktable:

   Root, Robert K., ed. The Book of Troilus and Criseyde by Geoffrey Chaucer.
        Princeton: Princeton Univ. Press, 1926.

_____

_____

2. Suppose that through your work on courtly love in Troilus and Criseyde, you became
   interested in the sources for Chaucer's version of this tale. What is the best book
   in the Library for a discussion of the sources and origins of Chaucer's Troilus?
   Justify your answer.

_____

_____

                    * * * * * *.* * * * * * * *

[This exercise is an excerpt from another assignment that focuses on aspects of
Shakespearean criticism.]

                    SOURCES AND DOCUMENTATION

Introduction
     Documentation enables your reader, or yourself, to locate the identified sources.
There is nothing worse than attempting to locate a publication through a fractured or
fragmented citation. Citations should, therefore, be accurate, complete, and clear.
The MLA Handbook presents a style for citations that is all of these, and it is the
style manual that you will use when documenting sources.[1]

     According to the MLA Handbook, citations also "lend authority and credibility to
your work."[2] Documentation in a paper or article can be used well or badly. Citations
may be unnecessary to strengthen your arguments, and so should not be used, or they may
be essential, so as not to give the impression that the thoughts expressed are your
own, when, in fact, they have been borrowed from another. Read the appropriate sections
in the MLA Handbook on plagiarism, documentation, and note logic.

     In this exercise, you will read an essay, "Shakespearean Criticism Today." In
the essay are a number of references to Paul Siegel's book, His Infinite Variety:
Major Shakespearean Criticism Since Johnson, of which pages 4-5, and 78-80, are
particularly relevant to the essay. Read these pages so that the relationships between
the source and the essay become clear.

                    Shakespearean Criticism Today

1   As Paul Siegel says in his introduction to His Infinite Variety, "each age
   has tended to see Shakespeare in its own way," but that at the same time each age
2 has also assimilated the criticism of the past.[1] As a result, contemporary
   interpreters of Shakespeare are free to choose from among critical opinions of the
3 past and to add their own interpretations.[2] Siegel points out that the contemporary
   critic can agree with the "neo-classical critics," the "romantic critics" and the
   "Victorian critics" at the same time as he disagrees with some of their responses.[3]
4 Thus, if critics are going to both react against and assimilate their predecessors'
   ideas, there is bound to be controversy about what is to be accepted, what is to be
   rejected, and what is to be modified and expanded upon so that it becomes something
   new.

_____

     [1] Modern Language Association, MLA Handbook for Writers of Research Papers, Theses,
and Dissertations (New York: MLA, 1977).

     [2] Modern Language Association, p. 49.

Discussion
The final discussion
consists of two evalua-
tions: of a given book,
and of a book to be
found on a related topic.
Compare to the final
section of the sciences
assignment in which use,
purpose, and function of
the tools are examined.

Many of the questions
following this essay are
concerned with such issues
as: Have the citations
been used well? Have they
been used effectively? Do
they strengthen the argu-
ment? Do they add cre-
dence and authority?
These are questions that
would be nonsensical in
the sciences assignment,
and, indeed, the sciences
assignment specifically
examines only citation
format.

Sources and Documentation

5   In this essay, I hope to show how several major critics of Shakespeare have both
6   borrowed from and rejected the ideas of their predecessors. For example, J. Dover
Wilson, the bibliographer and editor who is also a vigorous, delightful critic, goes
so far as to suggest that the relative importance of Falstaff and Prince Hal in
Henry IV is one issue upon which all critics agree:

> Falstaff may be the most conspicuous, he is certainly the most fascinating,
> character in Henry IV, but all critics are agreed, I believe, that the
> technical centre of the play is not the fat knight but the lean prince. Hal
> links the low life with the high life, the scenes at Eastcheap with those
> at Westminster, the tavern with the battlefield; his doings provide most of
> the material for both Parts, and with him too lies the future, since he is
> to become Henry V, the ideal king, in the play that bears his name. . . .[4]

7   Of course, in order to make such a generalization about "all critics"[5], Wilson must
not only know a great deal about Shakespearean criticism, but also risks the
8   assumption that some critic somewhere does not agree. However, this assumption
seems safe, particularly in light of Quiller-Couch's theory that the important
themes of Henry IV are built on the old structure of Morality plays, which
9   Shakespeare modernizes into a Tudor version in this play.[6] Human salvation was the
one topic that English drama concerned itself with before the first half of the
sixteenth century, and so not surprisingly it was this topic that Shakespeare
secularized for his purposes in Henry IV.

---

[1] Paul N. Siegel, ed., His Infinite Variety: Major Shakespearean Criticism
Since Johnson (Philadelphia: J. B. Lippincott Company, 1964), p. 4.

[2] Siegel, pp. 4-5.

[3] Siegel, pp. 4-5.

[4] "The Falstaff Myth," The Fortunes of Falstaff (Cambridge: Cambridge Univ.
Press, 1961), pp. 17-35, 43-48.

[5] Wilson, p. 80.

[6] Wilson, p. 80n.

A. Working with Sources and Documentation
       Based on the essay "Shakespearean Criticism Today," answer the following questions:[3]

1. In the first sentence, the writer both quotes and paraphrases. What do you find
effective and ineffective about both? How does the word "that" affect what the
writer's responsibility is for giving credit to his source?

_____

2. Why is sentence 2 footnoted? Does a footnote seem necessary? Is the footnote
form correct (in any case)?

_____

3. Is footnote 3 necessary for these quoted phrases? Is the footnote correct?

_____

4. Why is sentence 4 not footnoted?

_____

5. Should the writer try to avoid footnoting every sentence? How in paragraph 1 could
he avoid doing so? Would one footnote do for the entire paragraph?

_____

6. Is the writer guilty of any obvious plagiarisms in paragraph 1? Has he merely
paraphrased? Does all paraphrasing require footnoting?

_____

---

[3] Dr. Bruce Butterfield wrote the essay "Shakespearean Criticism Today" for this
assignment, as well as these questions.

Sources and Documentation

7. How does the writer's thesis (sentence 5) reflect the nature of Siegel's book? Has the writer merely copied Siegel's main idea, or does he have a legitimate topic of his own here?

   _____

8. In sentence 6, what phrase or phrases are obviously not the writer's own? Do these require footnoting? Should they perhaps be omitted?

   _____

9. How well does the writer introduce the long quotation in sentence 6? Is he making the best use of quotation here? How effective is the long quotation for the writer's purpose? Is it properly footnoted?

   _____

10. Is footnote 5 necessary? Is its form correct?

    _____

11. What are the complications involved (in sentence 8) in quoting or paraphrasing Quiller-Couch? Is the writer actually quoting? paraphrasing? plagiarizing? Some combination of these?

    _____

12. Is footnote 6 adequate? How would one quote from a quotation in the footnote to an essay that is a collection of essays? (Write the footnote that you would use.) Why is such quoting perhaps inadvisable?

    _____

13. Does sentence 9 seem paraphrased, quoted, plagiarized, or what? Does it need footnoting? Is so, how?

    _____

Notes

1. Our conceptual frameworks are largely derived from experience in teaching two upper-level courses, one on library researching in a humanities discipline, one on library researching in a scientific discipline. However, we have also found them effective approaches in our one-credit, semester-long, required library researching course where we have incorporated a three-unit sequence on researching the social sciences, the sciences, and the humanities.

2. For example, Jon Lindgren, "Seeking a Useful Tradition for Library User Instruction in the College Library," in *Progress in Educating the Library User*, ed. by John Lubans, Jr. (New York: Bowker, 1978), pp. 71–91; and Pamela Kobelski and Mary Reichel, "Conceptual Frameworks for Bibliographic Instruction," *The Journal of Academic Librarianship* 7 (May 1981): 73–77.

3. For example, Patricia B. Knapp, *The Monteith College Library Experiment* (New York: Scarecrow Press, 1966); and Elizabeth Frick, "Information Structure and Bibliographic Instruction," *The Journal of Academic Librarianship* 1 (September 1975): 12–14.

4. Discussions of distinctive features of the humanities and the sciences, drawn on epistemological and other grounds, can be found in: Ernst Cassirer, *The Logic of the Humanities* (New Haven, Conn.: Yale University Press, 1961); William T. Jones, *The Sciences and the Humanities: Conflict and Reconciliation* (Berkeley: University of California Press, 1965); Paul H. Hirst, *Knowledge and the Curriculum: A Collection of Philosophical Papers* (London: Routledge and Kegan Paul, 1974); R. S. Crane, *The Idea of the Humanities and Other Essays Critical and Historical*, 2 vols. (Chicago: University of Chicago Press, 1967); Albert William Levi, *The Humanities Today* (Bloomington: Indiana University Press, 1970); Stephen E. Toulmin, *Human Understanding*, vol. 1, *General Introduction and Part I* (Princeton, N.J.: Princeton University Press, 1972); and Moody E. Prior, *Science and the Humanities* (Evanston, Ill.: Northwestern University Press, 1962).

5. Frederick B. Thompson, "The Organization Is the Information," *American Documentation* 19 (July 1968): 305–308.

6. C. G. Jung, *Collected Works*, ed. by Herbert Read, Michael Fordham, and Gerhard Adler, vol. 6, rev. ed., *Psychological Types*, Bollinger Series 20 (Princeton, N.J.: Princeton University Press, 1971), pp. 473–481.

7. Harold I. Brown, "Objective Knowledge in Science and the Humanities," *Diogenes* 97 (Spring 1977): 95.

8. Thomas S. Kuhn, *The Structure of Scientific Revolutions*, 2nd ed., Foundations of the Unity of Science 2, no. 2 (Chicago: University of Chicago Press, 1970).

9. Jung, *Collected Works*, vol. 6, pp. 473–481.

10. *Scholarly Communication: The Report of the National Enquiry* (Baltimore, Md.: Johns Hopkins University Press, 1979), pp. 45–46; A. J. Meadows, *Communication in Science* (London: Butterworths, 1974), p. 89; Barbara M. Hale, *The Subject Bibliography of the Social Sciences and Humanities* (Oxford: Pergamon Press, 1970), p. 72; Lois Bebout, Donald Davis, Jr., and Donald Oehlerts, "User Studies in the Humanities: A Survey and a Proposal," *RQ* 15 (Fall 1975): 41–42; and D. J. Urquhart,

"The Needs of the Humanities: An Outside View," *Journal of Documentation* 16 (September 1960): 122.

11. Formal studies of the obsolescence of humanities literatures are few, and information concerning median citation age (apparent half-life) is frequently presented through comparisons with the more highly researched literatures of the sciences and social sciences. See Robert N. Broadus, "The Literature of the Social Sciences: A Survey of Citation Studies," *International Social Science Journal*, 23 (1971): 242; Clyve Jones, Michael Chapman, and Pamela Carr Woods, "The Characteristics of the Literature Used by Historians," *Journal of Librarianship* 4 (July 1972): 137–156; Hale, *Subject Bibliography*, p. 72; Bebout, Davis, and Oehlerts, "User Studies in the Humanities," p. 41; and A. Robert Rogers, *The Humanities: A Selective Guide to Information Sources*, 2nd ed. (Littleton, Colo.: Libraries Unlimited, 1979), pp. 4–5.

12. Robert H. Knapp, *The Origins of American Humanistic Scholars* (Englewood Cliffs, N.J.: Prentice-Hall, 1964), p. 155; and Bernard Berelson, *Graduate Education in the United States* (New York: McGraw-Hill, 1960), p. 55.

13. Edward T. O'Neill and Rao Aluri, "Library of Congress Subject Heading Patterns in OCLC Monographic Records," *Library Resources and Technical Services* 25 (January/March 1981): 76.

14. Rawski, for example, has characterized bibliographic patterns in the humanities as being "peculiarly obtuse" (Conrad H. Rawski, "Bibliographic Organization in the Humanities," *Wilson Library Bulletin* 40 (April 1966): 744). In the last several decades, humanists have expressed concern over the apparent disorganized state of their bibliographic tools. See, for example, Eric J. Carpenter, "The Literary Scholar, the Librarian, and the Future of Literary Research," *Literary Research Newsletter* 2 (October 1977): 150–152; Eric H. Boehm, "On the Second Knowledge: A Manifesto for the Humanities," *Libri* 22 (1972): 312–323; Lewis Shawin, "The Integrated Bibliography for English Studies: Plan and Project," *Pennsylvania Library Association Bulletin* 19 (February 1964): 7–19; and Carl H. Kraeling, "The Humanities: Characteristics of the Literature, Problems of Use, and Bibliographic Organization in the Field," in *Bibliographic Organization*, ed. by Jesse H. Shera and Margaret E. Egan (Chicago: University of Chicago Press, 1951), pp. 109–126.

15. The Institute for Scientific Information's *Arts and Humanities Citation Index* (*A&HCI*, 1978–) represents an important innovative effort to apply bibliographic order to the humanistic literatures. Significantly, its construction also illustrates problems of applying an indexing system developed for denotative literatures to highly connotative ones (for example, the necessity for creating pseudocitations and for enhancing titles). For a discussion of these issues, see Eugene Garfield, "Is Information Retrieval in the Arts and Humanities Inherently Different from That in Science? The Effect that ISI's Citation Index for the Arts and Humanities Is Expected to Have on Future Scholarship," *Library Quarterly* 50 (January 1980): 40–57.

16. Discussion of the functional components of scientific communication systems and the purposes they fulfill can be found in A. J. Meadows, *Communication in Science* (London: Butterworths, 1974); William D. Garvey, *Communication: The Essence of Science* (Oxford: Pergamon Press, 1979); Carnot E. Nelson and Donald K. Pollock, eds., *Communication among Scientists and Engineers* (Lexington, Mass.: Heath Lexington Books,

1970); and K. Subramanyam, "Scientific Literature," in *Encyclopedia of Library and Information Science*, vol. 26, ed. by Allen Kent, Harold Lancour, and Jay E. Daily (New York: Marcel Dekker, 1979), pp. 376–548.

17. Meadows, *Communication in Science*, pp. 89, 149–150.

18. For a review of half-life studies in the sciences, see Meadows, "Literature Usage and the Passage of Time," in *Communication in Science*, pp. 126–151.

19. O'Neill and Aluri, "Library of Congress Subject Heading Patterns," p. 76.

20. For a brief review of some general principles underlying this emphasis and their application to bibliographic instruction, see Kobelski and Reichel, "Conceptual Frameworks for Bibliographic Instruction," pp. 73–77.

21. See, for example, David P. Ausubel, Joseph D. Novak, and Helen Hanesian, *Educational Psychology: A Cognitive View*, 2nd ed. (New York: Holt, Rinehart and Winston, 1978); Robert M. Gagné, *The Conditions of Learning*, 3rd ed. (New York: Holt, Rinehart and Winston, 1977); Herbert J. Klausmeier, Elizabeth S. Ghatala, and Dorothy A. Frayer, *Conceptual Learning and Development: A Cognitive View* (New York: Academic Press, 1974); and David Klahr, ed., *Cognition and Instruction* (Hillsdale, N.J.: Lawrence Erlbaum, 1976).

22. For an example of a formalized statement of this approach, see Association of College and Research Libraries, Bibliographic Instruction for Educators Committee, "Bibliographic Competencies for Education Students," *College & Research Libraries News* 42 (July/August 1981): 209–210.

23. Peter H. Martorella, *Concept Learning: Designs for Instruction* (Scranton, Pa.: Intext Educational Publishers, 1972), p. 72.

24. G. O. M. Leith, "Implications of Cognitive Psychology for the Improvement of Teaching and Learning in Universities," *Educational Review* 31 (June 1979): 151.

25. Paul H. Hirst, *Knowledge and the Curriculum: A Collection of Philosophical Papers* (London: Routledge and Kegan Paul, 1974), pp. 47–48, 117–118.

26. Philip H. Phenix, *Realms of Meaning: A Philosophy of the Curriculum for General Education* (New York: McGraw-Hill, 1964), p. 11.

27. In reception learning, information is directly presented to the learner in more or less final form; in guided discovery, the learning process is promoted in the student by structured exposure to the problem and its solution.

28. Gagné, *The Conditions of Learning*, p. 113.

29. Tamar Levin, "Instruction Which Enables Students to Develop Higher Mental Processes," in *Evaluation in Education: An International Review Series*, vol. 3, ed. by Bruce H. Choppin (Oxford: Pergamon Press, 1979), p. 213.

30. Jerome S. Bruner, *The Process of Education* (Cambridge, Mass.: Harvard University Press, 1960), pp. 29–31.

31. David P. Ausubel, "Cognitive Structure and the Facilitation of Meaningful Verbal Learning," *Journal of Teacher Education* 14 (June 1963): 217–222; and Ausubel, Novak, and Hanesian, "Cognitive Structure and Transfer," in *Educational Psychology*, pp. 163–204.

32. Wilbert J. McKeachie, "Implications of Cognitive Psychology for College Teaching," *New Directions for Teaching and Learning* 2 (1980): 85–93.

33. Ausubel, Novak, and Hanesian, *Educational Psychology*, p. 167.

8

Computer-Assisted Instruction: An Overview

MITSUKO WILLIAMS and ELISABETH B. DAVIS

Since the development of modern computers in the 1950s, many innovative applications have been initiated in both academic institutions and industrial areas. The applications have been based on one or more of these functional features of computers: data storage and access, computation, and data processing.

Computer-assisted instruction (CAI) utilizes all these computer features and is generally defined as a "man-machine interaction in which the teaching function is accomplished by a computer system without intervention by a human instructor. Both training material and instructional logic are stored in computer memory."[1] Other definitions emphasize the individualized aspect of instruction in CAI.[2]

Another utilization of computers in the field of education is called computer-managed instruction (CMI); here, the primary function of the computer is to manage large amounts of data.[3] In CMI the computer is a tool to manage information rather than a means of providing instruction. The area covered by CMI includes data collection, diagnosis of student performance, prescription of directions (forward or remedial), resource planning and allocation, and reporting.

Although the term "computer-assisted learning (CAL)" appears in the literature from time to time, implying an emphasis on the learner rather than on the teacher, CAI and CAL are used interchangeably. CAI, CMI, and one other subcategory of educational computer utilization, called computer-assisted testing (CAT), are all basic, integral components of computer-based instruction (CBI).[4] Recently, CBI has been used by some to encompass all aspects of instructional processes in the educational context. In this chapter, however, CAI is used to emphasize the instruction of individual students, rather than the planning, management, and evaluation of entire educational systems.

Reflecting on the factors that have brought about the popularity of CAI since the 1960s, Richard C. Atkinson and H. A. Wilson state the following as most important: (1) interest in programmed instruction, (2) development of technology, particularly electronic data processing, coupled with the introduction of time-sharing communication systems, and (3) increased funding from the federal government as provided by the Elementary and Secondary Education Act of 1965.[5] The 1970s are regarded as the beginning of operational CAI programs, and librarians are also aware of the unique instructional medium used by such pioneers as Marina Axeen and Patricia Culkin.[6] Instruction as an ongoing library service was still in the early stage of development in the 1960s, and little significant growth of CAI in the library world occurred until the early to mid-1970s. CAI experimentation in the library instruction field apparently reached a plateau in the late 1970s. The high cost of equipment, diminished novelty, and the amount of time necessary for CAI program development were all possible causes.

Most computer-assisted library instruction programs to date have one common characteristic, despite differences in targeted audience, physical environment, content of lessons, conclusions, and future directions; these programs focus basically on how and why to use CAI in providing library instruction. This chapter investigates the theoretical basis for CAI, as well as presenting an overview of the educational climate in the United States that has nurtured CAI since the 1960s. In so doing, close attention is paid to the following: (1) learning

theory that supports CAI, (2) the general design of CAI programs, (3) review of the literature related to CAI in several
selected fields, and (4) current issues concerning CAI. Although hardware is a major component of any CAI system, it
is included here only as it affects program development.

Learning Theory

Much groundwork had been done in the 1950s to prepare for
the development of the new teaching method of programmed
instruction. The behavioral psychologist B. F. Skinner was the
major scientific force that supported this educational approach. He theorized that "the real focus in education should
be on consistent, immediate, positive reinforcement for appropriate behavior and for the attainment of delineated educational objectives."[7] Although sometimes blurred by a then
revolutionary teaching idea, Skinner's emphasis was on a
careful and sequential arrangement of teaching materials so
that the "learning experience will be presented at a size or
rate that the student can handle, and so that prerequisite
skills will have been mastered before more complex tasks are
attempted."[8] By the 1960s, other educators and psychologists
joined Skinner in noting the importance of educational materials and in contributing to the surge of programmed instruction in that decade.

Programmed instruction employs both linear and branching
approaches. The linear approach "analyzes a subject into its
component parts and arranges the parts in sequential learning
order."[9] The student's response at each step of the program is
judged, and feedback is given, indicating whether the response
was correct. The branching approach presents "alternative
answers to questions, and, on the basis of [the student's] decision, detours . . . to remedial study" or advances the student
to the next step of the program.[10]

CAI is sophisticated and complex programmed instruction
in which both approaches can be successfully incorporated.
Program development using the branching approach, however, can be, and often is, far more elaborate than that
which uses the linear approach. The teaching method that
supports CAI is student-centric and encourages a creative
approach to problem-solving. In most classroom environ-
ments, the student-centric system takes several homogene-

ous groups of students. With CAI, the student-centric system allows each student to set his or her own pace in the learning process.

Because of the computer's capability to store a large amount of data, a student's learning experience can be observed very closely. This capability to monitor and analyze the *process* of learning (how the student proceeded), as well as the *product* of learning (whether the student's answer was correct), clearly separates CAI from traditional classroom instruction.

Instructional Strategies

CAI programs generally consist of a combination of instructional strategies: drill and practice, tutorial, and dialogue.[11] Additional strategies are gaming, simulation, and problem-solving, but these appear to be techniques in the presentation of materials that can be applied to any of the three major strategies. Strategy selection must be based on the program's objectives.[12]

Drill and practice

Drill and practice is defined as "use of computer to guide, control and monitor by repetition a specific task or set of tasks."[13] The classic drill and practice format is probably best represented by the Stanford program, although other programs have also reported successful applications of this strategy in a variety of subjects.[14] The Stanford program consists of basic arithmetic skills such as addition, subtraction, division, fractions, and measures for students in grades one through six. It utilizes a number of branching strategies by either permitting the student to proceed to the next problem, or presenting the student with the same or a similar problem. Drill and practice strategy, although it can relieve teachers from time-consuming chores such as grading and recording, does not substitute for teaching in developing concepts and ideas. Victor C. Bunderson states that the widespread use of drill and practice in various programs is a "powerful vindication of the general concept that the educational work providing individual trials with feedback can produce marked performance gains," thus supporting the use of CAI for this particular strategy.[15]

Tutorial

Concept learning, although not appropriate as an objective in a program based on drill and practice strategy, can be successfully achieved through tutorial strategy, which is more complicated than drill and practice and incorporates a number of branching schemes. In the tutorial program, the student's previous set of responses (contingencies), rather than the response given last, determines the next step.[16] Contingencies may include demographic information, curriculum goals, and responses to test questions. Reading and biology programs developed by the School District of Philadelphia show examples of tutorial strategy.[17] In these programs, student performance and prior knowledge of learning ability act as contingencies. In tutorial strategy, students may also choose their own paths within the program, thus creating a learning environment that provides them more freedom.

Dialogue

Programs using dialogue strategy are not as well developed or utilized. However, dialogue strategy deserves attention because it is the most dynamic and individualized strategy of the three, fostering creative and intuitive learning. This strategy is sometimes referred to as the Socratic strategy.

A simplistic definition of dialogue strategy is that, in such a program, the student engages in a "conversation" with the computer, which may assume several roles, depending on the nature of the conversation.

The most well-known program using dialogue is the medical diagnostic program described by Leslie Jones.[18] The "patient" (computer) presents a set of problems (symptoms) to the student. In order to diagnose the illness properly, the student makes inquiries regarding the patient's case history and laboratory examination results. Upon receiving the information, the student then makes a diagnosis and prescribes treatment.

Program Design

The importance of developing a sound instructional design cannot be overemphasized. Some classroom instruction may be less effective than instruction provided by computer because of the difference in instructional design rather than the mode of presentation. According to a study conducted by Paul Dixon and Wilson Judd, students taught by classroom instruction with a well-developed instructional design learned just as well as those taught by CAI.[19]

In classroom instruction, generally only one teacher is involved in designing the lesson; CAI often takes a team approach. A team may include the subject specialist (instructor) and a programmer. Other personnel such as educational psychologists, other instructors, systems engineers, and artists may also join the team. Many library CAI programs were designed by librarians who learned programming on their own, but the team approach seems to be more efficient and economical in the long run.[20] Individual instructors, at the same time, should be encouraged to learn programming because it will foster an atmosphere for more creative use of CAI and help identify new areas that may be appropriate for CAI.[21] Following are specific steps for designing CAI programs:

1. State objectives.
2. Sequence objectives.
3. Select test and evaluation methods.
4. Formalize materials.
5. Review and evaluate program.
6. Plan for revision.

CAI programs, like traditional classroom instruction, require development of a well-defined set of objectives. Giving the objectives priority is also important and should be based on a careful analysis of the relationships of various skills or knowledge to be gained. The instructor must delineate each step of instruction and, at the same time, consider possible student responses at each step. Flowcharts are often recommended for developing and sequencing objectives. An instructional design and programming guide checklist, such as one suggested by Cherry McPherson-Turner, will also be helpful.[22]

The method of evaluation must be in accordance with the objectives developed. Collection and analysis of student performance data vary from system to system; so it is important to develop testing and evaluation plans that can be accommodated by the system to be used.

Formalizing and programming the material is the most time-consuming phase in CAI design. Here the programmer's knowledge and ability to use the features of the system play an important role. Incorporating various instructional techniques, such as gaming, simulating, and problem-solving, can enhance instruction and keep students from becoming bored. Lesson plans for certain subject areas that deal with quantitative materials are inherently easier to design, although not necessarily more suited for CAI, than those areas that deal with qualitative matters.[23] Unfortunately, library and bibliographic instruction fall into the qualitative category.

Another handicap associated with preparing CAI programs for library users is that librarians have little experience in formal teaching. As a result, they tend to provide CAI instruction in a page-turning manner (frame-by-frame presentation), which offers students little opportunity for interaction. In a study that measured student performances in two similar CAI programs, Allen Avner concluded that students who used a program with a great deal of interaction learned better than those who used a program with little interaction. The program content was the same; the "sole difference was that one set of materials required that the student give responses during the lesson that demonstrated understanding of the content being taught, while the other set allowed students to step through the material simply by pressing a key."[24]

No matter how careful the programming, CAI programs always seem to contain a fair number of "bugs" (problems) at the beginning. The debugging process is a tedious, but extremely important, task. Without this step, the program may not run in the exact sequence envisioned by the instructor, and, therefore, optimal learning may not occur. The evaluation of CAI programs is almost always done by computer, although the evaluation criteria, such as student performance, may vary from program to program. The evaluation of many library CAI programs was based on their effectiveness as compared with that of other instructional approaches. Despite the variation of items to be evaluated, CAI has the unique advantage of allowing a built-in evaluation system. The evaluation method can be programmed so that it takes place as each student accesses the program. Such an evaluation provides feedback for instructors to identify faults associated with the program before time and energy are wasted. To test the universality of the program, it can also be evaluated by students in other institutions.

Program revision, based on student performance data or on

student comments, is the next step after evaluation. Online monitoring of student performance enables the instructor to respond to content problems by editing and expanding the program.

CAI provides an excellent laboratory for cognitive psychologists in their research into the learning process. Determination of optimal learning conditions greatly depends on psychological research that yields quantitative predictions in many learning situations.[25] CAI designers must be alert to new findings in learning research and apply them to their programs. For this reason, a team approach that includes an instructional design specialist will become increasingly important.

CAI in the Literature of Various Fields

This selected review of the literature surveys developments in CAI, making use of state-of-the-art reports published since the late 1960s, as well as more recent research papers that identify significant trends and ideas.

The 1976 *Index to Computer-Based Instruction*[26] reported 1,837 separate CAI programs, 1,540 at the college/university level representing 137 different subjects, a clear indication of the interest and availability of CAI during the 1970s. The 1968 *Computer-Assisted Instruction Guide*[27] announced 226 CAI programs in 30 subject areas, evidence of the rapid growth of CAI in those eight years. A number of surveys of this swiftly increasing literature have been published during this more intense growth spurt. Several of the more helpful reviews follow.

Albert E. Hickey, ed., *Computer-Assisted Instruction: A Survey of the Literature*, 3rd ed. (Newburyport, Mass.: ENTELEK, 1968). This is a companion to the *Guide* in which Hickey surveys the literature reporting on CAI applications, centers, systems, learning theory, programming languages, and administration.

Derick Unwin and Frank Atkinson, *The Computer in Education* (London: The Library Association, 1968). This book presents 424 annotated entries dealing with the use of the computer in education, focusing on both administration and teaching.

John H. Feldhusen and Paul Lorton, Jr., *A Position Paper on CAI Research and Development* (Stanford, Calif.: Stanford

University, ERIC Clearinghouse for Educational Media and Technology, 1970), ED 036204. This is a valuable study of the research literature of CAI.

Karl L. Zinn and Susan McClintock, *A Guide to the Literature on Interactive Use of Computers for Instruction,* 2nd ed. (Stanford, Calif.: Stanford University, ERIC Clearinghouse for Educational Media and Technology, 1970), ED 036202. This review includes chapters and appendixes on meetings, symposia, conferences, professional organizations, and individuals closely connected with CAI.

Philip J. Schwarz, *The New Media in Academic Library Orientation 1950–1972: An Annotated Bibliography* (Stanford, Calif.: Stanford University, ERIC Clearinghouse for Educational Media and Technology, 1973), ED 071682. This is predominantly a review of media used in academic library orientations.

Henry M. Yaple, *Programmed Instruction in Librarianship: A Classified Bibliography of Programmed Texts and Other Materials 1960–1974, Occasional Papers No. 124* (Champaign, Ill.: University of Illinois Graduate School of Library Science, 1976). This extensive bibliography covers all levels of academic programs.

Deborah L. Lockwood, *Library Instruction: A Bibliography* (Westport, Conn.: Greenwood Press, 1979). This work includes mediated library instruction.

Medical programs

Medical education has long been a major contributor to CAI development. Just as medical bibliography has been at the cutting edge of automated bibliographic retrieval since MEDLARS became operational in 1964 and MEDLINE in 1971,[28] medical education has long taken advantage of the benefits to be derived through CAI. Because of the development of course materials and simulations in clinical situations, Jones states that medical educational institutions are most often considered leaders in CAI.[29] Jones conducted a survey in 1972 to identify existing CAI instructional materials and found that just under half of the medical schools responding were using CAI, although 31 others expected to use it in the future. One fourth of the dental schools responding were using CAI in their instructional programs, but only 17 of the 352 nursing and allied health schools were involved. Approximately one-third of the instructional programs were in clinical medical subjects, and 51 programs simulated the clinical experience in some respect. Although the role of CAI in medical education was not considered clearly defined as of 1974,[30] the innovative approach of CAI had been shown to be especially useful in the medical field for these reasons:

1. Health science/medical course content is basically concise, factual, and well defined.
2. CAI is especially suited for presenting repetitive situations of practice and mastery of identification, generation and testing of hypotheses, and formulation of judgments.
3. CAI is easily monitored and can be used in evaluating students' performance.
4. CAI is useful in clinical simulations and for training in decision-making.

In the medical field CAI was important enough to warrant the establishment of a biomedical CAI network linking three databases through a commercial time-sharing network to as many as 190 institutional users during the early 1970s.[31] Massachusetts General Hospital, the Ohio State University College of Medicine, and the University of Illinois Medical Center at Chicago were network members. This experiment was instrumental in demonstrating a substantial demand for CAI network services, and after it became self-sustaining, its support and operations were transferred to a user consortium.

Library programs

Discussions of CAI to teach library skills have appeared in the literature since the early to mid-1970s, probably the heyday of the CAI movement. Axeen used CAI to teach an introductory library skills course at the University of Illinois in the late 1960s, which is nearly always cited as one of the most significant and successful ventures.[32] Culkin used CAI to teach traditional library skills at the University of Denver, as well as to teach online search technique having the capability to tie in with an established bibliographic database.[33] The Denver program is a well-established watershed that has influenced all other CAI attempts in library instruction. Although the University of Denver is no longer active in CAI for teaching library skills, Culkin and Beverly Renford and Linnea Hendrickson conclude that CAI, whether used for direct public access to information or for the more traditional teaching of skills, is the wave of the future.[34]

A useful annotated bibliography on mediated library instruction, by Hannelore B. Rader, includes sections on CAI, on programs using various media formats with CAI, and on evaluation of mediated programs, among other topics.[35] This bibliography covers 1975 to 1979 and is updated yearly. Only four articles are cited in the 1975–1979 CAI section, a development that certainly corroborates the statement by Betty Hacker and Joel Rutstein that CAI is still only of peripheral interest in library instruction programs.[36] Hacker and Rutstein believe that CAI has little application for large numbers of users because of the expensive hardware and software associated with it, an opinion in direct opposition to Culkin, who writes of the computer's potential in reaching large portions of the user population quickly, effectively, and economically.[37] Stanley Benson reports that most of the librarians participating in strong course-related programs of academic library instruction thought that library instruction is more effective when delivered through personal contacts with classes and individual students than through CAI.[38] This provides more support for the drop in CAI reports appearing in the late 1970s and early 1980s. Cynthia Amann also reinforces this view; her survey indicates the scarcity of CAI programs in academic libraries, a situation caused, in her opinion, by restrictions in funding and personnel.[39]

Joan Hicks outlines the following advantages of CAI for veterinary medicine library users: lesson flexibility, time saved for librarians, ease of updating the lesson, evaluation of lesson capabilities, automatic data collection, and the capability of one lesson to be used simultaneously through a number of terminals.[40]

Mitsuko Williams and Elisabeth Davis report on the evaluation and effectiveness of CAI for teaching biology students to use the reference and bibliography collections.[41] Like Hicks, they used the computer to collect data, but they went one step further by using the computer to analyze and graph the results. Probably the most interesting aspect of this study was the finding that students prefer one-to-one instruction regardless of methods used.

A CAI project at the University of Nebraska-Lincoln by Kathleen Johnson and Barbara Plake investigated the relative effectiveness of CAI, of personal tutorials, and of the traditional orientation tours.[42] Johnson and Plake found that for the purpose of teaching card catalog use skills, CAI and the tutorial method were significantly better than tours or no instruction at all. These results were then compared with the Williams and Davis study. Johnson and Plake had serious questions about the cost-effectiveness of CAI and tutorials and concluded that other library instruction delivery programs, such as self-paced workbooks, were more educationally and financially satisfactory than those investigated in their study.

A small section on CAI was included in Mignon Adams's article on the individualized approach to learning library skills.[43] Adams recognizes the boom for CAI in library instruction in the 1970s and reiterates some of the advantages: novelty and enjoyment for students, little possibility of cheating, scoring and statistics gathered automatically, flexibility of subprograms within programs, and self-paced work according to need. Adams is also concerned with costs of CAI software development, as well as the purchase of hardware, and concludes that these costs really limit CAI applicability.

One of the most creative CAI approaches has been taken by Thomas Slavens in simulating the reference interview process for educating library science students.[44] Slavens built his program on the philosophy that steps in the development of CAI are like the steps in the development of any other lessons. CAI has the advantages of easier revision, of immediate, recorded feedback from students, and of evaluation and administration of diagnostic tests. Slavens advocates the use of CAI to remedy the problems of acute shortage of faculty, lack of individual instruction, varying levels in students' sophistication, and lack of self-instructional materials.

Other examples of CAI library programs are the report on teaching the Dewey Decimal Classification in a required introductory course, the CAI approach in teaching library skills to health care professionals, the application of CAI for deaf students, the comparison of effectiveness of two forms of programming for CAI (a comparison within one medium), and CAI on how to use the library card catalog for college students.[45]

Online training programs

The current activity in CAI is for teaching the use of online bibliographic retrieval systems. Elaine Caruso's excellent article and helpful bibliography for online searching enumerates, describes, and compares the computer training and/or learning aids that have been reported in the literature.[46] She identifies and distinguishes CAI programs that fall into three categories: (1) tutorials such as *MEDLEARN*, SCORPIO, TRAINER, DIALOG with PET, and ONTAP; (2) assistance programs such as CONIT, IIDA, and CCL; and (3) explanations and error diagnostics that are available within specific online retrieval systems, such as online HELPs and diagnostic messages. This last category is not discussed in the review since these aids are designed to improve performance of the search system and are not directly used to educate the searcher.

Caruso makes the important point that CAI systems should be financially supported, not only by funding for initial development, but also by revenues to maintain, advertise, and continue their development. She discusses the debate concerning the appropriateness of training for the intermediary versus the end user. This controversial issue is clearly defined with examples of the National Library of Medicine's advocate position for intermediary training against the British Library's stand that online search technique be taught within the subject curricula for the end users. Caruso outlines the various factors that have led to the current level of CAI use and development in online searching, and she summarizes the requirements that contribute to successful and economical CAI systems. She suggests ways that computer programs can assist the learning process, such as aiding in repetitive skill development exercises, in serving as a centrally updated resource, and in delivering continuing education for practitioners anywhere, anytime.

Additional attention to instruction methods in online searching appears in Rowena Swanson's survey, which concerns the following: (1) the demand for instruction in the use of online databases, (2) the comparison of purposive documentation (objectives, and so on) for the educational programs and resources, and (3) the evaluation mechanisms for nine representative instruction programs that are currently operational.[47] Particular attention is given to user expenses, program preparation costs, student/instructor ratios, end users and intermediaries, tests, and long-term feedback. Most programs of instruction combined several different educational methodologies. Swanson concluded that it is not possible to assess one approach as best or better than another because of the differing objectives, command languages, and databases. She does emphasize that self-instruction as exemplified by CAI is a useful tool in teaching the use of online searching. An extremely helpful table in her article compares the characteristics of online instruction programs, resources, and evaluation, allowing the reader easily to pick out those elements of instruction that are of the most interest in any particular situation.

Other programs

The April 1978 issue of *Educational Technology* is devoted to articles reporting on trends in CAI from a number of different viewpoints. It contains reviews of CAI in music education, in medical education, and in counseling. Although accurate statistics on CAI usage in schools and universities are elusive, Greg Kearsley's study reports that courses most heavily using CAI were found in the following subjects (in decreasing order of usage): mathematics, health professions, chemistry, computer operations and programs, biological sciences, English, foreign languages, physics, business, and psychology.[48]

A special issue of *Journal of Computer-Based Instruction*, February 1981, is devoted to computer-based music instruction, sampling the diverse applications of computers to current music instruction and research. Additional reports showing the impact and breadth of CAI applications from teaching the handicapped, to a Marine Corps electronics course, appear in the complete papers of the 1980 *Conference Proceedings: Computer-Based Instruction, a New Decade* (Bellingham, Wash.: Western Washington University, Association for the Development of Computer-Based Instructional Systems, 1980).

Thomas Bennett writes of computer use in directing and managing instructional programs (CMI) in schools, in conducting tests (CAT) and providing evaluative feedback to teachers, in providing information access to the blind, and in continuing education for adults in a variety of industrial, educational, and recreational areas.[49] Russell Skavaril and others report on the use of CAI to provide problems for an introductory genetics class.[50]

Current issues

CAI is an important technological tool with great potential for broad educational applications. However, several controversies and strongly held opinions are apparent from even a cursory glance at the literature. These arguments and problems, combined with the resistant attitudes of some members of the educational community, prevent CAI from completely penetrating all aspects of instruction.

The advantages and disadvantages of CAI are well documented and consistently reported. Probably the number one advantage is the capability to provide interactive instruction that is individually paced and directed for varying levels of skills, learning styles, and sophistication. Numerous studies have shown CAI to be at least as effective, or even more so, than other methods of instruction. At the very worst, there is no difference in learning using CAI versus other instructional techniques.[51] Although CAI is not widespread in teaching library science skills at present, it is considered very popular and useful in other disciplines, particularly the sciences, medicine, business, and economics.

Some benefits of CAI identified earlier have been disclaimed or counter-balanced by newly recognized unfavorable features. For example, many instructors who once viewed CAI as an ideal technology to reduce their teaching workload have found that CAI actually increased the amount of work, especially at the preparation stage. And claims that CAI offered more flexibility for students to schedule classes were, in fact, unrealistic because of terminal shortages in some institutions.

A recurring theme in the literature is concern over the cost-effectiveness of CAI. Jung Nievergelt explores this and other considerations in his state-of-the art review.[52] He concludes that more skill is needed for the teacher to use CAI effectively than is required by other media. For example, he estimates that 100 hours of preparation time is the average needed for several authors working together to produce one hour of student contact time. Nievergelt predicts that the cost of CAI programs will decline as mass consumption increases, but technological variations and institutional/organizational policies may hinder the free sharing of programs. Some proponents of CAI justify the high cost of production on the basis of better student performance, a benefit that cannot be easily translated into dollars.

Some feel that CAI is not an appropriate medium for educating large numbers of students; others claim that CAI is especially useful for reaching large groups. Some are concerned over the "impersonal" computer; others insist that CAI, if properly and carefully designed, is the most personal, individualized instruction available. In addition, Thomas Good and Jere Brophy say that classroom instruction is not as personal as it was thought to be.[53] Their study showed that teacher/student interaction is more frequent among high achievers than among low achievers; furthermore, the nature of this interaction between the teacher and the high performers is more positive than the interaction between the teacher and the low performers. In other words, with CAI the low performers have an opportunity for the sort of interaction that may be denied them in the classroom when they are competing against the high-performing student.

Trends

CAI, like other instructional methods, is only as good as the reliability and quality of its software and hardware. User frustration caused by faulty equipment or underdeveloped programs must be eliminated. CAI, if used exclusively, is not suitable for all people or for all situations. In the total educational system, CAI is most effective when it can supplement and complement, not replace, more traditional instruction.

Because of unique educational capabilities, the use of CAI will continue to increase as computers and terminals become commonplace in individual homes and institutions.[54] It has great potential for in-house training, for direct user access to information, and for end-user searching of bibliographic databases and online library catalogs. Karen Duncan, in her presidential address to the Association for the Development of Computer-Based Instructional Systems, says that "the major problems of cost, dissemination of information, faculty education, and effective courseware that have plagued us in the past are well on their way toward solution. CBE [computer-based education] is at last becoming a profitable venture that will have real impact on the educational system."[55]

In the Third Annual Dean Lecture on the Future of Computers in Education, Patrick Suppes stated that CAI will have a major impact on educational activity in the home in the near future.[56] According to Suppes, major improvements will be made by 1990 in processing natural language for input and output; by 1990 CAI will be delivered with the help of audio messages so that silent computers will be rare; by 2020 computers will have the capability of speech recognition, a development that will allow spoken dialogue between the user and the computer. Although 90 percent of all CAI activities currently take place in the United States, Suppes predicts that this figure will decrease as other countries, Japan, for example, begin sharp and rapid CAI growth.

Atkinson, another CAI authority, is quite optimistic about the future of CAI. He believes that advances in technology, current research trends, and a positive change in public attitudes toward computers portend significant developments for the medium. Attala agrees that the trend toward miniaturization will revolutionize CAI; Bitzer makes a plea for substantial federal funding for further CAI research and development. Hirschbuhl states that the major use of CAI will be at the preschool and professional development levels in the future.[57]

The effect of new technology and change in educational systems as represented by the development of CAI is a force to be reckoned with by librarians. The technological changes within libraries add to the necessity for librarians to assume a more active role in the educational environment. Printed books have been around for more than four centuries, and libraries even longer yet concentrated efforts in educating the users of books and library services began relatively recently. Because information format is shifting from print to machine-readable form, librarians should provide user instruction that is compatible with the new information structure.

Focusing on the role of librarians in the medical field, where significant growth of CAI has been observed, Linda Smith states that the medical librarian's involvement can be envisioned at three levels of CAI activity: research, development, and evaluation.[58] Librarians in other subject areas must also be ready to meet the challenges and seize the opportunities by exploiting the computer, not only as a housekeeping/computing tool, but as a dynamic medium for user education.

Notes

1. Alan B. Salisbury, "An Overview of CAI," *Educational Technology* 11 (October 1971): 48–50.

2. *Encyclopedia of Education*, 1971 ed., s.v. "Computer-Aided Instruction," by Lawrence M. Stolurow; and Lois N. Hansen, "Computer-Assisted Instruction in Library Use: An Evaluation," *Drexel Library Quarterly* 8 (July 1972): 345–355.

3. Frank Baker, "Computer-Managed Instruction: A Context for CBI," in *Computer-Based Instruction: A State-of-the-Art Assessment*, ed. by Harold F. O'Neil, Jr. (New York: Academic Press, 1981), pp. 23–64.

4. *Encyclopedia of Library and Information Science*, 1971 ed., s.v. "Computer-Assisted Instruction," by Karen Block; and Harold F. O'Neil and Judith Paris, "Introduction and Overview of Computer-Based Instruction," in O'Neil, *Computer-Based Instruction*, p. 1.

5. Richard C. Atkinson and H. A. Wilson, "Computer-Assisted Instruction," in *Computer-Assisted Instruction: A Book of Readings*, ed. by Richard C. Atkinson and H. A. Wilson (New York: Academic Press, 1969), pp. 3–4.

6. Patrick Suppes and Elizabeth Macken, "The Historical Path from Research and Development to Operational Use of CAI," *Educational Technology* 18 (April 1978): 9–11; Marina Esther Axeen, "Teaching the Use of the Library to Undergraduates: An Experimental Comparison of Computer-Based Instruction and the Conventional Lecture Method" (Ph.D. diss., University of Illinois at Urbana-Champaign, 1967); and Patricia B. Culkin, "CAI Experiment," *American Libraries* 3 (June 1972): 643–645.

7. Glen E. Snelbecker, "Learning Theory, Instructional Theory, and Psychoeducational Design," in *Behavior Modification and Instructional Technology* (New York: McGraw Hill, 1974), pp. 388–408.

8. Ibid., p. 392.

9. *Encyclopaedia Britannica*, 15th ed., s.v. "Programmed Instruction."

10. Ibid.

11. Patrick Suppes, "Computer Technology and the Future of Education," in Atkinson and Wilson, *Computer-Assisted Instruction*, pp. 42–44.

12. Victor C. Bunderson, "Courseware: Conceptions and Definitions," in O'Neil, *Computer-Based Instruction*, p. 101.

13. Salisbury, "An Overview," p. 48.

14. Patrick Suppes and Mona Morningstar, *Computer-Assisted Instruction at Stanford, 1966–68: Data, Models, and Evaluation of the Arithmetic Programs* (New York: Academic Press, 1972); John F. Vinsonhaler and Ronald K. Bass, "A Summary of Ten Major Studies on CAI Drill and Practice," *Educational Technology* 12 (July 1972): 29–32; and John R. Allen, "ELSE at Dartmouth: An Experiment in Computer-Aided Instruction in French," *The French Review* 44 (April 1971): 902–912.

15. Bunderson, "Courseware," p. 102.

16. Lawrence M. Stolurow, "Some Factors in the Design of Systems for Computer-Assisted Instruction," in Atkinson and Wilson, *Computer-Assisted Instruction*, p. 79.

17. James J. Diamond, *A Report on Project GROW: Philadelphia's Experimental Program in Computer-Assisted Instruction* (Stanford, Calif.: Stanford University, ERIC Clearinghouse for Educational Media and Technology, 1969), ED 035272.

18. Leslie Arnold Jones, "Study of a Computer-Assisted Student Assessment System for Basic Medical Sciences" (Ph.D. diss., University of Illinois at Urbana-Champaign, 1974).

19. Paul N. Dixon and Wilson A. Judd, "A Comparison of Computer Managed Instruction and Lecture Mode for Teaching Basic Statistics," *Journal of Computer-Based Instruction* 4 (August 1977): 22–25.

20. Joan Tomay Hicks, "Computer-Assisted Instruction in Library Orientation and Services," *Bulletin of the Medical Library Association* 64 (April 1976): 238–240; Kathleen A. Johnson and Barbara S. Plake, "Evaluation of PLATO Library Instruction Lessons: Another View," *Journal of Academic Librarianship* 6 (July 1980): 154–158; Mitsuko Williams and Elisabeth B. Davis, "Evaluation of PLATO Library Instruction Lessons," *Journal of Academic Librarianship* 5 (March 1979): 14–19; and R. A. Avner, "Production of Computer-Based Instructional Materials," in *Issues in Instructional Systems Development,* ed. by Harold F. O'Neil, Jr. (New York: Academic Press, 1979), pp. 133–180.

21. Chris Dimas, "A Strategy for Developing CAI," *Educational Technology* 18 (April 1978): 26–29.

22. Cherry McPherson-Turner, "CAI Readiness Checklist: Formative Author Evaluation of CAI Lessons," *Journal of Computer-Assisted Instruction* 6 (November 1979): 47–49.

23. Avner, "Production of Computer-Based Instructional Materials," p. 146.

24. Allen Avner, Carolynn Moore, and Stanley Smith, "Active External Control: A Basis for Superiority of CBI," *Journal of Computer-Based Instruction* 6 (May 1980): 115–118.

25. Greg P. Kearsley, "Some Conceptual Issues in Computer-Assisted Instruction," *Journal of Computer-Based Instruction* 4 (August 1977): 8–16; and Karen Block, "Cognitive Theory, CAI, and Spelling Improvement," *Journal of Computer-Based Instruction* 5 (May 1979): 86–95.

26. Greg P. Kearsley, "Some Facts About CAI: A Quantitative Analysis of the 1976 *Index to Computer-Based Instruction,*" *Journal of Computer-Based Instruction* 3 (November 1976): 34–41.

27. *Computer-Assisted Instruction Guide* (Newburyport, Mass.: ENTELEK, 1968).

28. Tamas E. Doszkocs, Barbara A. Rapp, and Harold M. Schoolman, "Automated Information Retrieval in Science and Technology," *Science* 208 (April 4, 1980): 25–30.

29. Jones, "Study of a Computer-Assisted Student Assessment System," p. 3.

30. Christopher R. Brigham and Martin Kemp, "The Current Status of Computer-Assisted Instruction in the Health Sciences," *Journal of Medical Education* 49 (1974): 278–279.

31. Harold Wooster, "An Experiment in Networking: The LHNCBC Experimental CAI Network, 1971–1975," *Journal of the American Society for Information Science* 27 (September–October 1976): 329–338; and Becky J. Lyon, "Mind Transplants, or the Role of Computer-Assisted Instruction in the Future of the Library," *Proceedings of the 1975 Clinic on Library Applications of Data Processing: The Use of Computers in Literature Searching and Related Reference Activities in Libraries* (Urbana-Champaign: University of Illinois Graduate School of Library Science, 1976).

32. Axeen, "Teaching the Use of the Library."

33. Beverly Renford and Linnea Hendrickson, "Computer-Assisted Instruction," in their *Bibliographic Instruction: A Handbook* (New York: Neal-Schuman, 1980).

34. Patricia B. Culkin, "Computer-Based Public Access Systems: A Forum for Library Instruction," *Drexel Library Quarterly* 16 (January 1980): 69–82; and Renford and Hendrickson, "Computer-Assisted Instruction," p. 153.

35. Hannelore B. Rader, "Mediated Library Instruction: An Annotated Bibliography," *Drexel Library Quarterly* 16 (January 1980): 116–133.

36. Betty L. Hacker and Joel S. Rutstein, "Educating Large Numbers of Users in University Libraries: An Analysis and a Case Study," in *Progress in Educating the Library User*, ed. by John Lubans, Jr. (New York: Bowker, 1978).

37. Culkin, "Computer-Based Public Access Systems," p. 69.

38. Stanley Hugh Benson, "Administering Course-Related Library Instruction Programs in Selected Academic Libraries" (Ph.D. diss., University of Oklahoma, 1979).

39. Cynthia Amann, "A Survey of Computer-Assisted Instruction in Academic Library Instruction," in *State-of-the-Art of Academic Library Instruction, 1977 Update*, pp. 73–78. ERIC Document Reproduction Service, 1979, ED 171 272.

40. Hicks, "Computer-Assisted Instruction," pp. 238–239.

41. Williams and Davis, "Evaluation of PLATO Library Instructional Lessons," pp. 14–19.

42. Johnson and Plake, "Evaluation of PLATO Library Instructional Lessons," pp. 154–158.

43. Mignon Adams, "Individualized Approach to Learning Library Skills," *Library Trends* 29 (Summer 1980): 83–94.

44. Thomas P. Slavens, "Computer-Assisted Instruction for Reference Librarians," *Journal of Education for Librarianship* 10 (Fall 1969): 116–119.

45. Lois M. Chan and Timothy A. Smith, "Computer-Assisted Instruction in DDC," *Journal of Education for Librarianship* 16 (Summer 1975): 33–40; Janette S. Closurdo, "Teaching Library Skills," *Hospital Progress* 55 (1974): 36, 40, 42; Jacob Arcanin and Geoffrey Zawolkow, "Microcomputers in the Service of Students and Teachers—Computer-Assisted Instruction at the California School for the Deaf: An Update," *American Annals of the Deaf* 125 (September 1980): 807–813; Carl F. Orgren, "Differences in Learning Under Two Strategies of Computer-Assisted Instruction for a Basic Reference Course in Library School," *Information Reports and Bibliographies* 8 (1979): 15–53; and Richard J. Wood, "Computer-Assisted Instruction Program on How to Use a Library Card Catalog: Description, Program and Evaluation." ERIC Document Reproduction Service, 1979, ED 167 156.

46. Elaine Caruso, "Computer Aids to Learning Online Retrieval," *Annual Review of Information Science and Technology* 16 (1981): 317–335.

47. Rowena Weiss Swanson, "An Assessment of Online Instruction Methodologies," *Online* 6 (January 1982): 38–52.

48. Kearsley, "Some 'Facts,' " p. 36.

49. Thomas H. Bennett, "Your Computer Wants to Tell You Something," *Serials Librarian* 2 (Winter 1977): 123–128.

50. Russell V. Skavaril, et al., "The Use of CAI to Provide Problems for Students in Introductory Genetics," *Journal of Computer-Based Instruction* 3 (August 1976): 13–20.

51. David D. Starks, Barbara J. Horn, and Thomas P. Slavens, "Two Modes of Computer Assisted Instruction in a Library Reference Course," *Journal of the American Society for Information Science* 23 (July-August 1972): 271–277.

52. Jung Nievergelt, "A Pragmatic Introduction to Courseware Design," *Computer* 13 (September 1980): 7–14, 16–21.

53. Thomas L. Good and Jere E. Brophy, "Analyzing Classroom Instruction: A More Powerful Alternative," *Educational Technology* 11 (October 1971): 36–41.

54. Lawrence A. Woods, "Applications of Microcomputers in Libraries," *Annual Clinic on Library Applications of Data Processing* (Urbana-Champaign: University of Illinois Graduate School of Library Science, 1981).

55. Karen A. Duncan, "Presidential Address, 1980 Annual Conference of the Association for the Development of Computer-Based Instructional Systems," *Journal of Computer-Based Instruction* 7 (August 1980): 1–4.

56. Patrick Suppes, "Third Annual Dean Lecture: The Future of Computers in Education," *Journal of Computer-Based Instruction* 6 (August 1979): 5–10.

57. Richard C. Atkinson et al., "Futures: Where Will Computer-Assisted Instruction (CAI) Be in 1990?" *Educational Technology* 18 (April 1978): 60–63.

58. Linda C. Smith, "The Medical Librarian and Computer-Assisted Instruction," *Bulletin of the Medical Library Association* 62 (January 1974): 6–18.

9

Teaching Information Structure: Turning Dependent Researchers into Self-Teachers

ELIZABETH FRICK

Colleges and universities have two functions: to teach students how to obtain information and to teach them to interpret that information. Academic librarians are concerned with the "obtaining" skill. Indeed, it seems that in colleges librarians alone are concerned with the presence of that skill in their students. Rarely does a professor get involved in the search process necessary to develop a bibliography or to hone the judgment needed to assess material through the bibliographic apparatus of various fields. Rather, the practice and teaching of research training has come primarily from librarians.

Jacques Barzun, in his gloomily titled article "The Wasteland of American Education," notes that higher education is no longer "trying to develop native intelligence and give it good techniques in the basic arts of man."[1]

At the risk of being accused of "library parochialism," I must class literature searching—information gathering, particularly—in a society with the communication complexity of ours, as a "basic art." Its neglect in higher education is to be deplored.

The slighting of this basic art, one that calls for clarity, control, and judgment, is especially regrettable, since information access and assessment have such far-reaching implications for the graduate's future intellectual development. The librarian should approach bibliographic instruction with this in mind.

The student who has simply been handed "material for research" has been cheated. That student has been given no opportunity to develop the ability to acquire information in this increasingly information-rich society. That student has not been given the skills that ought to be taken for granted with the awarding of the bachelor's degree in any college or university. Extending today's skills in information retrieval to tomorrow's questions will provide the student with long-range benefits. This is, in short, one of the most important gifts an institution can give its students.

This chapter is concerned with developing the ability to determine bibliographic patterns and structures. Why is this type of instruction necessary, what are the concepts underlying it, and how should it be undertaken? We are not concerned here with the development of reference librarians, but rather with the question of how best to give students the ability to acquire their own information, thereby enabling them to become independent learners. Of course, other ramifications of bibliographic instruction are involved. Questions such as the education of instructors to prepare them for the task of bibliographic instruction, who should give research instruction to undergraduates, the management of instruction in libraries, and the position of instruction librarians in the faculty-university setting all merit discussion. This chapter, however, focuses on a theory and method of undergraduate instruction in bibliographic research strategies and sources.

The "Why" of Instruction

Although efficiency is the most commonly offered reason for instituting a program of bibliographic instruction (it is more efficient to teach the use of sources to 25 students as a group than it is to teach each one appearing at the reference desk), such reasoning does not take us very far. "Efficiency" does not answer the deeper question, Why teach students at all? The most efficient method is to hand the student the information without comment. And "efficiency" does not deal with the occasional need to teach students individually, as in the "theses clinics" instituted in many libraries. But where this argument brings us most quickly to a dead end is in its lack of any theory around which to organize teaching methods.

In recent literature, the need for a conceptual basis for bibliographic instruction has been well expressed by Pamela Kobelski and Mary Reichel. They note the "students' inability to generalize from, become interested in, or remember material presented without conceptual frameworks."[2] They point to the importance of consolidation of learning "when previously learned material is reorganized with new material"[3] and argue that "without appropriate cognitive structures, students cannot consolidate material in a meaningful form."[4]

First, we need to develop a theoretical context for instruction; the conceptual framework must come before the instructional content. Theory provides a foundation for what is taught. It informs both the substance and method of teaching. It also informs those to be taught.

In its early days, the trend toward increased instruction, particularly at the undergraduate level, stressed the "how to" approach. At early Ypsilanti (Michigan) conferences, for instance, the questions heard most often were about recalcitrant faculty, about what reference titles to teach in the classroom, what slides to use, and, at a more normal level, the need for behavioral goals and objectives.[5] Major emphasis was on the how rather than on the why.

This emphasis was natural enough. Instruction librarians were battling for a foothold in the academic fortress. It soon became clear, however, that some theoretical underpinning, some understanding of "why" was necessary to give direction and substance to the instructional enterprise. The need for delineating goals beyond simple, mechanical objectives, such as "a student shall be able to find material relevant to his or her paper in the *Readers' Guide to Periodical Literature,*" was evident. I argued at that time that "consideration of the nature of the competencies we hope to develop in students should be of prime concern in designing an instructional program" and that those competencies should go beyond the skill needed to decipher a particular reference source.[6] The competencies that students should aim for are not those which produce an impressionable person but rather an "educable person," in Douglas Heath's phrase.[7] An "educable person" is one who is able to handle new ideas and to participate actively in his or her own education. If we wish to make this happen, then "somewhere in each student's course of study there must be a component which involves the rigorous assessment and understanding of information sources."[8]

How do we instill such understanding when most traditional methods have proved inadequate?

One response to the student's need to locate material for term papers has been to supply a bibliography of reference titles examining each title for its unique characteristics ("this title covers the years . . ." or "an annotated bibliography giving . . . , " and so on). A growing body of literature argues that this method, used alone, is insufficient and that it supplies only short-term gains. Students are left with skills sufficient for one paper only, and must return to the librarian for each new project.

The understanding of "why" is as important in a one-hour class on research methods for one particular paper as it is in a semester-long course on research sources. There is so much to teach. Where do we begin? Do we teach every source in the library beginning at A and ending at Z? Or do we teach only selected sources? Do we teach methodology as well as relevant sources in a class where we may be pressed for time? The importance of "why" is underlined when we realize that the task of instruction may be accomplished in a number of ways. Which is effective? Efficient? Based on accurate observation? Which works?

It has been argued that defining the "why" of instruction will lead not only to the question of *what* is being done and *how* it is to be done, but even to *who* should do it. In "Research Strategies: Bibliographic Instruction for Undergraduates," Sharon Rogers says:

[I]t is important to realize that the persistence of source-oriented, library-model instruction as taught by some library faculty reflects their academic backgrounds, and suggests that significant resistance to change in the conception of both what is to be taught and who should teach may well come from the librarians themselves. This is not to say that the academic background of librarians is inadequate for the

task, but rather that the success of the instructional process may require translation of knowledge from the academic library experience into the conceptual frameworks and habits of users. If this translation occurs, there may be no debate about who will assume responsibility for library instruction in the research process.[9]

In fact, Francis L. Hopkins sees bibliographic instruction as a "meta-discipline" best "carried out not from *within* disciplines [but] by librarians specifically trained in the interdisciplinary science of research."[10]

What, then, do we want to teach students engaged in bibliographic research? Students must acquire two basic skills in order to progress independently: (1) discrimination or judgment and (2) an understanding of bibliographic structure. Needless to say, one concept follows from the other.

Judgment

A class or course on bibliographic structure should help students discriminate among various aspects of a discipline's literature. Exploring and evaluating the literature expands the research process, allowing students to become contributing participants in their own education. Not only then are students able to continue their own education, but they see the chosen discipline as a living entity rather than a static corpus of facts and begin to develop judgment.

Discriminating between appropriate and inappropriate, scholarly and popular material is not only an important but a mandatory talent for college students. Book reviews, information about an author, the refereeing process in publication have always served as filters to help the student sift through a plethora of information. With the increased use of computerized searching, such screening methods run the risk of being by-passed. Evan Farber has said:

The increased amount of material available will surely be a problem, but an even greater one . . . is the disappearance of criteria that we take for granted now in order to make some prejudgment on quality. Criteria such as the reputation of the publisher, the significance of a journal's sponsor, the intended

audience of a publication, or reviews. Students can be taught
to look for these and to make some discriminations. But if
some predictions for the electronic library are correct . . . then
there's a big new problem. . . . All the outside means of guar-
anteeing some validity—refereed journals, the editorial staffs
of publishers, the book reviews—are based on a formal process
of publication. What happens when that formal process, with
the various screens that insure quality, breaks down?[11]

Only a student with a sense of structure can find the way
through masses of undifferentiated citations.

To learn discrimination in the use of material, the student
needs to understand the structure of the literature in order to
control its access.

Structural Understanding

Hopkins points to the need for structural understanding of a
discipline:

[I]n order to use library resources effectively, students need
to connect them with a basic understanding of how
knowledge is created, communicated, synthesized within
fields of inquiry, how knowledge differs structurally from one
field to another, and how bibliographic sources reflect the
various stages of the knowledge process.[12]

In an earlier mentioned article,[13] four levels of bibliographic
awareness are discussed that should be conveyed to students.
They are (1) a knowledge of specific titles that are useful for
specific tasks; (2) a knowledge of types of sources relevant to
types of questions; (3) a knowledge that each of the specific
disciplines inspires specific types of sources for reasons im-
bedded in their research goals, assumptions, and methods; and
(4) a knowledge that the structure of literature and information in a society or discipline both informs, and is informed
by, that society.

Having defined bibliographic awareness, we can now explore these interlocking levels of knowledge in such a way as
to provide a framework for classroom instruction. More specifically, what are these levels of understanding through

which the sophisticated student should organize the task of assembling a bibliography?

Using economics as an example, a student first notices that a title called *Index of Economic Articles* is a good place to look for articles on the chosen topic. This is a level of understanding that says "X title is good for articles on my topic." It is knowledge of specific titles. It is a useful bit of information, in no particular context other than that of an immediate need. With that piece of information, the student can write this paper. When assigned the next paper, say, for example, in political science, the student will get little help from the *Index of Economic Articles* and presumably must return to the "expert" (the professor, the librarian) to ask for the next direction.

With luck and some intelligence, the student's next question should be, Is there a source that looks like the *Index of Economic Articles*, but that deals with political science journals? Such a question demonstrates that the student has moved to the second level of understanding, a knowledge of types of relevant sources for specific types of questions. To belabor what may be an obvious point: Searchers who know that to find certain types of material, in whatever field, they should go to certain types of sources, have taken a major step toward becoming independent learners.

As that same student becomes aware that the most recent research in economics is often accessible only in working papers, over which there has, until recently, been little bibliographic control, he or she is beginning to understand the nature of the discipline and the dissemination of its research. The student may even reflect on the difficulty, for anyone who is new to the field, of using the classified system in the *Index of Economic Articles* and begin to get some insight into the nature of communication within the profession. The student's understanding of the bibliography of a field allows him or her to see the pattern of research and communication in a discipline's substantive portion.

When the student further reflects on the necessity of understanding the bibliographic organization of the field of economics before penetrating to the core of the literature, he or she is reflecting on the nature of the interaction between the discipline and society. At this level the student may ask questions about the impact of scholarship on society or about the awe and authority that this society accords its economists.

In achieving the sophistication and flexibility that this progression implies, the student begins to appreciate the bibliographic component of the chosen field as a significant aspect of that field and as one way to appreciate the significance of the field itself. Librarians would do well to read Thomas Kuhn's *The Structure of Scientific Revolutions*[14] to develop a better sense of significance of bibliography in understanding the dominating paradigms of a field.

The "How" of Instruction

How to achieve the four levels of understanding discussed above is very much open to experimentation. Following are models that have been tried with some measure of success. These methods have been adopted to fit a full course, a course-related, single-class presentation, or an integrated format. Depending on the length of time available for instruction and on the sophistication of the student, the librarian may touch on all the aspects examined above or may prefer to emphasize only some aspects, leaving the rest until another time. When teaching at the college level, it seems best to emphasize the understanding of types of reference sources and their relation to types of questions, thereby giving students a conceptual basis for approaching new bibliographic problems.

Issues of content are of primary importance. The question of what is to be taught determines the success of bibliographic instruction both for the student and for the program. What follows is an attempt to answer what Rogers has termed some of the "most interesting and crucial questions about search strategies," those surrounding the "issue of what is to be taught."[15] She boils the possibilities down to sources or process. The examples below are offered as a practical method to achieve both knowledge of sources and knowledge of process.

Course instruction

I prefer to be explicit with students concerning my reasons for presenting them with a course in bibliography, that is to say, my reasons for putting forth the energy, time, and ego that one always expends in teaching. Each course starts with a statement both of the broadest goals of the course (a statement that mirrors my reasons for presenting it) and of the structure of the course. The final course evaluation is based largely on these statements.

The stated goals given to the students are:

1. Students know which sources to use for a particular paper on which they are working.
2. Students know which types of resources they need for a given problem.
3. Students can read and assess information resources in a library.
4. Students can use other libraries intelligently.
5. Students know that there are other information banks than the library, for instance, community resources.
6. Students are logical and assured in information searches.
7. Students can transfer the knowledge of resources from one field to another field.
8. Students understand how libraries fit into learning.

The first of these stated ends is too often the only conscious goal of bibliographic instruction. The second goal begins to recognize the context within which the instruction is taking place and leads inevitably to the seventh and eighth goals. Once the instructor speaks of "types" of sources, the way is laid for the student to generalize from the particular sources presented and to consolidate the material into a cognitive structure useful for new problems.

I am not as forthright with my classes as I could be, usually from fear of intimidating them. Were I to be completely open about my goals for them, I would have to admit that I see the eighth goal as only a starting point. It is the beginning of a realization of the effect that the nature of a discipline has upon the reference sources in that discipline. An effect is exerted on the nature of all information sources by the context or society that produces them.

The explicit and implicit aims outlined above affect such drab realities as the order of the lectures, the nature of assignments, and the climate of the class. Let us take a Bibliography of the Social Sciences course (one that is designed for students who have already chosen a major) as a practical example of how one can integrate these eight goals into instruction.

The first lecture comprises not only a statement of the

goals of the course, an outline of its structure, and a presentation of the criteria on which the student will be judged, but a brief exploration of what we are talking about when we use the word *information*. Is it "facts" in the most popular definition? Is it a network of interacting facts? Or is it, as some have suggested, a process? What is the difference between information and knowledge? We then discuss the way in which scholarship and popular literature get published. What is the first place at which a piece of research appears? Where does it appear subsequently? Where does it get reported as it works its way into the fabric of "common knowledge"? Having constructed for the class one model of this literature pattern, and having illustrated others, a question arises that is of prime importance to the student doing research: At each point in the model, what is the literature access point? Which type of literature should an undergraduate access for a term paper—dissertations, articles, government reports, books? What type of reference source should the student use to get at an article—a book, a film script, a research report, a dissertation, an encyclopedic summary? The understanding is now in place on which to build a discussion of the logic of locating material for a given research problem. The student is ready to use this new knowledge of the literature to hear the first of many discussions on search strategies.[16]

Upon questioning, students willingly volunteer their own methods, some of which are disorganized or truncated, some of which have a logic all their own. We can then go over some of the models of a logical search that have been suggested in the literature as well as others suggested by the instructor. Each portion of these models is carefully related to specific types of reference sources. As well, perhaps for the first time, the students are explicitly told that through this searching logic and the concomitant logic of types of reference sources, they can become independent learners and self-educators. This knowledge of the available logic of the system allows searchers to move into fields in which they may have no substantive knowledge, for example, to move from searching in sociology, in which they may be proficient, to searching in geology, in which they may have little formal knowledge.

In subsequent lectures, the course looks at the different types of reference sources, moving from dictionaries to online literature searching. At every stage, the discussion of specific titles is preceded by a discussion of the value of that portion of the literature being accessed. Who does that portion of the literature serve and what are its functions? That leads to a discussion of the various formats possible in that type of reference source. The common characteristics in reference sources are just as important as their unique characteristics.

Periodical literature is a good example of this process. What are the various types of journal literature? Whom does each address?[17] What are the hallmarks of scholarly journals? Why do scholarly articles look the way they do with their peculiar abstracts, documentations, language? What is the "half-life" of literature? Which indexes provide access to the popular magazines? Which to the journal literature? When would each be useful? What is citation indexing and what are its ramifications?[18] What information would the "ideal index" provide? Students often give extensive lists in reply to the last question—a list that usually includes an answer to the question, Is the article any good?

Students then examine a bibliography of significant reference sources prepared by the instructor. They learn to examine the scope, format, and use of each. They may also compare the nature and usefulness of each type of source for the specific disciplines represented by members of the class. For instance, why are many bibliographies in the field of history so well constructed? Why is the form so well developed? Why, however, are the periodical indexes the most sophisticated in chemistry or biology? Why is economics reference literature often difficult for the uninformed to use? Why are the sciences so well represented in the online databases? Such questions make students aware of the distinctiveness of the literature of their chosen field and of the necessarily peculiar characteristics of the reference literature that provides access to that field. At the same time they are again made aware of the common pattern that emerges in handling all scholarly literature.

In this way, the course does not neglect the specific titles that students need to know in obtaining material for their term papers, but it also helps them move toward a recognition of the third level of understanding: awareness of the ways in which the literature and reference sources of a field reflect the nature of the discipline they serve. The perspective provided by this overview of the reference sources also helps students judge the sources they use. They are encouraged to employ critical judgment about the sources they use in their day-to-day assignments. The expectation is that students will develop both knowledge and judgment in research work, rather than simply learning a few specific titles by rote.

The syllabus of this social sciences course is designed to include sections on dictionaries and encyclopedias, handbooks, style sheets, the card catalog, periodical indexes and abstracts, newspaper indexes, citation indexes, union lists and published library catalogs, bibliographies, annual reviews, biographical sources, directories, statistical sources, legal sources, government documents, community and other similar sources, on-line searching, and computerized networks.

At each stage, method is the star. Logic is emphasized. The increased importance forecast for computers in future bibliographic work only enhances the message to students: The honing of inquiry logic is essential to good bibliographic research. At the same time we can promise the student that mastering the logic of the search makes room for creativity. Some magnificent finds can be made on the basis of inspired guesswork. Such payoffs are most frequent when they grow out of a sound assessment of bibliographic structure.[19] The guesswork becomes a creative leap, not a despairing plunge.

The course includes both required and optional readings and written assignments. The most important assignment is to compile a bibliography in the student's major field, preferably for an already assigned paper. The compilation of this bibliography gives students an opportunity, perhaps for the first time in their academic life, to experience excellence in bibliographic work.

Course-related instruction

In single, course-related classes, this same approach is adapted to a shorter time frame. Publishing patterns and search strategies are outlined briefly. Various items are discussed: periodical indexes, government documents, the card catalog, scholarly vs. popular periodicals, and so forth. The topics chosen for discussion depend on the class, the assignment, level of student sophistication, and the regular professor's wishes. At times it is more appropriate to begin with a demonstration of the depth and diversity of the literature, using sample articles and monographs, than to talk about how to judge its appropriateness to any given project and finally to move to assessing that literature through reference sources.

In a longer time frame, this latter approach can be used in

several ways. One model, demonstrated to me by a library colleague, is to offer three lectures in a course-related format. The regular professor sets aside three lecture hours for bibliographic instruction. The first hour is spent discussing the literature, who publishes it, in which formats it appears, how students can use it. The second lecture involves a discussion of access to the literature, the various bibliographies, indexes and abstracts, and so on. The final lecture examines some unique aspect of that particular literature. In one such set of lectures in the field of geology, the third lecture was used exclusively for a particularly difficult and important type of literature for the field, namely, maps. In another case, this session could cover government documents, international statistics, working papers, or any one of a number of specialized sources appropriate to the discipline.

Integrated Instruction

Integrated instruction, although presenting a problem of coherence because the librarian shares the lectern interchangeably with other faculty, has a great advantage in providing the opportunity to demonstrate relevance. In designing such a course, the teaching faculty, including the librarian, can adjust the syllabus explicitly to draw from the material a desired picture of scholarly communication as a foundation for scholarly research. Access as a function of research structure can be well documented. What one loses in being able to lecture nonstop in integrated instruction, one gains in being able to provide an example of the interaction of the library with the disciplines.

Conclusion

From no one other than a librarian is a college or university student likely to learn this fundamental truth: The manner in which you go about obtaining material for research on any single college paper is more important in the long run than the material you obtain. This is a difficult statement for some to accept. Learning how to learn, however, is what undergraduate education, especially, is about, and instruction in inquiry methods is the foundation of such learning.[20]

Theory, then, informs what we teach, how we teach, and even who teaches. Theory, in turn, is informed by the "why" of instruction. The "why" revolves around the long-term interests of the student in learning how to learn and in learning how to become an independent learner who can continue to function in a society where the ability to focus on the most relevant information in a maelstrom of increasingly difficult and important data is necessary.

One way to emphasize this point with students is to build into bibliographic classes components that stress a structured method of literature searching and an assessment of the reference sources used. This assessment must include both a judgment of the form and content of the sources and an understanding of the impact of that form and content on the accessibility of the literature in the field. The assessment also must include an awareness of the impact of the field on the form and content of its reference sources. The interrelationship of literature and bibliography is a concept crucial to the understanding of access to information. Once grasped, the understanding will ease a student's use of the world of information.

We are presented with an information environment in which knowledge of what one is about as a searcher is the only way to ensure quality. The really creative solutions to disciplinary questions will come from good minds that have such a thorough mastery of the logic that the process I have been discussing is second nature to them. Such mastery will free them to exercise subtlety and wit in dealing with information.

Notes

1. Jacques Barzun, "The Wasteland of American Education," *New York Review of Books* 5 (November 1981): 35.
2. Pamela Kobelski and Mary Reichel, "Conceptual Frameworks for Bibliographic Instruction," *Journal of Academic Librarianship* 7 (May 1981): 73.
3. Ibid.
4. Ibid., p. 74.
5. The later publication *Bibliographic Instruction Handbook* (Chicago: Policy and Planning Committee, Bibliographic Instruction Section, Association of College and Research Libraries, American Library Association, 1979), which developed from these earlier efforts, still reflects the emphasis on immediate behavioral goals and objectives, but the final aims have

shifted slightly. In addition to goals such as "the student recognizes the library staff," also included are broader goals such as "the student is able to evaluate materials and select those appropriate to his needs."

6. Elizabeth Frick, "Information Structure and Bibliographic Instruction," *Journal of Academic Librarianship* 1 (September 1975): 12.

7. Douglas Heath, *Growing Up in College* (San Francisco: Jossey-Bass, 1968), passim.

8. Frick, "Information Structure," p. 12.

9. Sharon J. Rogers, "Research Strategies: Bibliographic Instruction for Undergraduates," *Library Trends* 29 (Summer 1980): 78.

10. Frances L. Hopkins, "Bibliographic Instruction: An Emerging Professional Discipline," in *Directions for the Decade: Library Instruction in the 1980's* (Papers presented at the Tenth Annual Conference on Library Orientation for Academic Libraries Held at Eastern Michigan University, May 8–9, 1980), ed. by Carolyn A. Kirkendall (Ann Arbor, Mich.: Pierian Press, 1981), p. 20.

11. Evan Farber, "Quality Service, User Rights and Expectations, and Administrative Planning." Speech delivered at the Colorado Library Association's Annual Convention in Colorado Springs, October 20, 1981.

12. Hopkins, "Bibliographic Instruction," p. 18.

13. Frick, "Information Structure," pp. 12–13.

14. Thomas S. Kuhn, *The Structure of Scientific Revolutions*, 2nd ed. (Chicago: University of Chicago Press, 1970).

15. Rogers, "Research Strategies," p. 70.

16. The students look at a line method, a citation method, a document-centered approach, and pathfinders. They examine the merits and drawbacks of each. They also look at a number of writers who have diagrammed search logic. Among these are James M. Doyle and George H. Grimes, *Reference Resources: A Systematic Approach* (Metuchen, N.J.: Scarecrow Press, 1976); J. Gordon Brewer, *The Literature of Geography: A Guide to Its Organization and Use* (Hamden, Conn.: Linnet Books, 1973); Tom L. Martinson, *Introduction to Library Research in Geography: An Instructional Manual and Short Bibliography* (Metuchen, N.J.: Scarecrow Press, 1972); Thomas Kirk, "Problems in Library Instruction in Four-Year Colleges," in *Educating the Library User*, ed. by John Lubans, Jr. (New York: Bowker, 1974); and Elizabeth Frick, *Library Research Guide to History: Illustrated Search Strategy and Sources* (Ann Arbor, Mich.: Pierian Press, 1980).

17. For this purpose there are a number of fine articles on the uses of social science literature in general and of the literature of specific disciplines in particular. The articles in the *International Social Science Journal* (26), in an issue the theme of which is "Communicating and Diffusing Social Science," are especially helpful. The breakdown of periodicals by function and audience is outlined by Isac Chiva in "Scholarly Periodicals: Their Strengths and Weaknesses," on pp. 377–381 of that issue. It is an article I return to frequently, augmenting his breakdown with additional functions and audiences that I have isolated.

18. The study of indexes provides numerous enlightening lines of inquiry for the student. For instance, Richard Werking, in his brief but provocative

paper at Ypsilanti several years ago, pointed out that "many access mechanisms to the scholarly literature, as opposed to the scholarly journals themselves, are not generated by scholars or addressed to their perceived needs." He went on to point out two exceptions: the citation indexes and *Current Contents*, both of which reflect normal scholarly searching methods. Richard Werking, "Course-Related Instruction for History Majors," in *Putting Library Instruction in Its Place: In the Library and in the Library School* (Papers presented at the Seventh Annual Conference on Library Orientation for Academic Libraries Held at Eastern Michigan University, May 12–13, 1977), ed. by Carolyn A. Kirkendall (Ann Arbor, Mich.: Pierian Press, 1978), p. 44.

19. *Logic* is a relative word. Rogers in "Research Strategies," pp. 74–76, nicely uses Abraham Kaplan's *The Conduct of Inquiry* (San Francisco: Chandler, 1964) to emphasize the difference between "logic-in-use" and "reconstructed logic." It is an important distinction that leads to the process-oriented method I am describing in this chapter.

20. A number of authors have argued this directly, among them Raymond G. McInnis, *New Perspectives for Reference Service in Academic Libraries* (Westport, Conn.: Greenwood Press, 1978); Kobelski and Reichel, "Conceptual Frameworks"; Frick, "Information Structure"; Rogers, "Research Strategies"; Doyle and Grimes, *Reference Resources*. Thelma Freides, although she does not, in *Literature and Bibliography of the Social Sciences* (Los Angeles: Melville Publishing, 1973), link the study of access to instruction, indeed proceeds to instruct her readers in the access to literature through an understanding of the structure and uses of that literature. Howard R. Bowen in "The Residue of Academic Learning," *The Chronicle of Higher Education* (November 14, 1977), p. 13, said, "Most studies show that 50 to 80 percent of what is learned in courses is lost within one year. . . . Perhaps most important of all, the residues may include the tendencies, triggered by college, that encourage exploration and learning."

Selected Bibliography

Adams, Mignon. "Individualized Approach to Learning Library Skills." *Library Trends* 29 (Summer 1980): 83–94.

Allen, John R. "ELSE at Dartmouth: An Experiment in Computer-Aided Instruction in French." *French Review* 44 (April 1971): 902–912.

Amann, Cynthia. "A Survey of Computer-Assisted Instruction in Academic Library Instruction" in *State-of-the-Art of Academic Library Instruction, 1977 Update*, pp. 73–78. Stanford, Calif.: ERIC Document Reproduction Service, 1979, ED 171 272.

Arcanin, Jacob, and Zawolkow, Geoffrey. "Microcomputers in the Service of Students and Teachers—Computer-Assisted Instruction at the California School for the Deaf: An Update." *American Annals of the Deaf* 125 (September 1980): 807–813.

Association of College and Research Libraries. Bibliographic Instruction for Educators Committee. "Bibliographic Competencies for Education Students." *College and Research Libraries News* 42 (July/August 1981): 209–210.

———. Bibliographic Instruction Section, Policy and Planning Committee. *Bibliographic Instruction Handbook*. Chicago: American Library Assn., 1979.

Atkinson, Richard C., and Wilson, H. A., eds. *Computer-Assisted Instruction: A Book of Readings.* New York: Academic Press, 1969.

Ausubel, David P. "Cognitive Structure and the Facilitation of Meaningful Verbal Learning." *Journal of Teacher Education* 14 (June 1963): 217–222.

Ausubel, David P.; Novak, Joseph D.; and Hanesian, Helen. *Educational Psychology: A Cognitive View,* 2nd ed. New York: Holt, 1978.

Avner, Allen; Moore, Carolynn; and Smith, Stanley. "Active External Control: A Basis for Superiority of CBI." *Journal of Computer-Based Instruction* 6 (May 1980): 115–118.

Avner, R. A. "Production of Computer-Based Instructional Materials." In *Issues in Instructional Systems Development,* edited by Harold F. O'Neill, Jr., pp. 133–180. New York: Academic Press, 1979.

Axeen, Marina Esther. "Teaching the Use of the Library to Undergraduates: An Experimental Comparison of Computer-Based Instruction and the Conventional Lecture Method." Ph.D. dissertation, University of Illinois at Urbana-Champaign, 1967.

Baker, Frank. "Computer-Managed Instruction: A Context for CBI." In *Computer-Based Instruction: A State-of-the-Art Assessment,* edited by Harold F. O'Neil, pp. 23–64. New York: Academic Press, 1981.

Barzun, Jacques. "The Wasteland of American Education." *New York Review of Books* 5 (November 1981): 34–36.

Bebout, Lois; Davis, Donald, Jr.; and Oehlerts, Donald. "User Studies in the Humanities: A Survey and a Proposal." *RQ* 15 (Fall 1975): 40–44.

Bennett, Thomas H. "Your Computer Wants to Tell You Something." *Serials Librarian* 2 (Winter 1977): 123–128.

Benson, James, and Maloney, Ruth K. "Principles of Searching." *RQ* 14 (Summer 1975): 316–320.

Benson, Stanley Hugh. "Administering Course-Related Library Instruction Programs in Selected Academic Libraries." Ph.D. dissertation, University of Oklahoma, 1979.

Berelson, Bernard. *Graduate Education in the United States.* New York: McGraw-Hill, 1960.

Black, Max. *Models and Metaphors.* Ithaca, N.Y.: Cornell University Press, 1962.

Block, Karen. "Cognitive Theory, CAI, and Spelling Improvement." *Journal of Computer-Based Instruction* 5 (May 1979): 86–95.

Boehm, Eric H. "On the Second Knowledge: A Manifesto for the Humanities." *Libri* 22 (1972): 312–323.

Brewer, J. Gordon. *The Literature of Geography: A Guide to Its Organization and Use.* Hamden, Conn.: Linnet Books, 1973.

Brigham, Christopher, and Kemp, Martin. "The Current Status of Computer-Assisted Instruction in the Health Sciences." *Journal of Medical Education* 49 (1974): 278–279.

Broadus, Robert N. "The Literature of the Social Sciences: A Survey of Citation Studies." *International Social Science Journal* 23 (1971): 236–243.

Brown, Harold I. "Objective Knowledge in Science and the Humanities." *Diogenes* 97 (Spring 1977): 85–102.

Bruner, Jerome S. *The Process of Education.* Cambridge, Mass.: Harvard University Press, 1960.

———. *Toward a Theory of Instruction.* Cambridge, Mass.: Belknap Press, 1960.

Burke, Kenneth. *A Grammar of Motives.* Berkeley: University of California Press, 1969.

Cappuzzello, Paul G., and Rogers, Sharon J. *Information Gathering Skills for Pre-Service Teachers.* Toledo: University of Toledo Libraries, 1979.

Carpenter, Eric J. "The Literary Scholar, the Librarian, and the Future of Literary Research." *Literary Research Newsletter* 2 (October 1977): 143–155.

Carpenter, Finley. *The Skinner Primer: Behind Freedom and Dignity.* New York: Free Press, 1974.

Caruso, Elaine. "Computer Aids to Learning Online Retrieval." *Annual Review of Information Science and Technology* 16 (1981): 317–335.

Cassirer, Ernst. *The Logic of the Humanities.* New Haven, Conn.: Yale University Press, 1961.

Chan, Lois M., and Smith, Timothy A. "Computer-Assisted Instruction in DDC." *Journal of Education for Librarianship* 16 (Summer 1975): 33–40.

Chiva, Isac. "Scholarly Periodicals: Their Strengths and Weaknesses." *International Social Science Journal* 26 (1974): 377–381.

Closurdo, Janette S. "Teaching Library Skills." *Hospital Progress* 55 (1974): 36–42.

Computer-Assisted Instruction Guide. Newburyport, Mass.: ENTELEK, 1968.

Crane, R. S. *The Idea of the Humanities and Other Essays Critical and Historical.* 2 vols. Chicago: University of Chicago Press, 1967.

Culkin, Patricia B. "CAI Experiment." *American Libraries* 3 (June 1972): 643–645.

————. "Computer-Based Public Access Systems: A Forum for Library Instruction." *Drexel Library Quarterly* 16 (January 1980): 69–82.

Dimas, Chris. "A Strategy for Developing CAI." *Educational Technology* 18 (April 1978): 26–29.

Dixon, Paul N., and Judd, Wilson A. "A Comparison of Computer Managed Instruction and Lecture Mode for Teaching Basic Statistics." *Journal of Computer-Based Instruction* 4 (August 1977): 22–25.

Doszkocs, Tamas E.; Rapp, Barbara A.; and Schoolman, Harold M. "Automated Information Retrieval in Science and Technology." *Science* 208 (April 4, 1980): 25–30.

Dudley, Miriam. *Chicano Library Program*. Los Angeles: University of California Library, 1970.

————. "The Self-Paced Library Skills Program at UCLA's College Library." In *Educating the Library User*, edited by John Lubans, Jr., pp. 330–335. New York: Bowker, 1974.

————. *Workbook in Library Skills: A Self-directed Course in the Use of UCLA's College Library*. Los Angeles: University of California, College Library, 1973.

Duncan, Karen A. "Presidential Address. 1980 Annual Conference of the Association for the Development of Computer-Based Instructional Systems." *Journal of Computer-Based Instruction* 7 (August 1980): 1–4.

Encyclopaedia Britannica, 15th ed. S.v. "Programmed Instruction."

Encyclopedia of Education, 1971 ed. S.v. "Computers: Computer-Aided Instruction," by Lawrence M. Stolurow.

Encyclopedia of Library and Information Science, 1979 ed. S.v. "Computer-Assisted Instruction," by Karen Block; S.v. "Scientific Literature," by K. Subramanyam.

Farber, Evan Ira. "Library Instruction Throughout the Curriculum: Earlham College Program." In *Educating the Library User*, edited by John Lubans, Jr., pp. 145–162. New York: Bowker, 1974.

————. "Quality Service, User Rights and Expectations, and Administrative Planning." Speech delivered at the Colorado Library Association's Annual Convention in Colorado Springs, October 20, 1981.

Feldhusen, John H., and Lorton, Paul, Jr. *A Position Paper on CAI Research and Development*. Stanford, Calif.: Stanford University, ERIC Clearinghouse for Educational Media and Technology, 1970, ED 036 204.

Freides, Thelma. *Literature and Bibliography of the Social Sciences*. Los Angeles: Melville Publishing Co., 1973.

Frick, Elizabeth. "Information Structure and Bibliographic Instruction." *Journal of Academic Librarianship* 1 (September 1975): 12–14.

————. *Library Research Guide to History: Illustrated Search Strategy and Sources.* Ann Arbor, Mich.: Pierian Press, 1980.

"Futures: Where Will Computer-Assisted Instruction (CAI) Be in 1990?" *Educational Technology* 18 (April 1978): 60–63.

Gagné, Robert M. *The Conditions of Learning.* New York: Holt, 1965.

Garfield, Eugene. "Is Information Retrieval in the Arts and Humanities Inherently Different from That in Science? The Effect that ISI's Citation Index for the Arts and Humanities Is Expected to Have on Future Scholarship." *Library Quarterly* 50 (January 1980): 40–57.

————. "Primodial Concepts, Citation Indexing, and Historio-Bibliography." *Journal of Library History* 2 (July 1967): 235–249.

Garvey, William D. *Communication: The Essence of Science.* Oxford: Pergamon Press, 1979.

Good, Thomas L., and Brophy, Jere E. "Analyzing Classroom Instruction: A More Powerful Alternative." *Educational Technology* 11 (October 1971): 36–41.

Gross, Richard E., and McDonald, Frederick J. "Classroom Methods: III, The Problem-Solving Approach." *Phi Delta Kappan* 39 (March 1958): 259–265.

Hacker, Betty L., and Rutstein, Joel S. "Educating Large Numbers of Users in University Libraries: An Analysis and a Case Study." In *Progress in Educating the Library User*, edited by John Lubans, Jr. New York: Bowker, 1978.

Hale, Barbara M. *The Subject Bibliography of the Social Sciences and Humanities.* Oxford: Pergamon Press, 1970.

Hansen, Lois N. "Computer-Assisted Instruction in Library Use: An Evaluation." *Drexel Library Quarterly* 8 (July 1972): 345–355.

Heath, Douglas. *Growing Up in College.* San Francisco: Jossey-Bass, 1968.

Hess, R. C. "Guided Design, User Attitudes, & Group Problem-Solving Research." In *Proceedings for a National Conference on Teaching Decision-Making: Guided Design, 1980, May 28, 29, 30,* pp. 16.1–16.5. Morgantown, W.Va.: West Virginia University, 1980.

Hickey, Albert E., ed. *Computer-Assisted Instruction: A Survey of the Literature,* 3rd ed. Newburyport, Mass.: ENTELEK, 1968.

Hicks, Joan Tomay. "Computer-Assisted Instruction in Library Orientation and Services." *Bulletin of the Medical Library Association* 64 (April 1976): 238–240.

Hirst, Paul H. *Knowledge and the Curriculum: A Collection of Philosophical Papers.* London: Routledge and Kegan Paul, 1974.

Hodges, Theodora. "Citation Indexing: Its Potential for Bibliographical Control." Ph.D. dissertation, University of California, Berkeley, 1978.

Holman, Hugh C. *A Handbook to Literature,* 3rd ed. Indianapolis: Bobbs-Merrill, 1972.

Hopkins, Frances L. "Bibliographic Instruction: An Emerging Professional Discipline." In *Directions for the Decade: Library Instruction in the 1980's,* edited by Carolyn A. Kirkendall, pp. 13–24. Papers presented at the Tenth Annual Conference on Library Orientation for Academic Libraries Held at Eastern Michigan University, May 8–9, 1980. Ann Arbor, Mich.: Pierian Press, 1981.

Hurd, A. W. "The Workbook as an Instructional Aid." *School Review* 39 (October 1931): 608–616.

Jacks, Robert W. "The Status of the Workbook in Classroom Instruction." *Educational Method* 18 (December 1938): 105–109.

Johnson, Kathleen A., and Plake, Barbara S. "Evaluation of PLATO Library Instruction Lessons: Another View." *Journal of Academic Librarianship* 6 (July 1980): 154–158.

Johnson, W. P. "Then Came the Workbook." *Journal of Education* 131 (February 1948): 64–66.

Jones, Clyve; Chapman, Michael; and Woods, Pamela Carr. "The Characteristics of the Literature Used by Historians." *Journal of Librarianship* 4 (July 1972): 137–156.

Jones, Leslie Arnold. "Study of a Computer-Assisted Student System for Basic Medical Sciences." Ph.D. dissertation, University of Illinois at Urbana-Champaign, 1974.

Jones, William T. *The Sciences and the Humanities: Conflict and Reconciliation.* Berkeley: University of California Press, 1965.

Jung, C. G. *Collected Works.* Edited by Herbert Read, Michael Fordham, and Gerhard Adler. Vol. 6: *Psychological Types.* Bollinger Series, no. 20. Princeton, N.J.: Princeton University Press, 1971.

Kaplan, Abraham. *The Conduct of Inquiry.* San Francisco: Chandler, 1964.

Kaufman, Roger. *Identifying and Solving Problems: A Systems Approach.* La Jolla, Calif.: University Associates, 1976.

Kearsley, Greg P. "Some Conceptual Issues in Computer-Assisted Instruction." *Journal of Computer-Based Instruction* 4 (August 1977): 8–16.

———. "Some 'Facts' About CAI: A Quantitative Analysis of the 1976 *Index to Computer-Based Instruction.*" *Journal of Computer-Based Instruction* 3 (November 1976): 34–41.

Kirk, Thomas. "A Comparison of Two Methods of Library Instruction for Students in Introductory Biology." *College and Research Libraries* 32 (November 1971): 465–474.

————. "Problems in Library Instruction in Four-Year Colleges." In *Educating the Library User*, edited by John Lubans, Jr., pp. 83–103. New York: Bowker, 1974.

Kirkendall, Carolyn. *Academic Library Skills Workbook Listing.* Ypsilanti, Mich.: Project LOEX, 1979.

Klahr, David, ed. *Cognition and Instruction.* Hillsdale, N.J.: Lawrence Erlbaum Associates, 1976.

Klausmeier, Herbert J.; Ghatala, Elizabeth S.; and Frayer, Dorothy A. *Conceptual Learning and Development: A Cognitive View.* New York: Academic Press, 1974.

Knapp, Patricia B. *The Monteith College Library Experiment.* New York: Scarecrow, 1966.

Knapp, Robert H. *The Origins of American Humanistic Scholars.* Englewood Cliffs, N.J.: Prentice-Hall, 1964.

Kobelski, Pamela, and Reichel, Mary. "Conceptual Frameworks for Bibliographic Instruction." *Journal of Academic Librarianship* 7 (May 1981): 73–77.

Kraeling, Carl H. "The Humanities: Characteristics of the Literature, Problems of Use, and Bibliographic Organization in the Field." In *Bibliographic Organization*, edited by Jesse H. Shera and Margaret E. Egan, pp. 109–126. Chicago: University of Chicago Press, 1951.

Kuhn, Thomas S. *The Structure of Scientific Revolutions.* 2nd ed. Foundation of the Unity of Science, vol. 2, no. 2. Chicago: University of Chicago Press, 1970.

Lakoff, George, and Johnson, Mark. *Metaphors We Live By.* Chicago: University of Chicago Press, 1980.

Laszlo, Ervin, ed. *The Relevance of General Systems Theory.* New York: Braziller, 1972.

Lawrence, David. "Guided Design in the Basic American Government Course." *Teaching Political Science* 7 (April 1980): 321–328.

Leach, Edmund. *Culture and Communication: The Logic by which Symbols Are Connected.* Cambridge: Cambridge University Press, 1976.

Leith, G. O. M. "Implications of Cognitive Psychology for the Improvement of Teaching and Learning in Universities." *Educational Review* 31 (June 1979): 149–159.

Levi, Albert William. *The Humanities Today.* Bloomington, Ind.: Indiana University Press, 1970.

Levin, Tamar. "Instruction Which Enables Students to Develop Higher Mental Processes." In *Evaluation in Education: An Inter-*

national Review Series, edited by Bruce H. Choppin, vol. 3, pp. 173–200. Oxford: Pergamon Press, 1979.

Lewis, C. S. *Rehabilitation and Other Essays.* London: Oxford University Press, 1939.

Lindgren, Jon. "Seeking a Useful Tradition for Library User Instruction in the College Library." In *Progress in Educating the Library User,* edited by John Lubans, Jr., pp. 71–91. New York: Bowker, 1978.

Lockwood, Deborah L. *Library Instruction: A Bibliography.* Westport, Conn.: Greenwood Press, 1979.

Lyon, Becky J. "Mind Transplants, or the Role of Computer-Assisted Instruction in the Future of the Library." In *Proceedings of the 1975 Clinic on Library Applications of Data Processing: The Use of Computers in Literature Searching and Related Reference Activities in Libraries.* Urbana-Champaign, Ill.: University of Illinois Graduate School of Library Science, 1976.

McInnis, Raymond G. *New Perspectives for Reference Service in Academic Libraries.* Contributions in Librarianship and Information Science, no. 23. Westport, Conn.: Greenwood Press, 1978.

————. *Research Guide for Psychology.* Westport, Conn.: Greenwood Press, 1982.

McKeachie, Wilbert J. "Implications of Cognitive Psychology for College Teaching." *New Directions for Teaching and Learning* 2 (1980): 85–93.

McPherson-Turner, Cherry. "CAI Readiness Checklist: Formative Author Evaluation of CAI Lessons." *Journal of Computer-Based Instruction* 6 (November 1979): 47–49.

Mair, Miller. "Metaphors for Living." In *Nebraska Symposium on Motivation,* edited by Alvin W. Landfield, vol. 25, pp. 243–290. Lincoln, Neb.: University of Nebraska Press, 1977.

Martinson, Tom L. *Introduction to Library Research in Geography: An Instructional Manual and Short Bibliography.* Metuchen, N.J.: Scarecrow Press, 1972.

Martorella, Peter H. *Concept Learning: Designs for Instruction.* Scranton, Pa.: Intext Educational Publishers, 1972.

Maxwell, C. R. "The Workbook: A Recent Development." *American School Board Journal* 88 (March 1934): 16, 44, 46.

Meadows, A. J. *Communication in Science.* London: Butterworth, 1974.

Mellon, Constance A. *Program of Library Use Strategies.* Chattanooga, Tenn.: University of Tennessee at Chattanooga, 1980.

Mellon, Constance A., and Sass, Edmund. "Perry and Piaget: Theoretical Framework for Effective College Course Development." *Educational Technology* 21 (May 1981): 29–33.

Mulkay, Michael. *Science and the Sociology of Knowledge*. London: Allen and Unwin, 1979.

Nelson, Carnot E., and Pollock, Donald K., eds. *Communication Among Scientists and Engineers*. Lexington, Mass.: Heath, 1970.

Nievergelt, Jung. "A Pragmatic Introduction to Courseware Design." *Computer* 13 (September 1980): 7–21.

Nisbet, Robert. *Sociology As an Art Form*. London: Oxford University Press, 1976.

Nitecki, Joseph Z. "An Idea of Librarianship: An Outline for a Root-Metaphor Theory in Library Science." *Journal of Library History* 16 (Winter 1981): 106–120.

———. "Metaphors of Librarianship: A Suggestion for a Metaphysical Model." *Journal of Library History* 14 (Winter 1979): 21–42.

Oberman-Soroka, Cerise. "Question Analysis, Piaget, and the Learning Cycle." Paper presented at the 2nd Annual Conference on Reasoning and Piaget, Denver, Colorado, March 1981.

O'Neil, Harold F. *Computer-Based Instruction: A State-of-the-Art Assessment*. New York: Academic Press, 1981.

O'Neill, Edward T., and Aluri, Rao. "Library of Congress Subject Heading Patterns in OCLC Monographic Records." *Library Resources and Technical Services* 25 (January/March 1981): 63–80.

Orgren, Carl F. "Differences in Learning Under Two Strategies of Computer-Assisted Instruction for a Basic Reference Course in Library School." *Information Reports and Bibliographies* 8 (1979): 15–53.

Parker, Clyde A. "Improving Instruction in Higher Education: Meeting Individual Needs of Students." Proposal submitted to the Fund for the Improvement of Postsecondary Education, 1978.

Pepper, Stephen C. "Metaphor in Philosophy." In *Dictionary of the History of Ideas*, edited by Philip P. Weiner, vol. 3, pp. 196–201. New York: Scribner's, 1973.

———. *World Hypotheses*. Berkeley: University of California Press, 1942.

Perry, William G. *Intellectual and Ethical Development in the College Years: A Scheme*. Cambridge, Mass.: Harvard University Press, 1970.

Phenix, Philip H. *Realms of Meaning: A Philosophy of the Curriculum for General Education*. New York: McGraw-Hill, 1964.

Phipps, Shelley, and Dickstein, Ruth. "The Library Skills Program at the University of Arizona: Testing, Evaluation and Critique." *Journal of Academic Librarianship* 5 (September 1979): 205–214.

Piaget, Jean. *Science of Education and the Psychology of the Child*. New York: Viking, 1970.

Polanyi, Michael. *Personal Knowledge.* Chicago: University of Chicago Press, 1969.

Prior, Moody E. *Science and the Humanities.* Evanston, Ill.: Northwestern University Press, 1962.

Pullen, William R. *A Programmed Text on the Use of the Library for Georgia State University Students.* Atlanta, Ga.: Georgia State College Library, 1966.

Rader, Hannelore B. "Mediated Library Instruction: An Annotated Bibliography." *Drexel Library Quarterly* 16 (January 1980): 116–133.

Rawski, Conrad H. "Bibliographic Organization in the Humanities." *Wilson Library Bulletin* 40 (April 1966): 738–750.

Reigeluth, Charles M. *Meaning and Instruction: Relating What Is Being Learned to What a Student Knows.* Syracuse: School of Education, Syracuse University, 1980.

Renford, Beverly, and Hendrickson, Linnea. *Bibliographic Instruction: A Handbook.* New York: Neal-Schuman, 1980.

Rogers, A. Robert. *The Humanities: A Selective Guide to Information Sources.* 2nd ed. Littleton, Colo.: Libraries Unlimited, 1979.

Rogers, Sharon. "Class-Related Bibliographic Instruction: A Philosophical Defense." In *Proceedings from the 2nd Southeastern Conference on Approaches to Bibliographic Instruction,* edited by Cerise Oberman-Soroka, pp. 25–32. Charleston, S.C.: College of Charleston Library Associates, 1980.

———. "Research Strategies: Bibliographic Instruction for Undergraduates." *Library Trends* 29 (Summer 1980): 69–81.

Salisbury, Alan B. "An Overview of CAI." *Educational Technology* 11 (October 1971): 48–50.

Sarbin, Theodore. "Contextualism: A World View for Modern Psychology." In *Nebraska Symposium on Motivation, 1976,* edited by Alvin W. Landfield, pp. 1–41. Lincoln: University of Nebraska Press, 1977.

Scholarly Communication: The Report of the National Enquiry. Baltimore, Md.: Johns Hopkins University Press, 1979.

Schwarz, Philip J. *The New Media in Academic Library Orientation 1950–1972: An Annotated Bibliography.* Stanford: Stanford University, ERIC Clearinghouse for Educational Media and Technology, 1973, ED 071 682.

Shawin, Lewis. "The Integrated Bibliography for English Studies: Plan and Project." *Pennsylvania Library Association Bulletin* 19 (February 1964): 7–19.

Shibles, Warren A. *Metaphor: An Annotated Bibliography and History.* Whitewater, Wis.: Language Press, 1971.

Shulman, Lee S., and Tamer, Pinchas. "Research on Teaching in the Natural Sciences." In *Second Handbook of Research on Teaching*, edited by Robert M. W. Travers, pp. 1098–1148. Chicago: Rand McNally, 1973.

Silva, Dolores. "A Search-Paradigm for the Description of Problem-Solving Processes." *Educational Technology* 13 (August 1973): 36–39.

Skavaril, Russell V., et al. "The Use of CAI to Provide Problems for Students in Introductory Genetics." *Journal of Computer-Based Instruction* 3 (August 1976): 13–20.

Skinner, B. F. *The Technology of Teaching.* New York: Appleton-Century-Crofts, 1972.

Slavens, Thomas P. "Computer-Assisted Instruction for Reference Librarians." *Journal of Education for Librarianship* 10 (Fall 1969): 116–119.

Small, Henry G. "Cited Documents as Concept Symbols." *Social Studies of Science* 3 (1978): 327–340.

Smalley, Topsy N. "Bibliographic Instruction in Academic Libraries: Questioning Some Assumptions." *Journal of Academic Librarianship* 3 (November 1977): 280–283.

Smith, Linda C. "The Medical Librarian and Computer-Assisted Instruction." *Bulletin of the Medical Library Association* 62 (January 1974): 6–18.

Snelbecker, Glen E. *Learning Theory, Instructional Theory, and Psychoeducational Design.* New York: McGraw Hill, 1974.

Snow, Richard E. "Theory Construction for Research on Teaching." In *Second Handbook of Research on Teaching*, edited by Robert M. W. Travers, pp. 77–112. Chicago: Rand McNally, 1973.

Starks, David D.; Horn, Barbara J.; and Slavens, Thomas P. "Two Modes of Computer-Assisted Instruction in a Library Reference Course." *Journal of the American Society for Information Science* 23 (July–August 1972): 271–277.

Strawn, Richard R. *Topics, Terms, and Research Techniques: Self-Instruction in Using Library Catalogs.* Metuchen, N.J.: Scarecrow, 1980.

Suppes, Patrick. "Third Annual Dean Lecture: The Future of Computers in Education." *Journal of Computer-Based Instruction* 6 (August 1979): 5–10.

Suppes, Patrick, and Macken, Elizabeth. "The Historical Path from Research and Development to Operational Use of CAI." *Educational Technology* 18 (April 1978): 9–12.

Suppes, Patrick, and Morningstar, Mona. *Computer-Assisted Instruction at Stanford, 1966–68: Data, Models, and Evaluation of the Arithmetic Programs.* New York: Academic Press, 1972.

Swanson, Rosena Weiss. "An Assessment of Online Instruction Methodologies." *Online* 6 (January 1982): 38–52.

Thompson, Frederick B. "The Organization Is the Information." *American Documentation* 19 (July 1968): 305–308.

Toulmin, Stephen E. *Human Understanding.* Vol. 1: *General Introduction and Part I.* Princeton, N.J.: Princeton University Press, 1972.

Tyler, Leona E. "More Stately Mansions—Psychology Extends Its Boundaries." *Annual Review of Psychology* 32 (1981): 1–20.

Unwin, Derick, and Atkinson, Frank. *The Computer in Education.* London: The Library Association, 1968.

Urquhart, D. J. "The Needs of the Humanities: An Outside View." *Journal of Documentation* 16 (September 1960): 121–131.

Vinsonhaler, John F., and Bass, Ronald K. "A Summary of Ten Major Studies on CAI Drill and Practice." *Educational Technology* 12 (July 1972): 29–32.

Von Bertalanffy, Ludwig. *General Systems Theory.* New York: Braziller, 1968.

Wales, Charles E. "Data on New Educational Strategy: Guided Design." *Phi Delta Kappan* 60 (December 1978): 313–314.

———. "Improve Your Teaching Tomorrow with Teaching-Learning Psychology." *Engineering Education* 66 (February 1976): 390–393.

———. "Should Curriculum Planning Start with Subject Matter?" *Journal of Educational Technology Systems* 4 (1975): 23–32.

Wales, Charles E., and Stager, Robert A. *Guided Design.* Morgantown, W.Va.: West Virginia University, 1977.

Werking, Richard. "Course-Related Instruction for History Majors." In *Putting Library Instruction in Its Place: In the Library and in the Library School,* edited by Carolyn A. Kirkendall, pp. 44–47. Papers presented at the Seventh Annual Conference on Library Orientation for Academic Libraries Held at Eastern Michigan University, May 12–13, 1977. Ann Arbor, Mich.: Pierian Press, 1978.

White, Carl M. *Sources of Information in the Social Sciences.* Chicago: American Library Association, 1973.

Widick, Carol. "An Evaluation of Developmental Instruction in a University Setting." Ph.D. dissertation, University of Minnesota, 1975.

Williams, Mitsuko, and Davis, Elisabeth B. "Evaluation of PLATO Library Instruction Lessons." *Journal of Academic Librarianship* 5 (March 1979): 14–19.

Wood, Richard J. *Computer-Assisted Instruction Program on How to Use a Library Card Catalog: Description, Program, and Evalua-*

tion. Stanford, Calif.: ERIC Document Reproduction Service, 1979, ED 167 156.

Woods, Lawrence A. "Applications of Microcomputers in Libraries." *18th Annual Clinic on Library Applications of Data Processing.* Urbana-Champaign: University of Illinois Graduate School of Library Science, 1981.

Wooster, Harold. "An Experiment in Networking: The LHNCBC Experimental CAI Network, 1971–1975." *Journal of the American Society for Information Science* 27 (September–October 1976): 329–338.

Yaple, Henry M. *Programmed Instruction in Librarianship: A Classified Bibliography of Programmed Texts and Other Materials 1960–1974.* Occasional Papers no. 124. Champaign, Ill.: University of Illinois Graduate School of Library Science, 1976.

Young, Stanley, and Summer, Charles E., Jr. *Management: A Systems Analysis.* Glenview, Ill.: Scott, Foresman, 1966.

Zinman, John. *Public Knowledge.* Cambridge: Cambridge University Press, 1968.

————. *Reliable Knowledge.* London: Cambridge University Press, 1978.

Zinn, Karl L., and McClintock, Susan. *A Guide to the Literature on Interactive Use of Computers for Instruction.* 2nd ed. Stanford: Stanford University, ERIC Clearinghouse for Educational Media and Technology, 1970, ED 036 202.

Contributors

Patricia A. Berge is Coordinator of Reference at the University of Wisconsin-Parkside Library, Kenosha, Wisconsin.

Elisabeth B. Davis is Biology Librarian at the University of Illinois Library at Urbana-Champaign, Urbana, Illinois.

Elizabeth Frick is Head of User Services at the University of Colorado at Colorado Springs Library, Colorado Springs, Colorado.

Michael Keresztesi is Associate Professor at the Division of Library Science, Wayne State University, Detroit, Michigan.

Jon Lindgren is Head of Reference Services at Young Library, St. Lawrence University, Canton, New York.

Rebecca A. Linton is Head of User Services at Small Library, College of Charleston, Charleston, South Carolina.

Raymond G. McInnis is Head of Reference and Social Science Librarian at Wilson Library, Western Washington University, Bellingham, Washington.

Constance A. Mellon is Instruction Librarian at University of Tennessee at Chattanooga Library, Chattanooga, Tennessee.

Cerise Oberman is Head of Reference at Walter Library, University of Minnesota, Minneapolis, Minnesota.

Stephen H. Plum is a Reference Librarian at Feinberg Library, State University of New York College at Plattsburgh, Plattsburgh, New York.

Judith Pryor is Coordinator of Instruction at the University of Wisconsin-Parkside Library, Kenosha, Wisconsin.

Topsy N. Smalley is a Reference Librarian at Feinberg Library, State University of New York College at Plattsburgh, Plattsburgh, New York.

Katina Strauch is Head of Collection Development at Small Library, College of Charleston, Charleston, South Carolina.

Mitsuko Williams is Assistant Biology Librarian at the University of Illinois, Urbana-Champaign, Urbana, Illinois.

Index

BELOIT COLLEGE

025.56 T343

000

Theories of bibliographic educ   010101

0 2021 0008040 9